Cheap Web Tricks!

BUILD AND PROMOTE A SUCCESSFUL WEB SITE WITHOUT SPENDING A DIME

Anne Martinez

Osborne/**McGraw-Hill**

New York Chicago San Francisco
Lisbon London Madrid Mexico City
Milan New Delhi San Juan
Seoul Singapore Sydney Toronto

Osborne/**McGraw-Hill**
2600 Tenth Street
Berkeley, California 94710
U.S.A.

To arrange bulk purchase discounts for sales promotions, premiums, or fund-raisers, please contact Osborne/**McGraw-Hill** at the above address. For information on translations or book distributors outside the U.S.A., please see the International Contact Information page immediately following the index of this book.

Cheap Web Tricks!
Build and Promote a Successful Web Site Without Spending a Dime

1234567890 FGR FGR 01987654321

ISBN 0-07-219099-X

Publisher
Brandon A. Nordin
Vice President & Associate Publisher
Scott Rogers
Acquisitions Editor
Gretchen Ganser
Project Editor
LeeAnn Pickrell
Acquisitions Coordinators
Alissa Larson
Emma Acker
Technical Editor
Andrew Lardner
Copy Editor
Judith Brown

Proofreader
Susie Elkind
Indexer
Valerie Robbins
Computer Designers
Lucie Ericksen
Carie Abrew
Illustrators
Michael Mueller
Lyssa Wald
Series Design
Lucie Ericksen
Cover Design
Ted Holladay

This book was composed with Corel VENTURA™ Publisher.

Dedicated to frugal people everywhere,
who know that there's always a cheaper way

Contents

Acknowledgments

I'd like to take this opportunity to acknowledge the people who helped transform Cheap Web Tricks from an idea into a finished product. A book is created by many more people than the author who writes the text. It's a compendium of the expertise and effort of many people, who contribute in ways large and small, with the united goal of producing a final product that is useful and valuable to the reader.

The first round of thanks goes to the good folks at Osborne/McGraw-Hill, starting with Gretchen Ganser, who plucked the proposal for this book from the mass of submissions she receives and set it on the road to publication. Thanks also to Project Editor LeeAnn Pickrell, Acquisitions Coordinators Emma Acker and Alissa Larson, and Technical Editor Andrew Lardner, who, as a team, shepherded the manuscript from conception to completion, and to Lucie Ericksen, who created the design for the book.

Lucretia Johnson, president of Lucretia Design, Mike O'Guinn of Phonex Communications, and Shannon Brown of TheCastingSite.com, were kind enough to share their experiences as frugal Webmasters. David Cutler of Sandy Bay Networks, a veteran of the Internet game, contributed to Chapter 16. Thanks also to Neil Salkind of StudioB, my agent for this book.

1

Part One

Building Your Web Site

As for Number 2, desire, you've got that or you wouldn't be reading this book. Desire isn't usually a problem with Web site builders—this stuff is such fun and so interesting that desire is the easiest part. The time commitment, Number 3, depends upon the scope of your vision. You can have a decent one- or two-pager up in a single afternoon. If you've got something bigger in mind, it will indeed take longer. More extensive Web sites typically evolve over time. Webmasters (that's you now) often start small and add features and functions as schedules and interest permit. You don't have to do it all in one day, or one week, unless you want to.

Notice that I didn't include "Internet connection" in the requirements list. That's because I'm going to tell you how to get one for free a little later in the book. The omission of a Web hosting service (a place to put your pages) wasn't an oversight either. I'll point you to some freebie alternatives for that as well.

Before moving ahead, let's clarify one more thing: what is the difference between the Internet and the Web (also called the World Wide Web or WWW)? Although many people use these terms interchangeably, they aren't really the same. The Internet was around first, for one thing. The Internet is like an electronic roadway system connecting diverse destinations. It's a global network that connects millions of computers and millions of users, allowing them to exchange information. The information pathway consists of millions of miles of copper wire, fiber-optic cable, and satellites connected to hubs around the world. No one owns the Internet, or controls it. Each Internet computer, or host, is independent. Whoever owns the host decides which Internet services it will provide and which it will use, as well as if, when, and for how long it will be part of the Internet.

The World Wide Web is a subset of the Internet. If the Internet was a roadway system, the World Wide Web would be its collection of scenic overlooks. It's a system of Internet servers that support specially formatted documents, basically bringing a graphical interface to the Internet. WWW servers and the software (aka browsers) that are used to access them make it possible not only to jump from place to place by clicking on highlighted text, but also to view pictures, listen to sound, and even watch videos stored on the opposite side of the planet. This is the part of the Internet that allows us to create nifty and useful Web sites. Before the advent of the World Wide Web, the Internet was not nearly as pretty to look at.

Since we're going to be on such familiar terms with it very soon, we'll drop that long, formal World Wide Web stuff and from here on just refer to it as the Web. You'll know what we're talking about.

Steps to a Successful Web Site

The process of building and publishing a successful Web site is similar to initiating a journey through a black hole to another universe. Well, some people would like you to believe that, but really it's much simpler (and a whole lot less dangerous). It goes like this:

1. Decide what it is you want to accomplish with your site (publicize, sell, share).
2. Determine what your Web site will need to include to meet that goal.
3. Create an initial design, possibly on paper, possibly on your computer.
4. Put that design into HTML (I'll explain what this is later).
5. Publish those pages to the Web so everyone can see them.

Steps 1 through 3 pretty much consist of gathering your thoughts and organizing them into an overall plan. Although a good part of that is simply engaging your creative powers, it's important when undertaking this part to have an overall understanding of what's both feasible and well suited to your purposes.

As we go along, you are going to be surprised by just how much is feasible: there are many free tools and resources that will allow you to add apparently advanced features to your site with minimal effort. For example, you can add self-updating news headlines of specific interest to your visitors to any page of your site. And did I mention this service is free? Need a discussion forum? No problem. Heck, if you want to, you can even set up an entire online store without spending a dime.

As you read through this book, you'll get a better idea of what's possible and what tools are available to transform your vision to reality. You'll also be better able to choose a design that's within your (rapidly expanding) technical abilities, attractive to the people you want to draw to your Web site, and manageable to maintain over time.

JARGON ALERT: *HTML is an acronym for HyperText Markup Language, which is used to control the way Web page content is displayed.*

Once you get the hang of this Web site development stuff, steps 3 and 4 are often combined; you'll create your initial mock-up right in HTML. HTML is an acronym for HyperText Markup Language. Don't be intimidated by this techie sounding name; it really just means formatted text. If you can use a word processor, or even a text editor, you can write documents in HTML. In a word processing document you can endow particular words or phrases with special characteristics that make them different—more interesting and useful—than the surrounding text. For example, you might cause some words to appear in **bold** or *italics*. HTML is just an expanded version of this capability, which offers the same features plus a whole lot more and is standardized across the Web so that many different browsers and servers will all handle documents created using HTML the same way.

When a word processor user highlights a word and assigns it the characteristic "bold," the word processing program embeds invisible codes into the document that cause the word to appear in the designated format. The reader viewing the document never sees those special codes because even though they are present, they are not displayed. HTML works the same way. To make text appear in bold in an HTML document, the document author simply does this:

```
<bold>This is important!</bold>
```

When the document is displayed in a Web site visitor's browser, the formatting information is hidden, just like it is in a word processing document. The visitor only sees this:

This is important!

Easy, huh? Of course bolding is only one of many features the HTML document author can use. Using the same basic structure, you'll be able to cause particular words (or pictures) to appear larger or smaller; display a different document or jump to a different place in the same document; play a sound; align right, left, or center; use a different color or font; and so on. It gets a little more complicated when you start formatting your page into columns and sections, but the process is largely the same. Some day you might want to buy a book that describes absolutely everything you can do with HTML, but the crash course in Chapter 7 will be enough for most people's needs.

There are lots of handy-dandy tools to help you with the HTML part (step 4). You can actually write HTML with any plain text editor, but there are also quite a few programs (free and for purchase) that mimic a word processor, but are specifically geared to produce HTML (for example, you can select some text, click a "bold" button, and the formatting is inserted automatically for you). These are covered in detail in Chapter 5.

Step 5, publish your pages, consists of transmitting your documents and any associated images or other files to the Web server that will host them. Techies call this step *living* (pronounced "lye-ving"). This is most often accomplished through a software technology called *FTP* (File Transfer Protocol). The nitty-gritty of how it works doesn't matter to us; we only care that we tell an FTP program what files to transfer and where to transfer them to. Although there are other methods of living your pages, this is the most common. I will discuss using FTP in further detail in Chapter 9.

You can see from these steps that you're going to need a couple of pieces of software to produce your Web site: an HTML editor and an FTP program. Some programs combine both of these functions into one application. There's another type of software you're probably going to want as well, although it isn't absolutely necessary: a graphics program. Graphics programs allow you to create and manipulate the images that will appear on your Web site. This includes banners, buttons, logos, photos, and other artwork. You can actually do quite a bit of image creation and manipulation using tools freely available online, and I'll tell you how when we get to the point where you need to do so. Although such freebies offer limited functions, very few people know how to (or need to) take advantage of the full powers of a commercial graphics software package, so the free stuff will probably serve you just fine.

The Other Half: Promotion

At this point, you should have a decent idea of what you're in for as you set out to build your Web site, but getting the site up and running is only half of the story. You can build a fabulous Web site with eye-popping graphics, addictive content, and the most impressive products, but if no one ever visits it, what's the point? The vast majority of us build Web sites because we want people to come to them, whether it's to read our opinions, buy our products, support our cause, share our expertise in a particular hobby, or hire us to work for them. Okay, there are other reasons to create a Web page or two—for keeping your personal bookmarks online, for example—but those hardly qualify as successful sites. A successful site has visitors, preferably lots of them.

In Webmaster parlance, another word for visitors is *traffic*. The bad news is, despite what you may have heard about the Web being an instant gold mine for anyone who slaps up a couple of dashed-off Web pages, it isn't. Traffic won't come to your Web site if people don't know it exists, and they won't know it exists unless you make a concerted effort to tell them about it. So the second half of building a successful Web site is promotion, or building traffic.

To start with, your site may effectively be invisible, but there are lots of things you can do, without spending a dime, to bring it to the attention of the Web-surfing masses. For starters, you've got to get your site included in the search portals that Web surfers use on a regular basis. You probably already know about the bigger, all-encompassing search portals, such as Yahoo!, Excite, Alta Vista, and the like, but did you know there are lots of smaller search portals that can also funnel surfers in your direction? There are even search portals that hone in on a particular industry sector, or vertical market. These are call *vortals*.

You obviously must get your site included in as many of these portals

JARGON ALERT: *A vortal is a vertical portal—a search portal that exclusively serves a particular topic area.*

and vortals as possible, but getting listed is only half the trick; you have to get your site to come up on the results page when portal users enter search terms relevant to your site, and come up as close to the beginning of the returned results as possible.

There are lots of tips, tricks, and techniques to increase your Web site's presence and positioning in search portals. You could pay someone to apply them for you; there are quite a few companies that specialize strictly in search engine placement and positioning. But that's really not necessary and certainly isn't free. By the time you finish reading Chapter 10, you'll know as much as many of those who bill themselves as search engine experts. Plus, no one knows your site and your audience as well as you do, or has as great a desire to see it succeed, so this is a task that you should seriously consider undertaking yourself. Besides, there are lots of free tools that will make the job easier, tools I'll point you to and explain how to use in Chapter 10.

Because search portals are so key to traffic building, many Webmasters consider their promotional work done once they get listed in a few of them. But those Webmasters are making a mistake, because there's lots more you can do to advertise your site. You can trade links with other Webmasters, join a banner-swapping network, participate in a Web ring that connects sites related to a particular topic, issue a press release, seek out awards, and advertise in many subtle and not so subtle ways. I'll explain how to do each one of these and more in Chapter 11, where you'll discover that the only limit to the amount of promoting you can do is the amount of time you care to spend doing it.

It's important not to begin your promotional efforts too early. I'll say more about timing later on, but for now imagine that you follow a promising link to a Web site that sounds interesting, only to find that it consists of a bunch of "what's to come" promises and a series of "under construction" pages. Are you likely to stick around very long or come back later? If you're like most Web surfers, you'll head straight for the back button on your browser, never to return.

TIP: *Resist the temptation to start promoting your site the day you put up that first page. Wait until the site is ready.*

It's important to always keep in mind that you don't just want to attract people to your site; you also want them to stay as long as possible, and return over and over again. One of the great things about traffic-building efforts is that once your traffic starts to ramp up, it tends to climb with increasing speed before leveling out at a more sedate pace once again.

In Pursuit of Profits

There are lots of reasons people build Web sites, and underlying many of them is the aspiration of creating a profitable online venture. Although the Web has been vastly oversold as a frontier of effortless wealth, it is nonetheless a land of opportunity for the entrepreneur willing to work at success. There are few other formats where setting up a storefront can be accomplished with so little expense, especially when you consider that a Web-based business or storefront has potentially global reach from day one.

How do people make money through the Web? Pretty much the same way they do on terra firma—by selling products and services. On the product side, while some businesses may manufacture their own products and sell them through their own Web site, many product businesses on the Web are actually resellers. The Web is a natural medium for network marketing, not just by the traditional multilevel marketing players, but for traditional, well-known companies that never participated in network marketing before. It's also home to numerous companies that were launched from day one with the network marketing power of the Web as a central component of their business plan.

Much of the reselling is accomplished through affiliate programs. Affiliate marketing programs allow (almost) any Tom, Dick, or Harry who has a Web site to sell a particular vendor's products in exchange for a per sale commission. At first glance it might appear that all you have to do is add a few links to your Web site and the money will come rolling in, but experience shows that, for most sites, revenues from affiliate links are quite small. Consider that under the Amazon.com affiliate agreement in force as this was written, if visitors to your Web site purchased $5,000 of books from Amazon.com after following links from your site, you'd get $250 for your efforts. You're going to have to sell a whole lot of books to make a living that way.

On the other hand, participating in affiliate programs costs the Web site owner nothing, and there are often plenty of handy tools provided by the affiliate vendor that will automatically track your sales, create the necessary links for you, or even churn out a somewhat customized storefront. If you've got the space on your Web pages and nothing better to do with it, a few dollars here and there can add up over time. Plus, there are literally hundreds of affiliate programs to choose from. One or more of them may well be a perfect match for your Web site visitors. We'll explore them in detail in Chapter 13.

Fortunately, affiliate programs aren't the only way to make money on the Web. We'll talk more about revenue models in the next chapter as we dive into those first two steps toward building a successful Web site.

2

Chapter Two

Defining Your Mission Plan

Why plan ahead? You might be wondering if you really have to do much advance planning to build a Web site. Can't you just dive right in and start creating? The answer depends on how much time you have to do things over, and whether you will be satisfied with any Web presence or have your heart set on a good-looking, properly functioning one. To build a truly successful Web site, you're going to have to plan. But even though some people consider "plan" to be a four-letter word, it's much more desirable than another four-letter word—"redo."

It's usually pretty easy to tell which Web sites have been planned and thought out and which haven't. Web sites that have simply been thrown together in a rush reflect that, usually in their appearance and almost always in their usability. Such sites are also more difficult to maintain because maintenance issues are rarely considered during their hurried creation. Planned Web sites, on the other hand, have a clear, easily navigable structure, consistent use of style and theme, and are organized in a way that makes sense for the purpose at hand. As a result, they are also much easier to build onto and to maintain. As with so many other things in life, putting in a bit of planning time up front will save you oodles of time down the road—time you can spend adding cool new features to your Web site instead of fixing mistakes made in haste. You may be able to build a Web site without advance planning, but trust me, you don't want to.

Pinning Down a Purpose

The first step toward planning a successful Web site is to pin down exactly what it is you're trying to accomplish by undertaking this venture. You probably think you know already, but if you're like many Web newcomers, your initial goal needs refining. The goal "to make money" is a starting place, but so vague it's unlikely to end successfully. This is the kind of goal that would benefit from some careful sharpening of vision. On the other hand, "Because I think it's cool to have a Web site" might be dismissed by some as a frivolous reason, but not by me. Since you can do it for free, if it gives you pleasure, why not? Just be sure that, if this site is going to be affiliated with any business you currently own, that it's of sufficient quality to enhance rather than detract from that business's reputation.

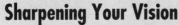

Sharpening Your Vision

Three questions to answer before you build your Web site:

1. Why do you want a Web site?
2. Who is your target audience?
3. What do they want/need?

Personal Reasons for Creating a Web Site

People create an online presence for themselves just because it's cool to be on the Net. They do it because they want to share personal interests, or put up photos or family news. Perhaps you have a hobby and you'd like to create a virtual meeting place to share and exchange information with other people who share the same interests. That hobby might be something as common as stamp collecting, or perhaps a bit more obscure, such as seeing how large a ball you can build out of rubber bands. Whatever it is, there are probably other people out there interested in the same thing. A Web site can help you find each other, and give you a chance to display your expertise and brilliance in the subject at hand.

Or maybe you have an inspirational story to share, or you feel strongly about a particular topic, be it religion, politics, or a health issue, and the Web is the perfect medium to get the word out.

Then again, perhaps you just want to have fun. Plenty of Web sites have been created simply for laughs. Consider the Dihydrogen Monoxide Research Division Web site (shown in Figure 2-1), which pokes fun at the scientific community by trumpeting the dangers of plain old water (H_2O).

NOTE: *Keep in mind that with a personal Web site, the more obscure your focus, the less traffic you're likely to have, no matter how fabulous your site is.*

Noncommercial Reasons for Creating a Web Site

By noncommercial, I mean sites that aren't intended to directly or indirectly produce a profit (though, heck, if opportunity knocks...) but are built for other purposes, such as sharing information or opinions. For

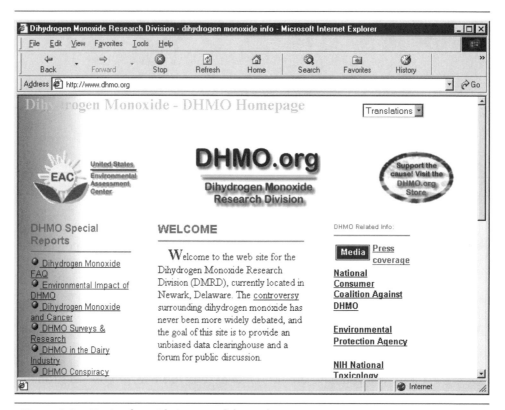

Figure 2-1 • Having fun with water and the Web

example, a Web site that disseminates information for a recreational sports team (such as the one shown in Figure 2-2) isn't personal, but it isn't business either. Such sites can be an efficient and effective form of sharing information with small to large groups.

Any nonprofit or grassroots group with an agenda can use the Web to get the word out and garner support. The site can serve as a connection point to the constituency—a place they can join a mailing list, learn which volunteer positions need filling, and gain a fuller understanding of the organization's mission. Besides its functional value as an information source, a Web site adds credibility to small organizations. It's very handy to be able to refer the media to the Web site, and sometimes television, radio, or print reports will refer people to the site for further information.

A nonprofit organization can also use a Web site as a fund-raising tool, through direct or indirect product sales, or simply by providing

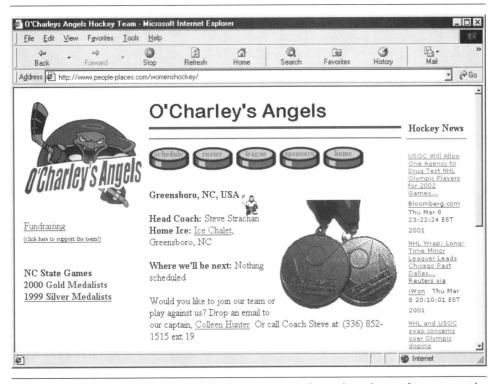

Figure 2-2 • The O'Charley's Angels hockey team uses the Web to share information with team members and fans.

an easy way to make contributions online. Figure 2-3 shows how one group of parents turned to the Web to aid their cause.

Business Reasons for Creating a Web Site

You might think the logic behind business Web sites is as straightforward as "if you have a business, you need a Web site," but that's not true. Even though you can publish a Web site for free, that's only half the job; promoting and maintaining the site over time remains ahead of you. Putting up a lousy-looking Web site or letting a nice one go fallow can reflect poorly on your organization.

Certain types of businesses will gain more from a Web presence than others. Local businesses that offer services to local customers have the least to gain, though they can still benefit. People just don't do much online shopping (yet) for this kind of thing. But if there's a targeted market at your doorstep that is comfortable online, a Web site can be a great way to connect with them. For example, in a college town, a Web

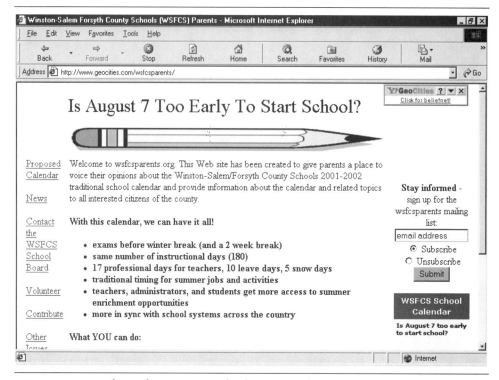

Figure 2-3 • North Carolina parents make their case online.

site may be an excellent way to attract students to businesses that cater to them.

Companies that have the potential to serve a national or global market have the most to gain. For example, by going online, a specialty store selling a hard-to-find item such as organic fresh-baked bread can expand its market to anywhere speedy shipping services can reach. A business that doesn't have enough demand in its local market to support operations may find that by expanding its target market via the Web, there are plenty of customers to be had.

Selling products or services to customers is one of the main business uses of the Web. An online site allows a business not only to expand its reach, but also to largely remove the limitation of business hours. With online ordering (or instructions for faxing orders), merchandise can be sold around the clock. Figure 2-4 shows the Web site of Phonex Communications, Inc., a Missouri company that sells headsets, telephones, and telephone systems both online and from a traditional storefront.

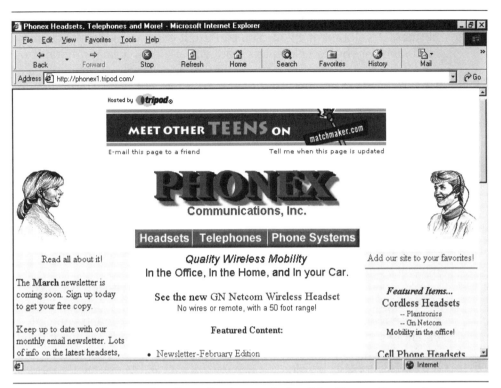

Figure 2-4 • Selling merchandise online has worked well for Phonex Communications.

A business Web site can also be used to distribute information to employees or customers. For employees, that might mean scheduling information, human resources policies, technical support, or company bulletins. If this is the purpose of the site, you can stash the material in a private area accessible only by employees so that it cannot be viewed by outsiders.

Information provided for customers would include materials to convince them to buy offline when it's more practical to do so (you're not going to be taking many online orders for dump trucks, for example), or technical support and materials to help them use products they currently own to their fullest potential.

Putting technical support documents and the answers to frequently asked questions online in an easily usable format can substantially reduce the support load on a business. Most software companies do this, and so do lots of nontechnical businesses. This gives customers 24-hour access to help, and they don't have to sit on hold listening to Muzak.

Your business Web site can also serve as an important part of your business development chain. You can use it to get direct feedback from customers, or you can glean less readily available information from the Web site statistics. For example, if you notice that you're getting a large percentage of your visitors from Australia, but not a proportionate percentage of orders from there, you might tailor products or services especially for them.

Self-employed businesspeople, independent contractors, or employees can use a Web site to make their presence known, as well as to establish expertise in a subject area. A technical writer, for example, might post samples of her work online, and create a technical writing FAQ (frequently asked questions) page that demonstrates her knowledge. If the writer then does the work of promoting the site well, potential clients will find her, and her name will become familiar within the technical writing community. Of course, there's lots more she could add to this site to make it even more attractive to potential visitors.

You don't have to be a big (or even medium-sized) business to take advantage of what the Web has to offer. It's actually a great equalizer, because it doesn't require huge amounts of capital (although you can certainly spend as much as you wish) or expertise to participate. It may not be the cash machine that some people would have you believe, but the Web still offers entrepreneurs a way to start marketing their products and services quickly and with little to no cash outlay.

After Why Comes Who

Once you've clarified your reasons for building a Web site, the next step is to identify your target audience. It's quite possible you'll have more than one. The hockey team Web site in Figure 2-2, for example, targets current players, fans, potential opponents, and new player recruits. A personal Web site may target family and friends, or perhaps rubber band enthusiasts. The parents' group Web site in Figure 2-3 includes local parents, media outlets, and local school officials among its intended audiences. A typical business site, such as the one in Figure 2-4, targets potential and existing customers. As discussed previously, there may be other audiences as well, depending on the reasons for building the site.

To pin down your target audience, which is crucial before undertaking the next step, sit down and make a list of the types of people you think might be served by your site. Be as detailed as possible. Instead of listing customers as a target audience, break that group into more specific components, such as new customers and returning customers. Both of those can be further subdivided as well. For example, new customers could be

broken into groups with different needs—college students, parents, and retirees (if they're all potential customers). Or your subgroups could be people who've bought the product before, but not from you, and people who've never purchased an item in the same category before. The first group would need competitive information on why your product is better; the second would need to be convinced to buy in the first place. The more specifically you define your audience members, the easier it will be to determine the most effective ways to serve them.

What Does Your Target Audience Want and Need?

Once you've pinned down the "who," next up is figuring out what your target audience(s) want and need that you might be able to provide online. Sit down and make an exhaustive list, placing yourself in the role of an audience member. This is a good time to solicit input from friends and customers. Don't worry about technical feasibility at the moment; for now, you're just generating ideas. If your final list doesn't contain more ideas than you can personally implement, then you haven't brainstormed enough.

Such a list for a product-oriented business Web site might include online technical support, after-hours ordering, product information (including pictures), assistance in choosing a product, contact information, guarantee policy, shipping details, articles on how to use a product, product news, directions (maybe even a map) to the physical storefront along with operating hours, catalog request form, feedback form, a forum for customers to exchange ideas related to your products, and anything else you can think of.

For the hockey team Web site, it included scheduling information, fund-raising, contacts, information on joining the team or competing against them, team news, general hockey news, hockey tips and techniques, resources related to playing hockey, a team roster, and action photos.

TIP: *Take a look at the Web sites of others in your market or field of interest to see what they're doing and what they include. To find them, visit a search engine such as Yahoo! and search using the keywords you imagine your target audience would enter when seeking out your products, services, or information.*

Once you've created your exhaustive list, go through it and rank each item as either an *a*, *b*, or *c* priority, with *a* being most critical and *c* being least critical. This will help you determine which features to implement first. This list will also play a role in your choice of Web hosting provider. Technical features and access vary among hosting services. Knowing which you want up front will save you the potential aggravation of relocating your site after you've already begun development. Chapter 4 will tell you everything you need to know about choosing Web hosts in an effort to save you from this particular nightmare.

Web Site Revenue Models

For-profit Web site revenue models have two parts: what the money is collected for and how it is collected. The four ways Web sites make money (or attempt to) are similar to revenue-producing methods employed by traditional (aka brick-and-mortar) businesses, by selling:

- Information
- Products
- Services
- Advertising

Web site–based businesses often use more than one of these methods at a time. As we explore these different options, I'll use both frugally built and not-so-frugally built sites as examples. I do this for two reasons: First, although there are clues, it's not always obvious how much money has been spent to set up a site. Second, just because someone else spent a lot to build a particular site doesn't necessarily mean you'll have to.

NOTE: *For a hobby Web site, the goal is often not to get rich, but simply to recoup the expense of the hobby.*

Selling Information

One of the more difficult models to use successfully on the Web is selling information. So much material is available for free that convincing visitors that yours is worth paying for takes some doing. Most Web users feel that information should be free and aren't willing to pay for it. Quite a few newspapers have attempted to create a paid

subscription service, but failed. However, some information is valuable enough that people will pay to access it.

The trick to getting Web surfers to open their wallets for information lies in providing content of very high value—much better than potential subscribers can get elsewhere for free. This might include a specialized database in a vertical market, or detailed articles that go into much greater depth than other articles covering the same topic. Information-based Web sites also offer the advantage of easy searching and organization of data. Plus, they can be kept more current than their printed counterparts.

For a Web site using this model to turn a profit, there's another often overlooked key component: the amount of effort and expense necessary to create and maintain the information. A Web site business that offers unique news and articles will have the expense of creating, purchasing, and producing that content. An online database of information will have to be updated regularly.

To summarize, for a Web site that relies on selling information to have a chance to turn a profit, the content must be

- Of very high value to the user
- Always current
- Affordable to maintain/produce

Hoover's Online (**www.hoovers.com**), which is a repository of detailed business profiles and information, uses the subscription model. The site also provides plenty of free content that draws additional visitors—some potential subscribers, but many not—which increases traffic flow substantially. Their subscriber base exceeds 250,000.

Syndicating Content

The above rules don't apply as rigidly if the Web site is in the syndication business. Syndication can be accomplished in a number of different ways, but basically involves reselling content, often branded under another company's name, or cobranded (both companies' names are present) with another company. The reason the rules can be bent is that content is often used as a magnet to draw users to a site, where they then buy products or services. A company that doesn't have the internal resources to produce its own magnet content will sometimes outsource that process by subscribing to a syndication service.

TIP: *Syndicating your content can also be an effective way to bring traffic to your Web site (more on this in Chapter 11, which covers promotion).*

Revenue from syndication can come from the Web sites that buy your content, or from people who have content they want widely distributed. Usually, syndication services choose one of these or the other, as using both can create ethical dilemmas.

Lineup (**www.lineup.com**) is a syndicator that specializes in streaming content. *Streaming* allows large media files, such as video or music, to begin to play before the entire file has downloaded. Lineup's content suppliers, which get paid on a per-view basis, include cartoonists, movie makers, news organizations, golf schools, and children's content creators. Lineup packages this content into bundles and offers individual items (streams) for purchase.

Content Aggregators

Another potentially valuable service a Web site can provide is content aggregation. This means collecting information from multiple diverse sources and bringing it together in a single place. Content aggregation is often done in combination with an advertising-driven revenue model, with the aggregated content used to bring traffic to the Web site, and the profit made selling advertising that is displayed to those visitors. I'll talk more about this in the "Selling Advertising" section later in this chapter. This is a primary revenue model for many portal sites.

A *portal site* is a Web site that serves as a gateway to a large quantity of information. If the information is tightly focused on a particular subject (or vertical market), the portal is sometimes called a vortal, which means vertical portal. For example, a parenting portal site could organize, rate, and comment on Web sites of interest to parents and provide direct links to those sites. When a parent needs information on breast-feeding at 3:00 a.m., instead of searching for the best resources on her own, she would go to the portal site that has already done that work for her.

Specialized content aggregators, particularly those that target businesses as customers, often make their money by selling access to the aggregated content directly to the client. Web-based services that monitor the Internet for mentions of a company, its products, and services, then consolidate their findings and deliver them to the subscriber at regularly scheduled intervals, fall into this category. News services that collect and organize headlines for their users are also content aggregators.

Information Payment Models

Web sites that sell information as their primary source of revenue have several different payment models to choose from. We already explored relicensing of content, which is the syndication process discussed previously. Other options include subscription, per-use fees, and the up-front fee.

Subscription payment models work the same way they do for non-Web businesses: users pay a set amount for access to the Web site's information resources for a predefined period of time. Hoover's uses this model. So does Art Today (**arttoday.com**), which aggregates clip art, fonts, Web graphics, sounds, and similar resources and gives subscribers access to download as many of these as they wish and use them royalty free.

Some Internet analysts think that pay per use is the natural payment model of the future. With this model, users are charged (usually a small amount) only for information or resources they access, on a per-use basis. A Web site selling information using a per-use model might charge by article viewed, or file downloaded.

The per-use payment model is used less widely than the subscription model. A key reason is the lack of a good system for collecting and processing small payments (called *micropayments*) in a cost-effective and convenient manner. Northern Light (**www.northernlight.com**) uses this system, charging from $1 to $4 per full text article retrieved from its "Special Collection." The technology demands of this payment model make it a less suitable choice for the frugal Webmaster.

The final model, up-front fee, can be used in conjunction with per-use or on its own. Users pay a set fee, one time, for unlimited access to the information. This is another method that's not in wide use on the Web because it can leave you open to having to provide a service even if it's no longer generating new revenue, for an extended period.

Selling Products

Online shopping is increasing in popularity as Web users get used to the idea of buying online. An Ernst & Young study of global online retailing, conducted in late 2000, found that despite concerns about online security and price sensitivity, consumers are buying things online in increasing numbers, and the amount they are willing to spend on online purchases is rising.

Product sales can be one of the most valuable revenue models to use if you have quality items to sell at competitive prices. Some Web site businesses manufacture their own products, but a larger portion are resellers. Amazon.com and CDNow are prime examples of companies that thrive by reselling other companies' products online.

You don't have to have the budget of Amazon.com to resell items that are made by recognizable, reputable companies. There are many affiliate programs that enable individuals and businesses with no inventory of their own to market and sell products through a Web site. We'll explore these in detail in Chapter 13.

Popular Online Products

Products that seem to sell best online include books, CDs, and computer hardware and software. Toys, sporting goods, and health and beauty product sales are picking up steam. Web buyers seem more willing to purchase low-cost items online than more expensive products. This is due to consumer fears over the security of online transactions combined with unwillingness to spend large sums on a product they haven't seen or touched first. You may be thinking, what about airline tickets? People buy those online, and they cost hundreds of dollars. Congratulations, you've spotted one of the exceptions to the rule. But if you think about it, tickets aren't something you need to see and touch. If you didn't buy them over the Web, you'd most likely be purchasing them by phone instead. There's no need to examine or test-drive the merchandise first.

This doesn't mean you shouldn't consider selling things that aren't in the list above, but when planning your Web site, you should keep in mind the types of products that are being sold successfully online. Items that have traditionally been sold by catalog or phone are good candidates. And as consumers become more comfortable with online purchasing, big-ticket items may well become a reasonable alternative.

Product Payment Systems

If you sell your own products, you're going to need a way to collect payment from customers. This can be accomplished through setting up a merchant account and using something called shopping cart software to facilitate browsing and purchasing of your products. It's not as complicated as it sounds, and I'll explain exactly how to go about it in Chapter 14.

In some cases, you might opt to take orders by fax or phone instead of online, which is another possibility. The main purpose of your Web site would then be to convince potential customers to buy from you, as well as perhaps to provide post-sales support. But if you do this, keep in mind that if you don't provide customers a way to complete the transaction online, they may go to someone else who does.

If you choose to go the affiliate route, which means that you basically serve as a salesperson for someone else's goods, the company you are selling products for will have a payment system in place that handles order and payment processing for you. Affiliate programs are covered in depth in Chapter 13.

Selling Services

The Web is an excellent channel for meeting customers who need the services you offer, and selling services is a popular entry point for new Web entrepreneurs. Although you could market local services such as house cleaning or pet watching online, services you can deliver without geographic limitations are better candidates. Figure 2-5 shows the Web site of Lucretia Design Group, which sells desktop publishing, graphic design, and Web site design services.

The key to success in selling services online is to establish your credibility and reliability. Remember the touch and feel barrier to product sales online? It applies to services too, which is why services are often marketed online, but the transaction is clinched through a telephone call.

Marketing services online seems more difficult than selling products, but you'd be surprised at the types of services people are willing to buy via the Web. One of the most personal services of all—counseling—can

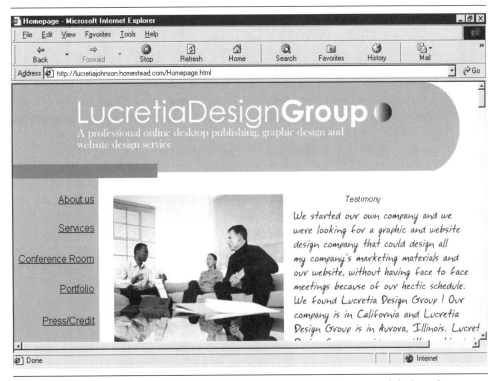

Figure 2-5 • The Web makes it possible to easily market services to a global market.

now be purchased and delivered online. Yahoo! alone lists over 80 providers of online therapy.

TIP: *Sites that sell products and services often provide additional information and resources (aka content) as a magnet to draw visitors to the site. The home page of Phonex Communications (Figure 2-4) demonstrates this practice.*

Selling Advertising

More than one site has been created with the plan of making a fortune by selling advertising space, but in reality, a Web site must have a huge amount of traffic to have a chance at a substantial income stream from this source. That said, smaller sites can derive revenue from ad space too; it's just not going to make you independently wealthy. Web sites without enough traffic to attract advertising on their own can often join advertising networks, which bundle sites together until they get enough total traffic to interest potential advertisers. We'll get more deeply into this in Chapter 15, but I'll give you an overview here.

Advertising is often sold as banner ads that display at the top of each page, or smaller buttons and text links located throughout the site. Another option is to allow advertisers to sponsor a particular area of your site. If you can convince your site visitors to sign up for your newsletter, advertising in that can be sold as well. There are many other ways to work in sponsors or advertisers; the only limit is your imagination.

Cost per Click and Cost per Thousand

Advertising spots are typically sold either by charging per display, or by actual click-through. A *display* (also called an *impression*) means that the ad was shown to a visitor, whereas a *click-through* means a user actually clicked on the advertisement and waited for the resulting page to load. Displays and click-throughs are typically sold in batches of 1,000 for a fixed rate. The acronym CPM stands for cost per mille. (Mille, also represented by the Roman numeral *M*, means thousand.) A Web site that sells banner ads at $15 CPM would get $75 for 5,000 displays of an ad.

As you might imagine, predicting the number of click-throughs for an advertisement is much trickier than promising a set number of impressions.

So click-through deals are usually made on a cost per click (CPC) basis, with the Web site owner receiving anywhere from 1 cent to 20 cents per click. Web site owners usually prefer CPM pricing, while buyers seem to favor CPC.

TIP: *When making your case for CPM pricing, remind advertisers that even when visitors do not click on the ad, they are being exposed to the advertiser's name, branding, and products. This may contribute to a purchase decision later on, even when an immediate click-through doesn't result.*

It's possible to directly hand-code advertisements into your Web page, but it's much more efficient and convenient to use ad serving software. This software will track impressions and clicks for you, as well as make it possible to rotate multiple advertisements through a single position on your site. There are quite a few options for ad serving software, and some of them are free. I'll tell you where to get them in Chapter 15.

Passion Counts

The most important thing I can tell you about choosing a subject and making a plan for your Web site is to choose something related to a topic or area you are passionate about. If you do that, the rest of the details can be worked into place. It doesn't matter if that passion is to turn a profit, to help people in need, or to keep your family more closely in touch with each other; if you care deeply about it, your chances of success rocket upward.

What I've explained so far may seem like a lot to keep in mind, but understanding the motives and opportunities for your Web site will help you design and build a successful Web presence. I'm not suggesting that you sit down, create a detailed blueprint, and stick to it for life. Nobody (at least, nobody I know) does that, and I wouldn't want you to be the first—it would be too boring. A successful Web site evolves over time, as opportunity and inspiration decree, and doesn't have to be designed and built overnight. It's a matter of uniting inspiration, perspiration, knowledge, and creativity.

As you get ready to dive into this new venture, now is the time to explore why you want to build a site. If your purpose is commercial, revisit your reasons with what you've learned about revenue models and the Web in mind. Go out on the Web, get some ideas, mingle and improve them, add expertise of your own, and cook up your own personal vision of what a successful Web site should be.

3

Chapter Three

Getting Connected

Y ou don't have to be connected to the Internet to create your
Web site—that can actually be done completely on your
personal computer—but it certainly makes life easier. A lot of
software for Web site creation includes a preview function that
shows your page as it should appear published, but for various
reasons these previews are sometimes inaccurate. Most Web
developers prefer to work a little bit, upload the results and look
at them live and online, and then add, revise, and upload again.
You're also going to want to go online to search out free tools and
research ideas, and of course, to publish your completed pages.

Free Internet Service

You may have an Internet connection of some kind already, but I'm
willing to wager that if you do, you're probably paying a monthly fee
for the privilege. The good news is that in many locations, especially
in the United States, you don't have to do that anymore if you don't
want to. There are companies that will provide you with a free dial-up
connection. What does the free Internet Service Provider (ISP) get out
of it? It varies among providers, but usually it's advertising. Sometimes
it's statistical information.

When you opt for a free connection, the ISP will provide you with
special software to install on your computer. You have to run this software
every time you want to access the Internet over the free connection. Most
of these programs display an advertising box somewhere on your screen
that will display rotating banner advertisements. Although this can be
annoying, you can usually reposition the box anywhere on your screen so
that it doesn't obscure your work. Figure 3-1 shows the screen users see
when they log on through Juno's Free Internet service.

Whether or not they display an ad box, most free ISPs will do two
other things: First, they'll set your start page to one that they've created.
Second, they'll customize your Web browser menu so that it includes
direct links to the ISP's products and services. This shouldn't negatively
affect any existing functionality; your Web browser will continue to
work as it always has.

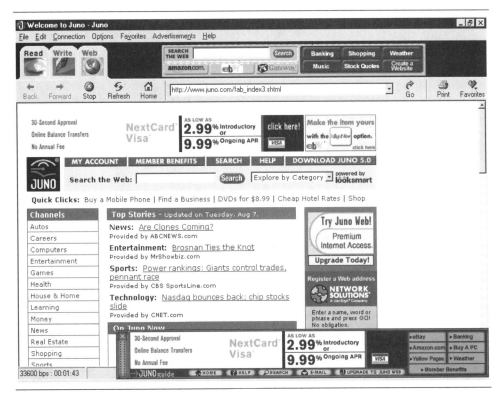

Figure 3-1 • **Free Internet sevice from Juno.com**

NOTE: *Unfortunately for Mac and Linux users, most free ISP software works on PC compatibles only. If you're not a PC user, you're going to have to search a bit harder to find a free connection.*

While many people consider viewing a particular start page or having an advertising bar on their screen a fair price to pay for a free connection, some free ISPs do something you might find much more objectionable: track your surfing. They record which Web sites you visit while online and what you do there. NetZero (**www.netzero.com**) does this, for example. If your chosen ISP does this, it should be disclosed in their privacy policy or user agreement, both of which should be available from the ISP's Web site. You should always read both of these documents before signing up with any service provider, whether a free ISP or not.

Once you install the software, which usually goes smoothly, you'll just click on the newly installed icon and you're off, taking a free ride on the Internet. Keep your paid service too until you're certain the free one will serve your purposes adequately.

An up-to-date list of free Internet providers can be found on the Cheap Web Tricks Web site (**cheapwebtricks.com/create/freeispdata1.shtml**). Providers in operation as this is being written include:

- **3web Network (www.3Web.net)**   Free dial-up access and e-mail in Canada. Future expansion into the United States, Latin America, and Europe.
- **Address.com (www.address.com)**   Unlimited free dial-up access. Instead of displaying an ad bar, runs periodic seven-second commercials to your screen.
- **MetConnect (metconnect.com)**   Free access in New York City area. No banner ads.
- **Juno (www.juno.com)**   Free dial-up access and e-mail across the United States. Unlimited; but especially heavy users may be restricted from connecting when congestion is a problem.
- **NetZero (www.netzero.com)**   Unlimited dial-up access and e-mail in the United States and Canada.
- **Nocharge (www.nocharge.com)**   Free unlimited dial-up access in northwestern United States. Supports Windows, Macintosh, Linux, Unix.
- **dotNow! (www.dotnow.com)**   Free unlimited dial-up access and e-mail in the United States, Europe, Australia, New Zealand, Mexico, and Japan. Charges a $9.95 set up fee.

Connection Options

Free Internet access services are almost always dial-up. That means you will connect to them over a standard telephone line using the modem that most likely came with your computer. This is how most people connect to the Internet. It's also the slowest (though least expensive) way to do it. If you have extra cash in your budget, it's worthwhile to consider one of the speedier alternatives. The choices include cable, special phone lines, or satellite. If you're connecting from a college dorm or corporate offices, you might even be lucky enough to have a really high speed connection like OC-3 or T1, in which case you can skip right on to the next chapter. For the rest of you, read on to learn your options.

Dial-Up Connections

You're probably most familiar with dial-up connections—using your computer and modem to call your ISP anytime you want to go online. This system has been around long enough that it's fairly stable and easy to use. The problem is speed. The fastest possible dial-up modem connection is 56 Kbps (kilobits per second), which means that transferring large files such as pictures can take a long time.

For a point of reference regarding speed, I'll use Bruce Springsteen's song, "Born in the USA." Stored on a computer hard drive as an MP3 file it takes up about 4,400 kilobytes (35,200 kilobits). Downloading it via a perfect 56 Kbps modem connection would take about ten and a half minutes. Because of the nature of phone line connections, there's really no such thing as a perfect 56 Kbps dial-up connection, which means transferring the file would take even longer. Older phone lines don't carry clear signals, and the more switches your connection travels through, the slower it becomes. If your ISP handles lots of calls, that can reduce dial-up connection speed as well.

Another drawback of dial-up service is that it ties up your phone line.

TIP: *Understanding connection speeds is also important when designing your pages. You'll want to construct them so they load quickly even for users with slower connections (more on this in Chapter 6).*

When someone in your house is online, no calls can come in or go out. You can solve this problem by putting in a second line for computer use, which of course entails additional expense. Another alternative is to use an Internet call answering program that will allow callers to leave a message in a voice mailbox and notify you that they've done so. You can get a basic version of the service for free, or pay a monthly fee for advanced features, including the ability to actually take the call if you choose to do so. Companies that offer free versions include CallWave (**www.callwave.com**) and BuzMe (**www.buzzme.com**).

Cable Modem Service

One of the most trouble-free and affordable ways to get dramatically faster Internet access is to sign up for cable modem service. Access is provided via the same cable (and usually the same company) that provides cable television service. Not all cable TV outfits have the capability to offer this service, but it's available in most major metropolitan areas. Two major vendors of cable modem access are @Home (**www.home.com**) and RoadRunner (**www.rr.com**). These vendors work in conjunction with local cable companies to provide high-speed Internet access.

To install cable modem service, you'll need to purchase or lease some additional pieces of equipment: a network interface card and a cable modem. Whoever installs your service can usually provide and install this equipment for you. During special promotions the equipment is often offered at great savings or even free.

A network interface card is a circuit board that goes inside the computer. The computer has to be opened to install it, which is really no big deal, though people who haven't done it before are usually intimidated by the idea. The computer has slots inside, and the network card is inserted into one of them. It's rather like plugging a cellular phone into a cigarette lighter in a car. If your computer is already part of an in-house network, your existing card will often do the trick. The network card includes a jack that the cable modem will plug into, just as a telephone plugs into a wall jack.

A cable modem is different (and more expensive) than the standard telephone modem used for dial-up access, but the concept is the same: you plug your computer into the modem and then attach the modem to the cable line. The modem acts like a translator between your computer and the cable network. Information your computer sends out is converted into a format that can travel over the cable, and incoming information is converted back into a format your computer can understand. If you have several computers networked together, they can share a single cable modem, although sometimes there's an additional charge for this.

So you plug your network card into the computer, the computer into the cable modem, and the cable modem is hooked up to cable service by your cable company. Run a little installation program, and you'll be able to download and view Web pages about 20 times faster than via a 56 Kbps modem connection. And you could download "Born in the USA" in 39 seconds. Monthly connection fees are running about $40 a month as this is being written. If you pay for a second phone line for your computer, you'll be able to drop that and recoup much of the expense that way.

High Speed Needs High Security

As much as we love high-speed Internet access, there's a potential drawback you should be aware of. Cable modem, DSL, and satellite connections are "always on." That means you can walk up to your computer and access the Internet without having to dial or make a connection. But (and the cable/telephone/satellite company often doesn't tell you this) it also means that your computer is more vulnerable to attack by unsavory hackers with nothing better to do than mess up other people's computers. Dial-up users are at risk too, but since they're not connected most of the time, and for technical reasons, the risk is lower.

Fortunately, it's pretty easy to protect yourself. Just install a piece of firewall software like ZoneAlarm from Zone Labs, and it will intercept and deflect any unauthorized attempts to connect to your computer. You can get a free (for personal or nonprofit use) copy at **www.zonelabs.com**. Business use requires paying a registration fee. Another popular (but not free) product is BlackICE Defender, which you can get at **www.networkice.com**.

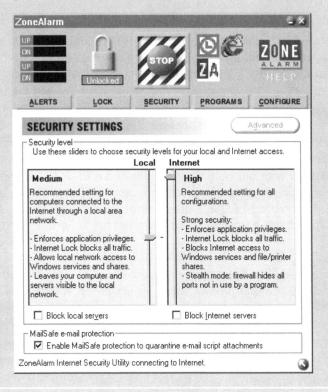

Plus, the physical cable connection and Internet access are a package deal, so there aren't any separate ISP charges.

On the downside, cable access is shared access. All the people in your neighborhood that have the service will be using the same physical cable. This means it's possible that as more people sign up for cable modem access, your access speed will drop. The other drawback is that you probably won't have much choice as to who you buy cable modem access from. There will probably be only one provider in your area.

Digital Subscriber Line (DSL)

Using special equipment and technologies, it's possible to transmit data over standard telephone lines at a much higher rate of speed than the standard dial-up connection allows, while simultaneously allowing standard telephone service without needing an additional line. This technology is called Digital Subscriber Line, or DSL. To make it work, special equipment is attached to the phone lines at your end and at the telephone company's office. You can only get DSL service if

- Your phone company offers it
- You are within a few miles of a phone company central office

Exactly what has to be installed and how it works will depend on which flavor of DSL you get. There are quite enough permutations to make you dizzy, each with its own acronym, of course: ADSL, SDSL, HDSL, VDSL. You don't really need to be able to tell them apart until you get ready to sign up for one, and then the one you get is largely dependent on what your phone company offers.

Unlike cable access, your DSL lines won't be shared with other customers, so access speed should remain fairly consistent, no matter how many of your neighbors use the same route to the Internet. Exact speeds vary depending on which type of DSL you get and other factors. Using a common ADSL type of connection, "Born in the USA" would download in about one and a half minutes.

NOTE: *The connection speeds given in this chapter are estimates. Expect your actual speed for any of these options to vary based on service provider, network conditions, and the weather in Pittsburgh (okay, maybe not that).*

Integrated Services Digital Network (ISDN)

ISDN technology has been around for over a decade, and before DSL and cable modems, if you wanted high-speed Internet access, it was this or nothing. Like DSL, ISDN lets you use the same lines, at the same time, for telephone and computer use. It also requires special equipment on both ends, and you'll have to be within 3.4 miles of a telephone company's central office to get it.

ISDN divides your phone line into three channels. Two of them are called B channels and are capable of transmitting up to 64 Kbps, for a combined total of 128 Kbps. At this rate, "Born in the USA" would take five minutes to download. The third channel is called the D channel, and is used to handle overhead/administrative data, so it isn't included in the transmission capacity calculations.

ISDN is notoriously difficult to set up, and usually expensive, so it's not one of my favorite options. Still, many people are very happy with it (once they get it going). In some areas it may be your only option for a faster connection.

Satellite Systems

One of the less used but still possible options for a speedier connection is satellite access. To use this, you need a satellite dish ($200–$300) and a clear view of the southern sky. You'll also have to install a special circuit board in your PC, which will be connected to the dish via a cable, and of course, pay a monthly fee for service.

This system promises a download speed of about 400 Kbps, which means 11 seconds to download our Springsteen tune. The biggest catch is that the satellite only sends data to you; you can't send data to it. This means that data will come into your computer (via the satellite) at a high rate of speed, but outgoing data is routed through a standard modem and dial-up connection. Most Web surfers have a vastly larger amount of data coming in—Web pages, file downloads, and so on—than going out (e-mail, file uploads), so this is not quite as big a drawback as it might seem at first.

The main provider of this service is DirecPC (**www.direcpc.com**), the same company that sells DirecTV. Service is available pretty much anywhere in the United States and Canada where you have a clear view of the relevant section of sky, even in remote locations.

How to Decide

I haven't gone into detail on every possible form of Internet service connection. That would be another book—one that would be most useful to telecommunications professionals and insomniacs. For Web site development, a dial-up connection will suffice, though it may try your patience at times. It's also currently the only option you can use for free. If you crave something faster, cable modem or DSL are probably the best choices.

Now that you know the various ways you can get online to publish your site, the next big question is, where are you going to put it? Once again, you've got options galore. The next chapter will help you choose the one that's best for your particular circumstances.

4

Chapter Four

Finding a Home for Your Web Site

O ne of the first and most important decisions you'll make about your Web site is where to put it. The pages, images, and other components you create will need to reside on a computer (called a *Web server*) that is constantly connected to the Internet, preferably with a fast connection. That server runs special software that enables it to dish up your pages to anyone who happens by. If this sounds like it will be expensive, that's because it can be, and some people pay a small fortune for it. But you can also choose an option that won't cost you a dime.

Cost is an important matter, but there are other factors to consider as well. You'll need to choose a hosting arrangement that will

- Serve up your pages fast and reliably to all comers
- Provide an easy-to-use method for you to publish and modify your files
- Answer your technical support inquiries
- Allow you to install or even provide add-on features you want, such as shopping cart software

There are all manner of extras you might decide you need, but these are the basics that need to be in place. Take some time to choose your Web site's home with care. The wrong hosting service can cause you substantial headaches, and moving your site later, while possible, is an aggravation (trust me) you can certainly do without.

Free Web Site Hosting

There is a plentiful supply of companies willing to host your site for free. Why do they do this? Because they have plans for how it will benefit them as well. But it can still be a good deal for you. There are two kinds of free Web hosting: online communities that provide free space for Web pages and Web space provided by an ISP as part of an Internet connection service.

Free Hosting Communities

The best way to get a free home for your Web site is to sign up at one of the many free page communities. These provide basic space for your pages (sometimes unlimited), usually don't charge anything even if you have more traffic than you envisioned in your wildest dreams, and often provide free tools and add-ons that make it possible to add customized features to your site without any programming knowledge. Figure 4-1 shows the home page for a free hosting community.

What does the service provider get out of hosting your online venture? A common way that free Web hosts make their money is to run advertisements on your site. These may come in the form of a banner ad that runs across the top of each page, or a (more annoying) pop-up window that appears whenever users access your site. Some

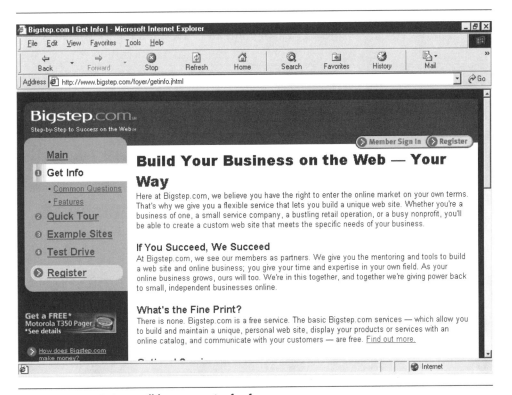

Figure 4-1 • BigStep will host your site for free.

sites will give you a bit of control over the type of ads that run, and most promise not to display pornographic or similarly objectionable ads.

Web surfers are used to viewing pages with ads at the top, and they will have no way of knowing that the ones on your site aren't put there by you. Figure 4-2 shows what a page with a banner ad on top looks like.

A few free Web hosts don't run advertisements on your pages, but have other ways of making a profit. One method is to sell you add-ons. These can be features for your site, such as shopping cart software, a special Web address, or elimination of the ads on your pages.

Free hosting services are inventing new revenue-generating ideas every day, often centered around advertising. Most of this stuff is no big deal to budget-conscious Web site builders, especially since paid hosting often costs $20 a month or more.

When choosing a company to host your site for free, the key considerations are the type and location of the ads they run, the amount of Web space allotted to you, the free add-ons they offer, and whether or not you are restricted to using only their site-building tools.

Figure 4-2 • Joseph Gatch's Web site showcases his artwork.

   Choose a type of ad display that doesn't drive you crazy and won't drive your visitors away. Pop-up ads can be especially obnoxious. A few services will let you choose the ad style you prefer. If you want add-ons, such as a message board, as part of your site, you may be able to hook them in directly from your free Web host. If not, you can get them elsewhere.

   Some free Web hosting services offer or require you to use their proprietary site-building tools. If it's only an option, that's fine, but if you are required to use them, consider looking elsewhere. While you might find such tools a big plus at first, they tend to restrict what you can do with your pages. Their use also means you don't have a copy of your Web site in your possession. This makes it harder to move the site somewhere else in the future if you find it necessary. You can actually save the pages to your hard drive as you view them, like any other visitor would in a Web browser, but this is a rather second-rate way of obtaining them. For these reasons, many site builders prefer Web hosts that allow them to upload files using ftp (file transfer protocol) software.

> **TIP:** *All Web site addresses start with **http://**, which indicates to your computer that documents found at the address that follow are to be retrieved and displayed using a process called HyperText Transfer Protocol. Today most Web browsers don't require you to type in the http:// part of a URL; for ease of presentation, I'm not going to show it in the Web addresses provided in this book, either.*

   If your Web site is related to a local topic or organization, look for free Web hosting provided by a locally focused portal. Sometimes a newspaper or television station provides free hosting for community organizations and nonprofits. Portals like this will often give an extra boost to your marketing efforts. Figure 4-3 shows such a community.

   There are hundreds of free hosting communities to choose from. Here's a list of a half dozen larger communities to get you started. You can find more to consider by visiting the Cheap Web Tricks Web site (**cheapwebtricks.com**) or through Yahoo!'s free Web hosting index (search for "free Web hosting").

- **BigStep** (**bigstep.com**)   Free Web hosting for businesses and nonprofits; add-on services, including credit card processing.
- **Geocities** (**geocities.com**)   Yahoo!'s free Web hosting community; lots of add-on features available. Pay a small fee to get rid of the ads, or live with them.

- **Homestead (homestead.com)** Free Web hosting for personal, small businesses, and organizations. You must use their site-building tools.
- **NetColony (netcolony.com)** Free Web hosting and ftp access so you can upload pages or use their site-building tools; lots of add-ons.
- **CheapWebTricks (cheapwebtricks.net)** When I discovered I could provide a free Web hosting alternative for you, I figured, why not? Get matching e-mail if you wish.
- **Tripod (tripod.lycos.com)** Free Web hosting with lots of add-ons.

Be sure to check out a few sample sites before you sign up for any service, and read the terms of use. That will tell you if commercial sites are allowed (some free services don't allow business use) and any other restrictions you may have to comply with.

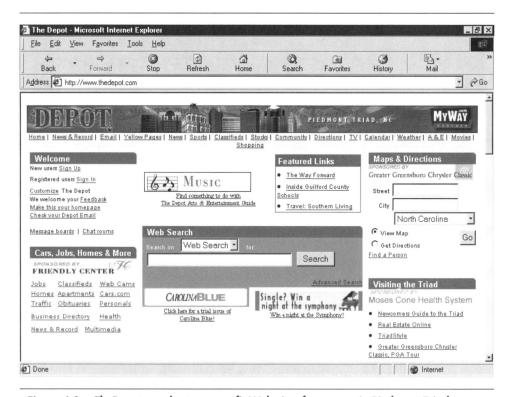

Figure 4-3 • TheDepot.com hosts nonprofit Web sites for groups in Piedmont Triad, North Carolina, for free.

ISP-Provided Page

If you connect to the Internet via America Online (AOL), MSN, or another Internet Service Provider, chances are you are allotted space for a personal Web page as part of your monthly fee. You can use this to build your Web site. This is my least favored free alternative though, for several reasons.

First of all, most people end up changing Internet service providers periodically. Although you can take your Web pages with you, you can't take the address associated with them. That means you'll have to promote your new address (wherever you put your pages next) all over again. Visitors to your old address will receive a "page not found" error and move on to other Web sites. There is a way around this problem using something called URL forwarding, which I'll explain later in this chapter.

Second, many ISPs don't allow commercial use on their hosted pages. If your Web plans include turning a profit, this simply won't do. Finally, hosting is typically an afterthought for ISPs, whose main business is connecting you to the Web. Although there are exceptions, most ISPs have their hands full providing customers with a reliable Internet connection and spend fewer resources on creating a substantial Web hosting community.

Paid Web Site Hosting

Even though there is a broad selection of sites that will host your site for free, you might choose a for-pay package instead. If you shop carefully, you can probably find a free hosting service that will meet your needs, at least for the first year or two. After that, if your site has grown tremendously, you might need to move to a more robust, paid hosting service.

One of the main things you will get with paid hosting that rarely comes with free services is POP e-mail. POP e-mail is not just a forwarding service, but rather it gives you an actual storage space (mail box) where your mail is collected. You can then retrieve your mail using any method you wish, or have it forwarded to another account. Paid hosting usually comes with a great deal of e-mail flexibility directly related to your domain. Also, your e-mail address can be linked to your Web site address, which is less common with free services. For the Web site cheapwebtricks.com, the Webmaster e-mail address is webmaster@cheapwebtricks.com. On a free hosting service, the

Webmaster would probably be using another e-mail account, such as cheapwebtricks@yahoo.com, for e-mail.

Something else that often comes with paid hosting is traffic statistics. Statistical information about who visits your Web site, how often, and how they got there is invaluable in promoting a Web site. Fortunately, there are ways to get this information (through free services), even if your Web hosting service doesn't provide it.

As with the statistics, there are other features that come packaged with paid hosting that you can get elsewhere if you're willing to deal with the inconvenience of not getting all your goodies from one source. The third frequently used item is the ability to install your own scripts for add-ons. These scripts, sometimes called CGI (common gateway interface) programs, allow you to add features like a guest book, polls, and message forums to your site. Once again, if you choose to go the free route, you can get these add-ons, without having to install and configure them yourself, using remote free resources. Doing so will give you less control over exactly how they work, but at the same time save you from technical tinkering and resource overhead you would need in order to install them yourself.

JARGON ALERT: *CGI is an acronym for Common Gateway Interface, which is a standard for communications between programs and Web server software. CGI programs are often used to add interactivity to a Web site.*

Hosting Packages

Paid Web hosting is typically sold as a bundle of services for a set monthly fee. Each package includes, at a minimum:

- **Disk space for storing your files**   You'll need less than you might imagine. A small Web site of a dozen pages can get by with 1MB (megabyte); a medium-sized site, 25MB; a large site with over a hundred graphics or multimedia files might need 100MB or more.
- **POP e-mail accounts**   Makes it possible to use *yourname@ yourdomain*.com, and retrieve that mail from your Web server, instead of using a separate e-mail address that is unrelated to your domain name.
- **Data transfer allotment**   Every time a visitor comes to your site, the pages and images are sent (transferred) from your hosting

service to the visitor's computer. The more visitors your site has, the larger data transfer allotment you will need. A small site for an individual or organization, with light traffic and a few graphics, would use less than 100MB of data transfer a month; a fairly heavily visited site with many pages, 500MB per month; and a hugely popular site more than that.

- **FTP access**   This allows you to upload files you've created on your own computer, using password-protected connection.
- **Technical support**   Either by e-mail only or by e-mail and phone.
- **A selection of tools**   Helps you to upload and manage your site.

Some packages will also include these features:

- **Your own CGI-BIN directory**   This is a special location where you can install those scripts I mentioned earlier.
- **Web site statistics package**   To generate statistics you can use, a program is run against raw log files, and a graphical display of the information is created. It tells you how many times your site has been visited, which pages are most popular, and it tracks this information over time. You should be able to view the graphical display online. This report may be generated daily, weekly, or monthly, depending on the hosting service.
- **Server Side Includes (SSI)**   You can direct the Web server to preprocess certain pages before delivering them to visitors. This allows the Web site builder (you!) the flexibility to dynamically combine information from different sources into a single display page.
- **Telnet access**   This gives you password-protected access to the actual operating system on your Web server. Most Webmasters don't need or use this, as most development tasks can be accomplished through Web interfaces and ftp.
- **E-mail aliasing**   You can create e-mail addresses that automatically redirect received mail to another address.
- **Autoresponder**   A program linked to a particular e-mail address automatically sends a predefined response to any address it receives e-mail from. These are often used to distribute frequently requested information, such as a schedule or product list.
- **Mailing lists**   Software for creating and managing e-mail subscriber lists is included in some hosting packages.
- **FrontPage support**   This means that the hosting service has installed special modules that support special proprietary features of the Web site design tool Microsoft FrontPage.

- **Secure server access**   Special software used to process transactions that involve sensitive information, such as credit card numbers. Only needed for sites that will sell things online. More on this in Chapter 14.

> **TIP:**   You can also get almost all of these things via either free Web hosting providers or free services available online, but you will have to spend more time shopping around. Novice Web designers often find that the free versions are easier to install and manage, and better documented.

The costs for Web hosting packages vary widely. Prices have dropped dramatically as the Web has grown, and with diligent shopping you can find a reasonable starter package for under $10 a month. For large data transfer allotments and more features, prices ranging from $20 to $50 per month are common. Figure 4-4 shows how one Web hosting provider bundles its services into different levels and prices.

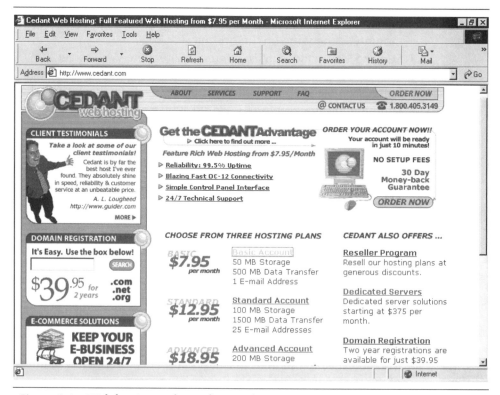

Figure 4-4 • Web hosting packages from Cedant

Setting Up Your Own Web Server

The third Web hosting possibility is to set up your own server and Internet connection. This is the most expensive option of all and most technically demanding and time-consuming. The frugal among us probably won't even consider it, but in case you're considering taking the plunge, the basics you'll need are

- A computer running your choice of Linux, Unix, or Windows operating system.
- Web server software, such as Apache, NCSA HTTPD, or Microsoft's Internet Information Server (IIS).
- A high-speed, preferably always on, Internet connection.

You can obtain the server software, and even some computer operating systems, for free, but the rest is going to cost you. Perhaps more daunting than the expense is the expertise involved. Although anyone willing to dig and learn can set up an Internet server, getting it to run smoothly and securely takes substantial specialized knowledge beyond the scope of this book. You'll probably want to pick up a specialized book on the topic, such as *IIS 5.0, A Beginner's Guide* by Rod Trent (Osborne/McGraw-Hill, 2001) and *Apache Server 2.0: A Beginner's Guide* by Kate Wrightson (Osborne/McGraw-Hill, 2001).

For details on how to set up your own Web server using Windows 98 Second Edition, try the ServerWatch tutorial "Build Your Own Home Server," which can be found at **serverwatch.internet.com/articles/buildserver/**. If you're considering a Linux-based Web server, LinuxPlanet's "Setting Up Your Own Web Server" (**www.linuxplanet.com/linuxplanet/tutorials/212/7**) will get you started.

Flavors of Hosting

When you start shopping for a Web host, you're likely to encounter several terms describing hosting alternatives: virtual hosting, nonvirtual (or subdomain) hosting, and dedicated hosting. Sometimes the word "server" is used instead of "hosting," as in virtual server. Here's what they mean:

- **Subdomain hosting**   Your Web site is hosted using a custom subdomain name. Your address would be something like http://*mysite*.bigwebhost.com or, alternatively, http://bigwebhost.com/*mysite*. Although it will have a unique address, your Web site

will be physically sharing a computer with other Web sites. This
is also called *nonvirtual hosting.*

- **Virtual hosting**   Your Web site is hosted using your own domain
  name. Your address would be something like http://*mysite*.org.
  Your Web site will be physically sharing a computer with other
  Web sites (but not a domain name).

- **Dedicated hosting**   This is similar to virtual hosting, but on a
  computer that serves your Web site alone. This is usually only
  used by Web sites with extremely high traffic or mission-critical
  applications.

Your Web Site Address

No matter where you put it, your Web site will have an address that will
allow people to locate it. The technical term for a Web address is URL,
which is short for Uniform Resource Locator. A URL is like the address
of your home: a unique identifier that tells people exactly what to type
into their Web browser if they want to visit your site. When I suggest
an online resource to you, I give you its URL so you can type that
into your browser and view the resource. A URL can be long, like
people-places.com/womenshockey/index.html or short, like *yourname*.org.
That's because, like your home address, a Web site address (aka URL)
can have multiple parts that get more specific as they go along. You can
tell people you live on Maple Street, or 1234 Maple Street, or 1234 Maple
Street in apartment 2B. A Web site address can tell people where to find
the Web site, or where to find a specific page or section of it.

JARGON ALERT: *URL is short for Uniform Resource Locator.
It's the address you type into your browser to visit a particular Web
page and looks something like http://cheapwebtricks.com/
index.shtml.*

How Domain Names Work

At the heart of every URL lies a domain name, which is constructed
following special rules. You really don't have to know all the ins and
outs of the domain naming system in order to build and promote a Web

site, but a good grasp of the basics will make it easier to choose your initial Web hosting alternative and, later, to analyze where visitors to your Web site came from—information that you can use to make your site even more successful. So here's how it works.

JARGON ALERT: *IP (pronounced as separate letters) stands for Internet Protocol and is the addressing scheme used on the Internet. An IP address consists of four numbers separated by periods and uniquely identifies each computer directly connected to the Internet.*

Every computer connected to the Internet has a unique identifying number, called an IP (Internet Protocol) address. An IP address looks something like this: **216.115.108.243**. While numbers are the language of computers, human beings find it much easier to remember addresses made up of alphabetic characters, like this: **yahoo.com**. Type either one of these into the address bar on your Web browser, and you'll end up in the same place: the Yahoo! Web site. What was that IP address again? If you're like most people, you can't answer without rereading it. But odds are you can easily recall its alphanumeric alternative: yahoo.com.

JARGON ALERT: *A domain name is an English-like substitution for an IP address (or collection of IP addresses). Domain names are easier than IP addresses for humans to remember and type without error.*

Yahoo.com is a *domain name*. The system of using an alphanumeric name instead of an IP address for identifying a computer on the Internet is called the *domain name system*. A basic domain name consists of two parts, separated by a period (or *dot*). The rightmost part—"com" in our example—is called the top-level domain (TLD). You can't just pick any TLD you can think of. Top-level domains are chosen and administered by a central authority, currently the Internet Corporation for Assigned Names and Numbers (ICANN), and are intended to have particular meanings (although they aren't always used in the intended way).

Some of the more commonly used TLDs and their meanings are shown in the following table:

TLD	Used By	Example
com	A commercial entity	yahoo.com
org	Nonprofit organization	adoption.org
net	Network-related organizations, such as ISPs	bellsouth.net
gov	U.S. government organizations	nsf.gov
edu	Educational institutions	mit.edu
mil	U.S. military organizations	army.mil

Since Yahoo! is a business, it has a top-level domain of "com." Most of the above TLDs are not linked to any particular country, but many countries do have their own TLD designation. For example: uk = United Kingdom, ru = Russia, au = Australia, us = United States, tv = Tuvalu.

The section of the domain name to the left of the TLD, called the second-level domain, identifies a subdomain within the top-level domain—often but not always an individual computer. Unlike the TLD portion, this portion does not have to be selected from a limited list. It can be any combination of alphanumeric characters (up to 67 characters in most cases) that isn't already in use by another computer, for example, womenshealth, 123-go, or yahoo.

Remember that I said a basic domain name consists of two parts? As you've probably guessed, domain names can also have more pieces. The good news is that once you understand how a basic, two-part name works, you can decipher any domain name. That's because the domain naming system is hierarchical, like this:

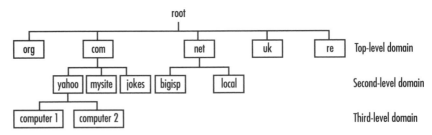

As you can see in the above illustration, each subdomain of a domain name further subdivides the level above it. So, a domain name like computer1.yahoo.com would identify a machine called computer1, which is part of the second-level domain yahoo, which is a member of the top-level domain com.

The purpose of this nesting business is to make it possible for one computer to find another on the Internet in an efficient way. Imagine for a moment that all the addresses of everyone in the world were listed in a single monstrous phone book. Looking up the address of a friend in another state would take a very long time, especially if you had to wait in line behind thousands of people wanting to use the same phone book. If you could go to a phone book just for the area your friend lives in, you wouldn't have to share it with so many people, and there would be a lot fewer pages to look through.

This same system works for the Internet. When your computer needs to find another computer on the Web, it starts with a root server at the top of the hierarchy, which tells it where to find the address information for all members of the specified TLD (com in our computer1.yahoo.com example). This leads to the phonebook for yahoo domain, which quickly spits out the IP address of computer1. By distributing the lookup job like this, the process of locating any one of the millions of computers connected to the Web can be accomplished in a matter of milliseconds.

How does a particular computer get a particular domain name? Someone picks it out and registers it through one of the internationally recognized domain registration authorities, called domain registrars. Figure 4-5 shows the home page of one of these companies. The price of registering a domain name varies depending on choice of TLD and which registrar is used. As this was written, com, org, and net domains could be registered for $35 per year or less. A bit later in this chapter I'll tell you why you might want to get one, and how to do so.

Sharing a Domain Name

Every Web site doesn't have its own domain name. Remember how I said that a domain name is at the heart of every Web site address (URL)? By adding more information to a URL, you can use it to identify different Web sites within a single domain.

Returning to our earlier analogy comparing Web addresses to home addresses, if the domain name is the street part of the address (Maple Street), then additional parts of the URL can identify which building (Web site) on the street, and which apartment (section of the Web site) within the building. So, if the organization that owns the domain name people-places.com uses it to host multiple Web sites, one Web site could have the URL people-places.com/womenshockey/, while another is people-places.com/homerepair/. So you don't have to have your own domain name to have a Web site—you can use someone else's. As I mentioned earlier in this chapter, this is called nonvirtual hosting, or subdomain hosting.

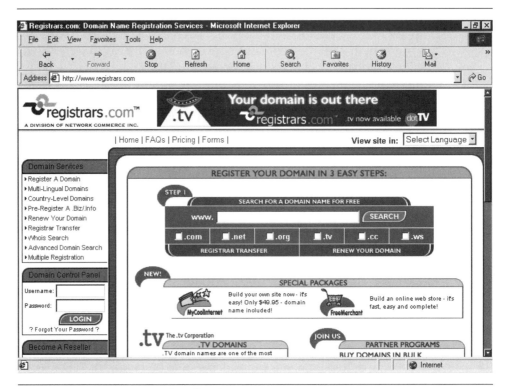

Figure 4-5 • Registrars.com handles domain name registrations.

Sometimes, instead of providing you with a URL like this, a hosting service will create a subdomain for you that accomplishes the same thing (sharing a domain name) but results in a differently formatted address. In this case, the URL would be something like homerepair. people-places.com. Web site builders sometimes prefer an address using the second method because they feel it makes it less obvious that they are sharing a domain. Most free hosting services provide subdomain hosting with addresses like these. Paid hosting services typically give you a choice of sharing their domain name or using your own.

Your Own Domain Name

You might decide that it's worthwhile to own your own domain name, whether or not you use a free hosting service. There are two major benefits of doing so:

- Greater control over choosing a memorable address for your site
- The option to move your site to another hosting service while retaining the same address

When you share a domain name, your Web site address will be longer and less unique. For many Web site builders, this isn't a problem, especially when it saves you domain registration fees. But in some cases, especially for commercial Web sites, a distinctive and short Web site address is a big plus. A short address is easier to promote, simpler for potential clients and visitors to remember, and can be used as part of efforts to increase brand awareness of your group or business. It also tends to look more official when included in promotional materials or on business cards. If having an address like annemartinez.com rather than annemartinez.homestead.com is important to you, consider registering your own domain name.

The second reason, keeping your address even if you change Web hosts, is more compelling. Let's say you decide to use bigfreeWebhost.net as your free hosting service, and they give you the address *yoursite*.bigfreewebhost.net. You build and publish and promote your site and everything is going along great, but then, six months or a year down the road, you decide you need greater flexibility than this host provides. Or perhaps bigfreewebhost.net goes out of business. It's a simple enough matter to move the pages that make up your Web site to another host, but when you do, you're also going to have a new Web address—something like *yoursite*.anotherwebhost.net.

Suddenly none of your previous visitors will be able to find it. If you've included the Web site address on promotional materials, business cards, and so on, you're going to have to reprint those with the new address. All the effort you've spent getting your site included in search engines will have to be repeated, using the new address. This can be a major drag, and potentially expensive. If you have your own domain name, you can simply change the IP address associated with it if you change hosting services. Your visitors never need know or be bothered by your change of Web hosts.

That said, many Webmasters have set their sites up on a free Web host, using the address that was given to them for free, and are happily cruising along with no complications (and no registration fees) years later. It's a personal choice for you to make.

Choosing a Domain Name

If you do decide that your own domain name is a must-have, then choose one with care. The best domain names are short, memorable, and related to the purpose of your Web site. They're also probably already taken.

Sorry for the bad news, but I'd be remiss if I didn't warn you. There are a few pieces of good news in this department as well. Although the obvious domain names have pretty much been snapped up, by employing a little creativity you can probably come up with one that will do the job admirably and is still available. Second, the powers that decide such things are in the process of adding more top-level domains, which means that all of the possible subdomains beneath them will be open to the first comers. You may not be able to get stevesart.com, but maybe you can get stevesart.biz, when that TLD becomes available. Here are some more guidelines to follow:

- When choosing a domain name, pick something that is easy to type and hard to misspell. For example: NHL.com instead of NationalHockeyLeague.com.
- Although dashes are allowed (as in "computer-services") avoid them if you can.
- Don't try to snag someone else's registered trademark as your domain name. Whoever owns that trademark may try to take it from you, and they'll probably succeed. But even if they don't, the resulting legal fees and aggravation can pile up over several years.
- If your ideal domain name is already taken, think of variations that will work nearly as well. For example, if test.com is taken, try 2test.com, or testcentral.com.

If your creative powers need a kick start, try a few of the online domain name suggestion services from the directory located at **dmoz.org/Computers/Internet/Domain_Names/Name_Search/Name_Generators/**. These let you enter a few words related to your topic, and then they suggest domain names that incorporate them.

NOTE: *Although it's unlikely you'll want to go to this extreme, Barnes and Noble took the step of registering several versions of its name, including misspellings. For example, barnesandnobel.com, barnesandnoble.com, barnsandnobl.com, bn.com, and a dozen other permutations of the company name will all take you to the bookseller's Web site.*

To check on whether a potential domain name is still available, you'll want to use a tool called WHOIS. The easiest place to get this is to go to the Network Solutions Web site WHOIS page at **www.networksolutions.com/cgi-bin/whois/whois**. Enter the domain name, without the **http://** or **www**, and click the Search button. If the domain is already registered, the current ownership information will be displayed on a page like the one shown in Figure 4-6. If it's not already taken, you'll get a message telling you it's still available instead.

Registering a Domain Name

Once you settle on an available domain name, it's time to register it before anyone else has the same great idea. There used to be just one company (registrar) performing this service, but now you can choose from a variety of domain name registrars. Two of the most used are **registrars.com** and Network Solutions (**networksolutions.com**). These companies can register domains in the com, org, net, and a few other popular TLDs. If you're after a TLD associated with a specific country (for example uk, us, or ru), you can find the proper registrar through the Internet Assigned Number Authority (IANA) at **www.iana.org/cctld/ cctld-whois.htm**.

TIP: *If you are signing up for paid Web hosting, many hosting services will offer to register your domain name for you for free. It's a better idea to do it yourself so you can be sure it's registered in your name, not theirs, and so you know where to go if you need to change the registration information later.*

We're not going to go through each step of the process, because the actual forms you'll fill out will vary depending on which registrar you use. You'll have to enter the domain you want to register, choose a registration term (one year up to ten years), enter your contact information, and payment information.

You'll also encounter a section asking for domain name server (DNS) information for whoever will be hosting your Web site, which will include space for two IP addresses. If you've already selected a hosting service, enter the information they supplied. If not, leave it blank—you can come back and fill it in later.

Figure 4-6 • WHOIS identifies the domain yahoo.com as already taken.

Free Domain Names

Since this is a book about free stuff, you've probably been wondering if it's possible to get a domain name for free. The answer is yes, and no. I've seen a few free domain registration offers come and go, and usually they just have too many strings attached to be worth serious consideration.

For example, as of this writing, Domain Names for Free (**www .domainnameforfree.com**) was hawking free domain names, but you'd have to buy other services from them in order to receive one. Another offer, from **www.freebonds.ws**, will charge you $70 to register a domain name in the .ws TLD, and then send you a $75 U.S. government savings bond. Of course, if you cashed that bond in as soon as possible, which would be six months after the issue date, it would be worth about $38.

The bottom line is that you don't need your own domain name to run a Web site, and if you decide you want one anyway, the cost is so minimal to register it yourself that it's just not worth the risk and hassle of any of the "free" domain offers that are currently out there.

The Rest of the URL Story

Now that you know all about the domain part of Web addresses, it's time to wrap up our discussion of how URLs work. You might have noticed that some URLs consist of just a domain name (for example, cheapwebtricks.com), while others have some extra stuff stuck on at the end, like this: cheapwebtricks.com/create/freeisp.shtml. The first URL will bring you to the home page of the Cheap Web Tricks Web site, while the second brings you to a specific page of the site. In this example, the second URL would display the page called freeisp.shtml, which is in the Create section of the cheapwebtricks.com site.

URL Forwarding

One service that is worth a serious look is domain name forwarding. And yes, you can get it for free.

URL forwarding (also called domain forwarding or URL redirection) allows you to connect a custom domain name with a particular Web site, even if the company hosting your site doesn't provide that service. So if you sign up for free Web hosting that provides you with a URL like bigfreehostservice.com/really/ridiculouslylongurl/joesmith, you can replace it with a shorter, custom URL (like joe.freeurl.com) that automatically forwards to the longer one. This allows you to move from host to host and keep the same URL for your Web site. So, for example, if you are using free Web space provided by your ISP, and you change ISPs, thus losing that free space, you could simply change the redirecting service URL to forward people to your Web site's new location. Visitors will never even know that your site has moved; they will keep using the same URL to reach you that they always have.

You can use a URL forwarding service with a domain you registered and own. If you don't have one, some services will provide you with a subdomain of their domain (still shorter than old ridiculouslylong). Using free domain forwarding services in operation as this was written, the above URL could effectively be replaced with something like go.to/joesmith, joesmith.vdirect.com, or .joe.millionaire-inc.com. In some cases, the redirect service will also provide a matching e-mail account.

Browse through a variety of URL forwarding services before choosing one. Some will put advertising on your page, others don't. If you intend to register a domain name of your own, shop around among registrars because some (such as **lowcostdomains.com**) offer free domain forwarding if you register through them. Here are a few forwarding services to get you started. You can find more through Yahoo! by searching on "free URL forwarding" (include the quotes).

- **cjb.net**   Forwarding with no ads, unless you opt to display them in exchange for cash. Example: poetry.cjb.net
- **freeurl.com**   An extensive selection of custom domain forwarding URLs, some with advertising, some without. Example: yourname.freeurl.com
- **Jaze Web Services (iscool.net)**   A variety of interesting domain names offered, including iscool.net, isfun.net. Example: joe.iscool.net
- **v3.com**   Your choice of go.to, come.to, or i.am addresses with companion e-mail. Example: go.to/mysite

As always, don't just pick the first service you come across, but compare several until you find the one you like best. Be sure to read the terms of usage to avoid any ugly surprises later on.

The Bottom Line

We've covered a lot in this chapter, but it's important that you understand your options so that you can choose wisely. To summarize what we've discussed:

- Free Web hosting is widely available and will suffice for many Web sites.
- Free Web hosting typically comes with an address like either *yourname*.freehost.com or freehost.com/*yourname*.
- If you don't like your free hosting address, you can register your own domain name and/or use URL forwarding to attach a domain name you do like to your site.
- All hosting services, free or paid, have terms of use you must abide by or they will turn off your site. This usually means no pornography, but sometimes also includes a ban on commercial sites. Always read the terms of any service before signing up.

Up to this point, we've talked about clarifying your Web site goals, getting connected to the Web, and finding a home for your site. Next up on our hit list is a discussion of site-building tools. The next chapter will explore exactly what tools you'll need and where to get them without spending a dime.

5

Chapter Five

Choosing Site Creation Tools

There are several ways you can create your Web site without spending a dime. No fancy tools are required, though they can make the job easier. It's even possible to create a Web site using nothing but your Web browser (such as Netscape or Internet Explorer). Many of you, though, will prefer the flexibility and low-level control offered by building Web pages using more traditional methods that employ other tools. This chapter will cover the tools you will need for the method that is best for you.

Instant Web Pages

Homestead has a rather amazing free Web site design tool called SiteBuilder that runs completely within your browser. (There's a version you can download and run on your own computer, too.) The tool allows you to create, customize, and save Web pages for your Homestead site. You can insert special features (called *elements*) such as a poll, message board, map, photo albums, and even commission-based links to online stores. Here's how you do it:

1. Go to the Homestead Web site (**homestead.com**), which is shown in Figure 5-1.
2. Sign up for a free Web site.
3. Choose the Use Page Wizard option and follow the directions (see Figure 5-2).

Yes, it's really as simple as that. Although Homestead's SiteBuilder will only work on computers running the Windows operating system, there is a stripped down "Express" version that runs on any system, including WebTV and Macintosh.

Some site builders may find Homestead's products to be the perfect option for their first Web venture. A graphical interface like the one Homestead SiteBuilder uses can be helpful when creating those first Web pages, but it can quickly become tedious and constricting. It's also important to realize that if you build your Web site using Homestead's

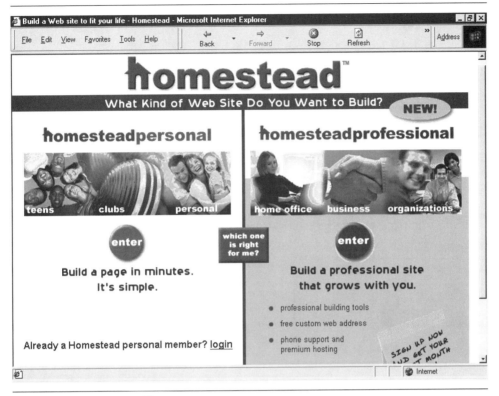

Figure 5-1 • Homestead home page

proprietary elements, moving your site to another location in the future will be difficult if not impossible; you are locked into staying with Homestead for the foreseeable future. This doesn't mean that you shouldn't use them; it's just a consideration to keep in mind.

Advanced Site Building

You may prefer to build your Web site using tools that allow you to modify the code behind the page directly, in any manner you wish to,

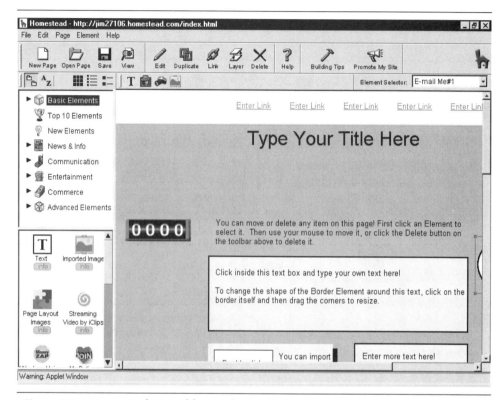

Figure 5-2 • Homestead SiteBuilder can be run via a web browser.

with a lot less hand-holding along the way. By the way, that doesn't mean you can't still use Homestead as a host for the site.

If sticking with an all-in-one tool isn't always the easiest or the best option, what will you really need?

- An authoring tool to assist you in creating the pages
- An FTP (File Transfer Protocol) program so you can move your files to and from your Web site host at will
- A graphics package or individual tools that let you create and tinker with images (less critical, but very useful)

Whatware?

When it comes to software, the word "free" is not always as straightforward as it seems. As you begin to troll the Web for free software, you're going to encounter several different kinds of "free." The definitions below will help you sort out what's what.

- **Freeware** This is copyrighted software that is given away by the author for the purposes the author allows, which often means free for personal use only; commercial users must pay.
- **Public domain software** These programs have been placed in the public domain by their creators. They are not copyrighted. They are free, and you can do anything with them you wish.
- **Shareware** Think of this as software on the honor system. Shareware is not free, but you get to try it for free. If you like it and use it regularly, you are supposed to send a check to the program's publisher, usually for a small amount. The registration fee typically gets you product support and often free updates.
- **Crippleware** This is shareware or a demo version of a commercial program that stops working if you don't become a registered user within a specified period of time, or has critical functions, such at the ability to save your work, disabled.

Authoring Tools

At the opposite extreme of the strictly graphical Web site-building tool is the plain text editor. Using any program that allows you to enter and manipulate text, such as Windows Notepad or SimpleText on the Macintosh, you can create Web pages. It's slow and tedious though. You have to remember every HTML tag yourself and type them in one at a time. Hardly anyone creates Web pages this way anymore, not even die-hard geeks. And why would you want to? There are a number of full-featured HTML (HyperText Markup Language—the "code" Web pages are written in) editors available for free.

HTML Editors

I mentioned in Chapter 1 that writing in HTML consists of placing tags like <BOLD> </BOLD> around ordinary text. There are many of these tags, and they can be combined in lots of different ways. Since typing things like <BOLD> over and over again can quickly grow tiresome, and remembering all of the HTML tags and their attributes is a challenge, it's a perfect job for a computer program. Thanks to some enterprising individuals, there's a generous selection of these programs (called HTML editors or authoring tools), available for free online.

Why are people and companies willing to give these away? The reasons vary, but most commonly, the free software is a scaled-down version of another, for-purchase product that the seller hopes you'll buy. Potential economic gain isn't the only reason. The author of one such program, Arachnophilia, asks that you

> "…stop whining for an hour, a day, a week, your choice, and you will have earned your copy of Arachnophilia. Say encouraging words to young people, make them feel welcome on the planet earth (many do not),…"

and then goes on to say that if you don't want to comply with this, you can have the software anyway.

HTML editors vary in the features offered. Even the most basic ones include such things as

- Automatic completion of tags
- Ability to select tags from a list
- Color coding in the document so that the formatting is easier to pick out
- Buttons that can perform common tasks with a single click
- A choice of available attributes for any specific tag, allowing you to select those you desire (and the program generates the final tag for you)

Many programs go much further. Often they provide both text and graphical interfaces, and allow you to toggle between them, giving you the best of both worlds in Web development. You have as much control as possible, yet you can easily switch to a view that will show you what your page will look like to a visitor. Figures 5-3 and 5-4 show the text and graphical views of the same Web page, using a free HTML editor.

Site-Building Packages

HTML editors are sometimes packaged with additional programs and features designed to simplify the tasks of creating and managing a Web site. For example, such a package might have built-in FTP capabilities (I'll explain a bit further in a minute), which allow you to upload your pages without using a separate program. Another might offer a link-checking facility, which simplifies the task of checking your pages for broken or dead links to other pages. A third might check your HTML for errors and suggest corrections or provide project management tools. Such packages are full-blown Web site authoring tools, and rival many that are commercially available.

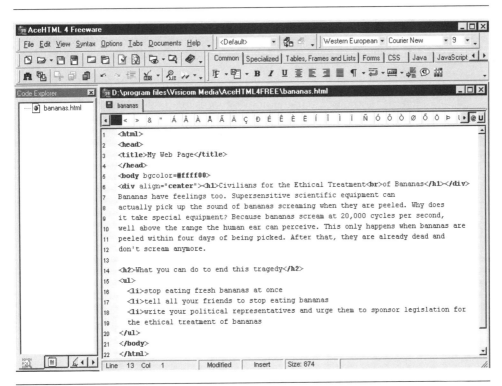

Figure 5-3 • **A Web page being worked on using the AceHTML free authoring tool**

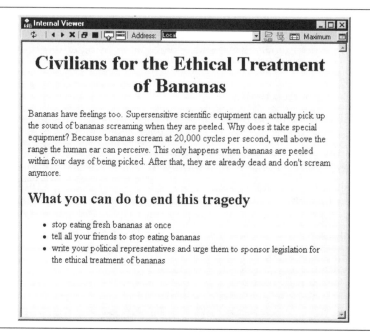

Figure 5-4 • The same Web page using AceHTML's preview feature

Here are some of the free authoring tools available at the time of writing:

Free Authoring Tools	Description
AceHTML **freeware.acehtml.com**	Free HTML editor complete with templates, JavaScript, extended replace, and more. Runs on Windows.
CutePageHTML editor **cutepage.com**	Both code and visual editing modes; includes tools to create buttons, menus, and more. Runs on Windows.
EasyHTML **javascript-page.com/easyhtml**	Color-coded HTML tags, built-in preview, helper buttons to automate common tasks. Runs on Windows.
Screem **screem.org**	An acronym for Site Creating & Editing Environment; includes preview window, tag lists, spell check, and more. Runs on Linux.

NOTE: *I tried to find free Web site building tools for Mac users too, but sorry to say, they're hard to come by. You may be able to run the Windows programs under a PC emulator, if you happen to have one, or take advantage of free trials of commercial packages.*

Commercial Authoring Tools

You really, really don't need to shell out a single dollar for a Web authoring tool. But if someone offers to give one to you, or you have a compelling reason to open your wallet, three popular commercial packages are FrontPage, Dreamweaver, and HomeSite.

FrontPage is Microsoft's site-building tool. It's pretty popular among new Web developers. The program includes many site management features along with basic HTML editing capability. You can also use it to add a database interface or insert special components such as a message board into your pages. Be forewarned that if you use any of the proprietary components, you'll only be able to publish your site to a hosting service that has installed special programs to support those components, or they won't work. Plus, some special features you can use are only viewable by visitors using Microsoft's Internet Explorer browser. It retails for about $150 and runs on Windows computers. Figure 5-5 shows what the interface looks like.

Dreamweaver is a Macromedia product. It's been a favorite among designers who prefer a graphical interface, although the most recent versions are more friendly to hand-coders, too. This is a robust package with text and design modes and includes tools to facilitate collaboration among multiple designers working on a single site. All the standard project management and site management features (link checking and so on) are included. It integrates well with Macromedia's other products. The street price is about $280. It runs on Windows or Macintosh computers.

HomeSite is a little less well known than the other two, but advanced Web designers have been using it for years for its straightforward and efficient Web design capabilities. HomeSite was originally a product of the Allaire Corporation, which has since merged with Macromedia. It's not as heavy on bells and whistles, and the price of $90 reflects that. It runs on Windows computers. Figure 5-6 shows what the development interface looks like.

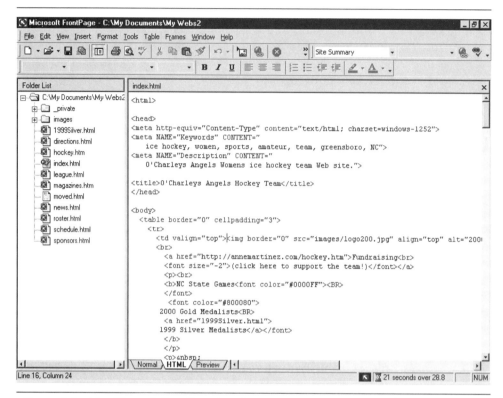

Figure 5-5 • The Microsoft FrontPage interface

If you need a commercial authoring program that will run on something other than Windows or Macintosh—say, Linux—your options are very limited. Consider WebSphere Homepage Builder (**www-4.ibm.com/software/webservers/hpbuilder**) and CoffeeCup (**www.coffeecup.com**), both of which are very inexpensive. CoffeeCup is also available in a Windows version.

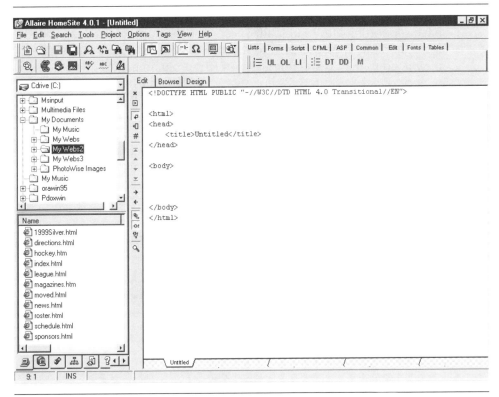

Figure 5-6 • The HomeSite interface

FTP Programs

FTP stands for File Transfer Protocol. It's a method used to send and receive files over the Internet. You're going to be doing a lot of this as you work on your Web site. The initial pages you create will need to be uploaded to your hosting service, and every time you modify one, you'll need to upload the new version.

In addition to the HTML pages, from time to time you're going to have supporting files to upload. These include graphics (such as your logo), and any files you plan to make available for your visitors to download to their own computer. An FTP program makes this process a piece of cake. Figure 5-7 shows what one looks like.

Although, like any other piece of software, an FTP program can be fluffed up and bloated with dozens of unnecessary extras, its basic functions are straightforward. You'll need to enter the FTP login information for your hosting service (they will provide this to you), and then click the Connect button. Once the connection is made, you select which files you wish to transfer and where you want to transfer them

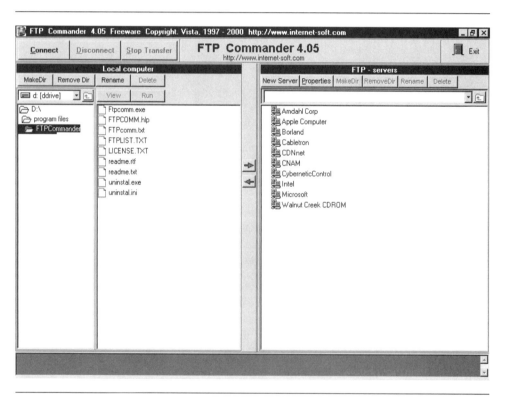

Figure 5-7 • The FTP Commander startup screen

within your Web site, click another button, and you're done. I'll walk you through the process in Chapter 9. Meanwhile, grab one of these free FTP programs so you'll be ready to go:

Free FTP Programs	Platform
ws_ftp LE **wsftp.com**	Runs on Windows. Look on the product download page for the LE (light edition).
FTP Commander **internet-soft.com/ftpcomm.htm**	Runs on Windows.
FTP Now **surf.to/ftpnow**	Runs on Windows.
FTPWizard **cyberkare.com/products.html**	Runs on Mac.
Comfortable FTP **www.giga.or.at/pub/nih/cftp/**	Runs under Linux, X Windows.

Even if you settle on an authoring package that includes built-in FTP capabilities, you might wish to have a separate FTP program. It's nice to have a simple, uncluttered interface for uploading files without needing to run a full-blown authoring environment.

Graphics Tools

Good-looking graphics make a Web site interesting and eye-catching. They're indispensable for displaying your logo, showing what a product looks like, or sharing your firstborn's first smile. To use them effectively, you're going to need a few more software tools.

Graphics Editors

A graphics editor lets you create and modify images. Full-blown packages used by graphics designers cost hundreds of dollars. Adobe PhotoShop, one of the hottest sellers around, goes for $500+. But you know I don't expect you to spend that much. In fact, you don't have to spend anything at all. Here's a list of free graphics editors that allow you to create and manipulate images:

Free Graphics Editors	Description
Adobe Create a Graphic **webservices.adobe.com/graphic/ main.html**	Completely Web-based graphics editor lets you create images from scratch or upload and modify an existing image. Works with Netscape Navigator or Internet Explorer.
GIFWorks **www.gifworks.com**	Another completely online tool that helps you create Web site graphics, even animated ones! Shown in Figure 5-8, GIFWorks works with Netscape Navigator or Internet Explorer.
ImageForge Freeware Edition **www.cursorarts.com/ca_imffw.html**	Create and edit images using many drawing tools. Windows compatible.
Photogenics Demo Version **www.paulnolan.com/home.html**	Graphics package for creating and manipulating images. Runs on Linux, Windows, or AmigaOS.
VCW Vicman's Photo Editor **www.vicman.net/vcwphoto**	Full-blown image editor that supports 30 different image formats. Windows compatible.

TIP: *In the interests of expediency, you can probably get by for a bit without your own graphics editor, especially if you make use of freebies in the graphics gadgets listed throughout this chapter.*

Image Crunchers

Graphics can be one of the coolest features of a Web site, but they can also be its greatest drawback. That's because images take a whole lot longer than text does to appear on a visitor's computer screen. To keep from driving impatient surfers away, you need to make the files containing your graphics as small and compact as you possibly can, so they will appear more quickly. This is accomplished by compressing the files. The challenge is to make the file smaller without substantially reducing the quality of the image.

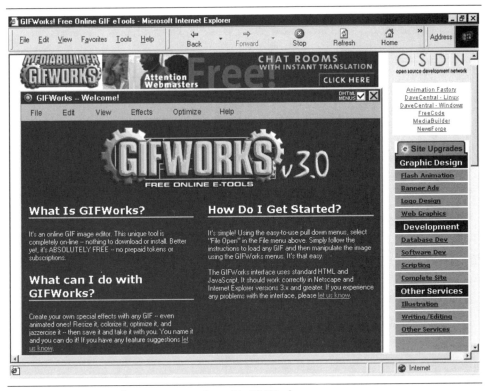

Figure 5-8 • **Free online image creation with GIFWorks.**

Some graphics editing programs contain a compression feature that automatically springs into action when you choose "Save for Web." There are also quite a few stand-alone programs that will do it more quickly, and in some cases, more efficiently. Try these for starters:

Free Compression Programs	Description
Adobe Optimize an Image **webservices.adobe.com/optimize/ main.html**	Online image compression tool works with many different file formats.
GIFBot **netmechanic.com/GIFBot/ optimize-graphic.htm**	This online tool, shown in Figure 5-9, lets you specify a GIF graphic either on the Web or on your hard drive and creates a selection of compressed alternatives for you to choose from.
JPEG Wizard Online Optimizer **www.jpegwizard.com**	Shrink your JPEG graphics with either the online or downloadable version of this tool.

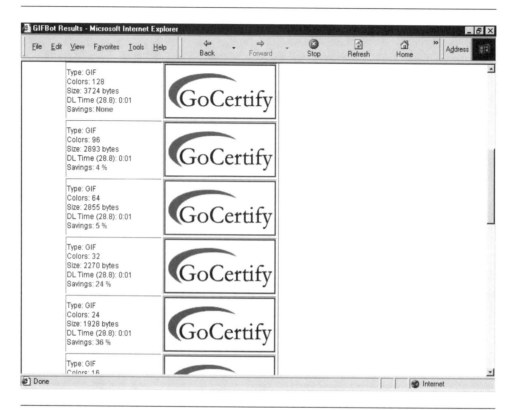

Figure 5-9 • GIFBot offers a choice of optimization levels.

Other Graphics Gadgets

A graphics editor and image cruncher may be the graphics tools a
Web builder turns to most often, but there are a bunch of other free
and handy graphics gadgets that can make your life easier. Here are
two of my favorites:

Free Miscellaneous Graphics Tools	Description
Cool Archive Logo Generator **coolarchive.com/logogen.cfm**	Create a nifty logo in GIF or JPG format for free, online.
CoolText **cooltext.com**	Make spiffy buttons, logos, and bullets online to your specifications.

As more and more Web site building tools appear online for free, it's easier than ever to create a professional-looking Web site. In the next chapter, we'll run through a few design basics. Then it's time to let loose all of those great ideas that have been building up in your mind and start creating your Web pages.

6

Chapter Six

Effective Web Site Design

Other than abstract artwork, there isn't much that won't come out much better if built with a design plan in mind. Even advanced works of art are usually created only after an underlying structure is envisioned and sketched into place. While a Web site doesn't require a detailed set of blueprints in the way building a home does, an underlying design plan is critical to creating a Web site that visitors will return to again and again.

A Model for Web Site Structure

You already started on your Web site building plans in Chapter 2, when you clarified the motive behind your site, identified its potential audiences, and considered what those audiences will want and need from you. Now it's time to actually lay out the structure of your site so that it will provide those things. Figure 6-1 shows a model for you to follow.

As you can see, this model looks at a Web site as a hierarchy with three levels: home page, main topic pages, and detail pages. A Web site can have more levels, or fewer, but it will still follow the same basic structure. A three-level structure is very common.

The Home Page

The front door to any Web site is its home page. Every Web site has one, and it serves as an introduction and quick directory to what lies deeper within. It's the first view most visitors will have of your creation.

If you want people to stick around, your home page should immediately identify your site's purpose and give visitors an idea of the kind of

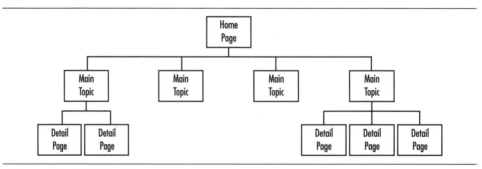

Figure 6-1 • Web site layout

content your site contains. It also has to tell visitors how to find that content. It would be a shame if a visitor left when you had the answer she was seeking, and she just couldn't tell it was there.

To add to the challenge, the majority of this information should be conveyed in the top four inches or so—that's the amount of the page that most users will see without having to scroll down.

Main Topic Pages

The second row of Figure 6-1 consists of a set of main topic pages, one for each key area of the site. The home page will link to each of them. The number of main topic pages will depend on how you decide to organize your information, using the analysis you conducted in Chapter 2. (You did do that, didn't you?)

Detail Pages

The final row of our Web site structure model consists of detail pages. These pages provide further information about the related main topic. A main topic might have many detail pages, or none.

Navigation

You can have all kinds of great stuff on your site, but if people can't find it, it might as well not be there. It should be so astoundingly easy to find information on your Web pages that a grade-schooler could do it. If you make it simple enough for a kid, most adults will be able to handle it, too. As a general rule, no page should be more than a few mouse clicks from any other. Aim to keep it to one or two. If you follow the Web site structure we've been discussing, this is simple to accomplish.

Navigation, or the way people find their way from Point A to Point B on your site, is accomplished through the use of hyperlinks. A *hyperlink* is a special spot—either an image or a bit of text—that will immediately transfer users to another Web location when they click on it. They're called *links* for short.

Navigation links are often grouped together, either along the top of a page, like these:

or down one side, like these text links:

Proposed Calendar
News
Contact the School Board
Volunteer
Contribute
Other Issues
Contacts

Sometimes an image map is used. An *image map* is a graphic such as the one shown in Figure 6-2. Depending on which part of the image users click on, they will be taken to a different page within the Web site. In Figure 6-2, clicking on a particular state brings up a list of information on Civil War battles fought in that state.

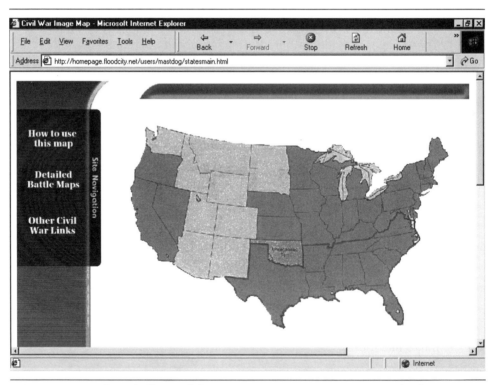

Figure 6-2 • Civil war buffs can click on any state to connect to a page with information on battles fought there.

When adding navigation links to your pages, follow these four basic rules:

- Every page should contain a link to the home page.
- Every page should contain links to the page directly above it and the pages directly beneath it in the Web structure.
- Be consistent between pages. Use the same style and color scheme for links, and keep them in the same position on the page whenever possible.
- Provide a text alternative to graphical links. A good way to do this is to add text-based links at the bottom of every page.

Don't get too clever. Some Web builders make an effort to find or create nifty images for use as navigation aids, only to discover that visitors are left guessing as to what each image signifies. Keep it simple and make it obvious what the link leads to.

If your site doesn't include a huge number of pages—for example, if it only has two layers instead of three—consider creating a master set of navigation links that will work on any page.

The Model in Action

The Cheap Web Tricks site (**cheapwebtricks.com**) was built following the model structure and navigation rules just described. Before the first page was written, the site was mapped out following the structure model in Figure 6-1. Figure 6-3 shows the result.

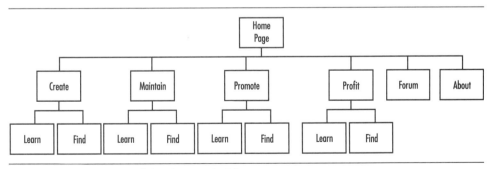

Figure 6-3 • Structure of the cheapwebtricks.com

Within the top few inches, the home page, shown in Figure 6-4, tells users:

- What the site is about: how to "create, maintain, promote, and profit from your Web site ~ without spending a dime ~"
- Who would want to use the site: people with a low budget or no budget
- What they'll find there: totally free tools and articles

You'll also notice the navigation links across the top (HOME, create, maintain, promote, profit, forum, about), which link to the main topic pages.

Figure 6-5 shows one of the main topic pages, "Create," from the second row of the structure chart in Figure 6-3. Once again, the top few inches make it clear what this page is about. Note that it has the same navigation links in the same position across the top, including a link to the home

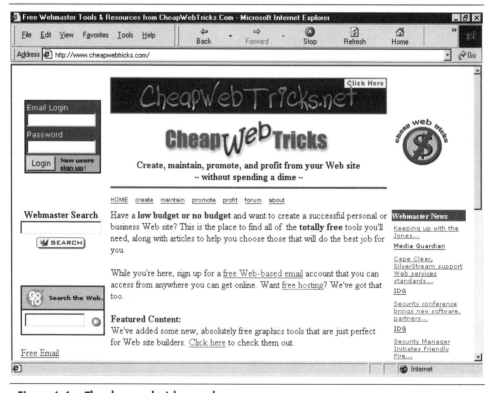

Figure 6-4 • The cheapwebtricks.com home page

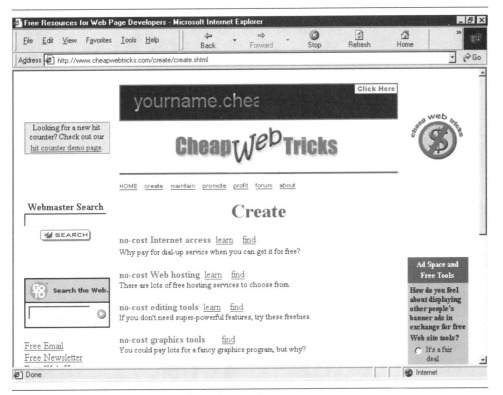

Figure 6-5 • A main topic page from cheapwebtricks.com

page. The body of the page contains descriptions of the detail pages beneath it in the structure chart, along with links to them.

A detail page that lies at the third level of the cheapwebtricks.com structure is shown in Figure 6-6. The familiar navigation links are in place, and the subject of the page is obvious.

TIP: *Keep in mind that the home page isn't always the first page visitors see. Depending on how they arrive at your site, they may encounter another page first. For example, they may arrive via a link that is connected to a specific detail page of your site, having been directed there by a search engine or someone who thought that particular page would be of interest. Make those first four inches of every page count!*

Figure 6-6 • A detail page from cheapwebtricks.com

Information You Must Include

There are certain items you absolutely must include on a commercial Web site. On a personal Web site, they're not quite as critical, but still important to have.

Contact Information   Make it easy for people to contact you. If you hide behind your Web site by deliberately or accidentally omitting this information, visitors will not trust the site, its contents, or you. An e-mail address is the bare minimum. Any commercial venture should include the company address and phone number as well.

Ordering Information   This seems like a no-brainer, but more than one manufacturer has put up a site touting its products, and neglected to tell people where to get them. An online ordering capability is ideal, but if that isn't in the works yet, an order form that can be faxed, phoned, or mailed is better than nothing.

Copying Web Content

It's very easy to copy other people's creations on the Web. With a simple right-click of the mouse it's possible to save any Web graphic to your hard drive to do with as you wish. It's also illegal, immoral, and fattening. Okay, maybe not fattening, but it's definitely a bad thing to do and can get you into deep (and expensive) legal trouble.

The person who creates an image (or text or sound file) owns the copyright to it, and you have no right to use that content without their permission. Many things on the Internet are free, but that doesn't include other people's Web site content. Copying someone else's work may get you sued, and certainly won't impress your site clientele if/when they discover your lack of ethics. So save yourself a big headache and don't do it.

The topic of intellectual property on the Internet is an interesting one. If you want to learn more about it, visit **ecommerce.ncsu.edu/ topics/ip/ip.html**, an enlightening site put up by the North Carolina State University.

While copying someone's work is illegal, observing an idea or concept and taking it one step further is legal and in many cases a shrewd move.

Copyright Notice   You don't technically have to have this, but it helps ward off potential page pirates. You own the copyright to your site simply by virtue of having conceived of and created it. A simply worded copyright notice placed at the bottom of each page reminds visitors of that fact, and will work in your favor in the unlikely event someone copies your content for their own use. Something like "(C) Copyright 2000 Rebecca Evans. All Rights Reserved" will do fine.

Defining the Structure for Your Site

As you can see, defining a well-organized and easy-to-navigate Web site is surprisingly straightforward. It doesn't require any magical skills or a four-year degree; all it takes is some common sense, a little know-how (which you now have), and a solid understanding of the purpose of your Web site and who it will serve.

To define the structure of your own site, use the model presented in Figure 6-1. Start by drawing the box for the home page on top, and then lay out your main topic pages underneath, and the detail pages beneath those.

Did I mention that you should do this in pencil? Unless you like scribbling things out and starting over from scratch, I strongly recommend it. You're going to discover that as you go along, your ideas will change, reformulate, and solidify, only to change again. The act of actually diagramming your ideas lets you make these adjustments on paper, where they are easy to fix (if you listened to me and used pencil) before you spend time turning them into actual Web pages that need to be corrected later.

Consider showing your planned layout to a friend who knows something about Web site design, or even to potential users of your site. Their feedback will help you refine the plan further.

Creating Eye Appeal

Once you have the underlying structure and navigation in place, it's time to consider the finer details of the design of the site. If you've got a great eye for color and shape, you're a step ahead of many new Web site builders, but even if you don't, you can still build an appealing Web site by following a few guidelines.

Choosing Colors

One of the easiest things you can do to make your Web site appear more professional is to create a consistent appearance. We already talked about consistency in navigation, but you'll also want to settle on a color scheme and stick with it. This will give your site a cohesive look and feel that makes it an organized unit rather than a bunch of unrelated bits slapped together by an amateur.

There are entire books on color theory, and if you read them you'll probably learn a lot. But if you don't have the time or inclination to do that, follow these three basic rules:

- *Use sharply contrasting colors for text and the page background.* Don't put light text on a light background or dark text on a dark background. Watch out for garish combinations as well. Light pink on a dark green background may be sharply contrasting, but it's also unreadable. When in doubt, black text on a white background is always safe.
- *Pick two or three colors and stick with them.* Settle on a background color and one or two accent colors and use them consistently throughout your pages.

- *Avoid tiled/patterned backgrounds.* Although they can be kind of cool, more often than not they make it difficult to read the text. If you must use one, make sure the pattern is very lightly colored—more like a subtle watermark than Christmas gift wrapping.

All you need to do to see the importance of following these rules is to surf the Web and find a few sites that don't follow them. Some sites, like the ones with purple text on a black background, actually make your eyes hurt. Personal sites are often the worst offenders.

If you want to play around with different color combinations, there are several sites on the Web that were created to help you do just that.

- PageTutor's Color Picker (**www.pagetutor.com/pagetutor/ makapage/picker/index.html**) lets you choose colors for text, links, and background, and displays the results on your screen. You can also download a copy to your computer for use offline.
- Webmaster's Color Lab (**www.visibone.com/colorlab/**) lets you choose colors by clicking on them, and then places those colors side by side on the screen. This site also contains links to articles on color use and theory.

Browser-Safe Colors

There's another, very annoying thing you should know about colors and Web sites: the same color value doesn't appear the same way in different browsers or on different machines. That is, an image viewed by a visitor using Netscape on a Macintosh computer may appear to be a different color than that same image viewed on an IBM-compatible computer using Internet Explorer.

The good news is that there are 216 colors that will appear properly to all visitors of your Web site, without regard to their choice of browser or computer. These colors are called browser-safe, or alternatively, Web-safe. Most graphics programs will let you limit your color choices to just these 216 colors, and it's a good idea to do so. The color pickers mentioned above use this same collection of colors (called a *palette*).

TIP: *A few site authoring tools, including Homestead's SiteBuilder and Microsoft FrontPage, will let you choose from a selection of themes and will automatically apply your choice to every page of your site. A theme typically includes a background color, background image, button styles, and navigation style and placement.*

Using Fonts and Text

The appearance of the text on your Web pages is controlled by the use of fonts. A *font* is a particular typeface rendered in a particular way (such as italic, bold, or underline). You get to choose which fonts are used to render the text of your Web pages. Be careful not to abuse this power, or your visitors will suffer.

- *Stick with one or two fonts throughout your site.* A common method is to use one font for headlines and another for body text.
- *Go easy on the colors.* Multicolored text creates visual confusion. If you want to use multiple text colors, use them consistently, with a purpose—such as to make a particular element of your site stand out—not just because it looks pretty.

Besides following these guidelines, take care to avoid overwhelming visitors with large, unbroken blocks of text. Reading text on a computer screen is more fatiguing than reading printed publications, so make it as easy on your viewers as possible. Break large sections of text into smaller units, and don't run text all the way from one side of the screen to the other. Even newspapers break their content into columns to make it easier on the eyes.

For similar reasons, don't create overly long pages of text; instead, divide your content into multiple pages and use headings to help viewers jump directly to the section that most interests them.

Design for a Variety of Viewers

A common trap that Web site builders fall into is to design a site that looks fabulous on their screen, completely forgetting (or ignoring) the fact that visitors who come to the site will be using an assortment of different platforms. We already saw how this can happen with color choice, but there are other pitfalls to watch out for.

Monitor Size and Resolution

When you go to a Web page that is wider than your screen, it was probably designed by someone with a lovely 21-inch monitor without regard for the many visitors who would be viewing it on a 15 incher. The opposite can happen as well. A Web site that looks peachy on a 15-inch screen can be a mess on a larger monitor, often because

a background image contains a vertical bar and wasn't created wide enough, so the Web browser has automatically repeated the pattern (called *tiling*). Figures 6-7 and 6-8 show what this looks like. The solution is simple: make that background image wide enough for the larger screen.

A monitor's screen resolution affects the appearance of your site as well. Screen resolution, which defines the sharpness of an image, is set by computer users to whatever resolution they prefer. A higher resolution means more stuff fits on the screen. Screen resolution is defined using pixels. A *pixel* is a single point in a graphic image, like a tiny dot. A monitor that is set to a resolution of 640 x 480 will display an area 640 pixels across by 480 pixels tall, for a total of just over 300,000 pixels. That same monitor, set to 800 x 600, will cram 800 pixels across by 600 pixels down (for a total of 480,000 pixels) into the same area. This changes the way your Web site will appear on that monitor. A higher resolution allows more to fit on the screen. Figures 6-9 and 6-10 show the same Web site on the same monitor at different screen resolutions.

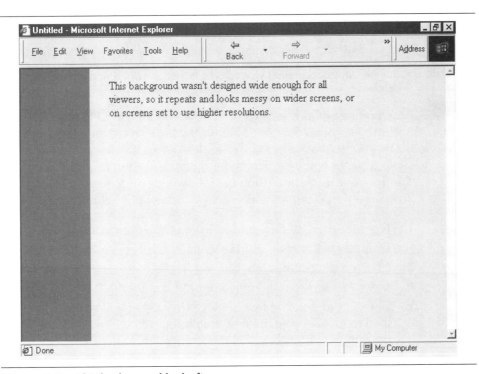

Figure 6-7 • **This background looks fine.**

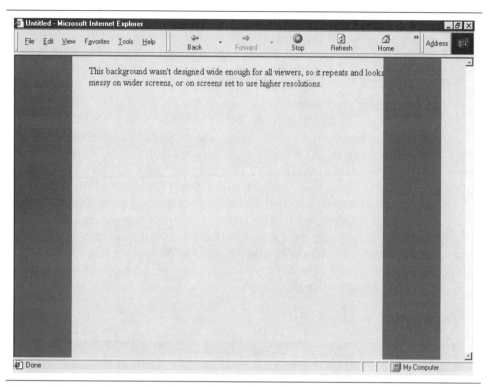

Figure 6-8 • But the same background viewed on a larger screen, or at a higher resolution, does not appear as the designer intended.

Common resolutions for PCs are 640 x 480, 800 x 600, and 1024 x 768. Currently, many surfers (PC and Mac users) have their screens set to 800 x 600, so that's a good size to design for. If you want to know what your pages will look like under different screen resolutions, you can adjust your resolution using the following instructions.

To change the screen resolution on a Windows PC, follow these steps:

1. From the Start menu, choose Settings and then Control Panel.
2. Double-click on the Display icon.
3. Click on the Settings tab.
4. Move the Screen area indicator until it reads "800 by 600 pixels."
5. Click OK to save the new setting. The screen will go black and then reappear using the new resolution setting. You will have the option to Cancel or OK the change.

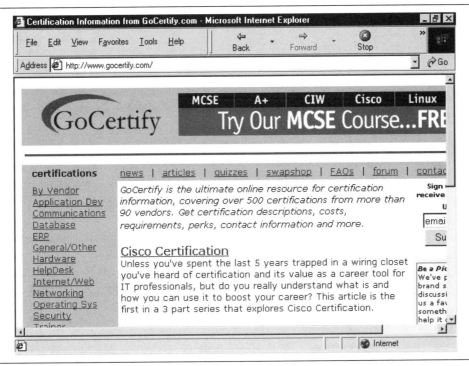

Figure 6-9 • GoCertify.com viewed with screen resolution set to 640 x 480

To change the screen resolution on a Macintosh, follow these steps:

1. From the Apple menu, choose Control Panels and then Monitors.
2. Click the Monitor button.
3. Select the resolution setting you want from the list.
4. Close the box by clicking the upper-right corner. The screen will go black and then reappear using the new resolution setting. You will have the option to Cancel or OK the change.

If you're using a PC, another option is to download the free utility BrowserSizer (**applythis.com/browsersizer**). This handy program allows you to change the resolution of your Internet Explorer or Netscape Navigator browser window only, without changing the screen resolution for your entire system.

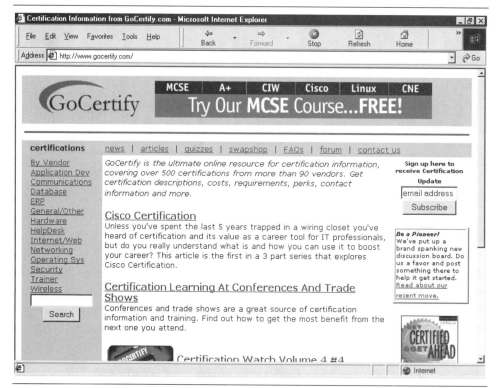

Figure 6-10 • GoCertify.com viewed with screen resolution set to 800 x 600

Web Browser Differences

Another common problem in designing sites for a variety of users is the number of Web browsers out there. They don't always display the same page the same way, and if the difference is dramatic, you can inadvertently (and unknowingly) cut out half of your potential audience. You can avoid this problem to some extent by sticking with HTML, which is known to work the same way in all browsers, or at least most of them. But to be extra safe, you should check how your pages appear in the most commonly used browsers. Right now that means Netscape Navigator and Microsoft Internet Explorer. Both are free, and anyone determined to build a successful Web site should have one of each on their computer. You can get Netscape Navigator at **home.netscape.com/download/**. The latest version of Microsoft Internet Explorer can be found at **www.microsoft.com/windows/ie/**. If your Web site targets an audience that is known to use a different browser, be sure to check your pages using that one as well.

TIP: *I suggest you avoid using those "best viewed with ..." logos encountered on so many sites. For people with a different browser, that's an immediate invitation to shove off. The chances that they will get the other browser and return to your site to view it in its full glory range from nil to none.*

Wise Use of Graphics

There's no question that graphics add considerably to a Web site's eye appeal, so you're probably going to want to use some. The key word in the previous sentence is "some." Every graphic you add to your page will increase the amount of time a visitor has to wait to view the page. Since Web surfers are notoriously impatient, it's important to keep that wait time to a bare minimum. Here's how you can do that:

- *Use small images.* They download more quickly.
- *Compress images.* Use the image crunching programs described in Chapter 5 to make the actual file size of your images as small as possible.
- *Provide text alternatives to image links.* Some visitors will have their browser set so that it does not load images. If your design relies on images for navigation, they will be lost, and when that happens they will leave. I'll explain how to do this using HTML alt tags in the next chapter.
- *Always specify the image size.* I'll tell you how to do this in the next chapter. For now, just remember that doing so will make your page load more quickly and smoothly.
- *Choose the proper image format for graphics you create.* There are several different file formats you can choose from (explained in a moment). By choosing the format that's most appropriate for the type of image you are creating, you will end up with a smaller final file size.

GIF vs. JPG vs. PNG

As you continue your journey into webmasterhood, you're going to discover that graphical images used on Web pages come in one of three varieties: GIF, JPG, or PNG. Which format a particular image uses is apparent in its file name, which will end in either .gif, .jpg, or .png (for example, myphoto.jpg).

When you create an image for use on your site, you will have to choose which format that image will utilize. How do you decide? In a nutshell, GIF files (GIF stands for Graphics Interchange Format) are best for images with fewer, more distinct colors. It's best for line art and simple icons. It also supports animated graphics. The JPG (aka JPEG for Joint Photographics Expert Group) format allows more colors (including shades of gray). It works best for photographs and photolike images. GIF (pronounced "jiff" or "giff") and JPG (pronounced "jay-peg") are the most widely used image formats on the Web.

NOTE: *In 1995, UNISYS announced that it holds the patent on the compression algorithm used in the GIF file format and would require people to pay licensing fees for the privilege of using it. Despite dire warnings from uninformed Web page authors claiming otherwise, this doesn't mean that anyone who creates or uses a GIF image has to pay royalties. It's authors of programs that output GIF images that are on the hook.*

PNG (pronounced "ping") stands for Portable Network Graphics. It's the latest graphics file format, and for that reason not all browsers support it fully. It's also much less widely used, but it may become more popular. It was created as an alternative to GIF, and offers more features that mostly propeller-heads care about. The rest of us will probably benefit from it too if it becomes widely accepted, but for now, GIF and JPG are still the way to go for most of us. Table 6-1 summarizes the differences between these formats.

Format	Uses
GIF	Images with a few distinct colors, including line art and simple colors. Supports animation.
JPG	Images with lots of colors and or shades, such as photos and lifelike images. No animation.
PNG	Upcoming format. Combines best features of GIF and JPG. Use sparingly for now, but keep an eye on it for future use.

Table 6-1 • Key Features of Common Image Formats

If you don't choose the ideal format, it's not a disaster. What will happen is that your file will probably be larger than necessary, which means it will take longer to download. It's also likely that your image will not be as sharp and distinct as it could be.

Accessibility

There's another important aspect of Web site design that you'll want to consider—accessibility by visitors with disabilities. Yes, visually impaired, deaf, and otherwise challenged individuals surf the Web too. According to Microsoft Corporation's accessibility Web site, about 8 percent of the people who use the Web have a disability.

Many people with disabilities use special tools to help them navigate the Web. Visually impaired individuals, for example, often use a special Web browser that reads the pages aloud. There are specific things that Web site builders can do to make it possible for people with disabilities to access a Web site. Most of them have to do with providing alternate ways to access content, or avoiding methods that are likely to create barriers. For example:

- An audio or video segment should have an associated text transcript or caption.
- Images should make use of the alt tag to provide a text alternative.
- Graphs and charts should have a summary attribute that describes their content.
- Flickering and flashing content, such as text that blinks, should be avoided.

IBM gives extensive tips and guidelines on their accessibility site at **www-3.ibm.com/able/accessweb.html**. You can also find a wealth of resources and information on the topic at the WebABLE site (**webable.com**).

TIP: *To check whether your pages are accessible, and receive suggestions on how to improve them, use Bobby (**www.cast.org/ bobby/**), a free software tool that will check your pages and assess them for accessibility features.*

As much as we all want to make our sites accessible to everyone, it would be dishonest to claim that implementing all of the suggested accessibility guidelines is easy. But even if you can't manage to make your pages accessible to everyone, each step you do take to facilitate access is a step in the right direction.

7

Chapter Seven

Creating Your Web Pages

Finally, the moment you've been waiting for: it's time to start creating your Web pages! You've actually been building your site ever since Chapter 2, when you clarified your goals, purpose, and target audience. In Chapter 6, you used that information to lay out an overall structure; now it's time to start filling in the boxes of that structure by creating pages in HTML.

HTML (HyperText Markup Language) is called a text markup language because it works by taking plain text and adding formatting information (or, marking it up) using tags. It's easy to tell what is a tag and what isn't because the tags are enclosed in angled brackets, like this:

```
<TAG>
```

The other thing about tags is that, with a few exceptions, they come in pairs, with the text that should be affected by them in between. For example:

```
<B>This text appears bold</B>
```

Notice that the second (or closing) tag has a / before the actual tag name. Whenever you see a tag with a / in it, you know it's the closing tag of a pair. Tags can be nested to create additional effects, like this:

```
<B><I>This text appears bold and italic</B></I>
```

Although tags don't have to be written in all uppercase letters, people often write them that way to make them stand out from surrounding text.

NOTE: *XHTML, a new extension of HTML, is case sensitive, and all XHTML attributes and element names (tags) must be written in lowercase. But in HTML, it's strictly personal preference.*

HTML is all about using these tags to create well-organized, interesting documents for viewing on the Web. In Chapter 1, I explained that

HTML is simply a way to add structure and format (in other words, mark up text) to control how text pages will appear when viewed on the Web. When the document is viewed in a plain text editor or HTML authoring tool, the tags are visible and the effects they create are not. But when that same document is viewed using a Web browser such as Microsoft Internet Explorer or Netscape Navigator, the opposite is true: the tags are hidden and the formatting created by them appears instead.

TIP: *You can view the HTML behind any Web page by right-clicking on the page and selecting View Source from the pop-up menu.*

A Web Page You Can Put Up Today

The first thing we're going to do with HTML is create a Web page you can put up today. In fact, it will only take you a few minutes. This first page (shown in Figure 7-1) isn't very fancy, but it can serve as a placeholder for your Web presence, and it demonstrates HTML in action.

Figure 7-1 shows how the page appears when viewed in a Web browser. If you look at the same page with an HTML editor or plain text editor, it looks like Figure 7-2.

The name of the page, index.html, tells you a few things about this particular document. First, because it ends in .html, you know it's an HTML document and so does any computer program that reads it. Sometimes .htm is used instead, but it means the same thing. Second, the "index" part of the name identifies this page as the main page of this Web site. In our example, it's the only page, but even when there are hundreds of pages in a site, it's a convention to name the home page index.html. Other pages are named anything the author wishes (ending in .html or .htm). This particular page contains the following elements:

- A headline: Future Home of Jim's Dynamite Web Site
- An image named JimDilbert.jpg
- A paragraph of text

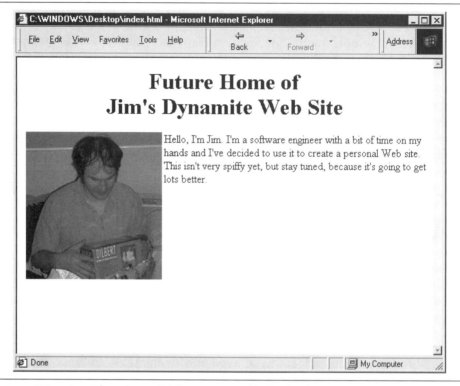

Figure 7-1 • A quick and easy Web page named index.html

```
index.html - Notepad
File  Edit  Search  Help
<HTML>
  <BODY>

    <H1 align="center">Future Home of<BR>
      Jim's Dynamite Web Site
    </H1>

    <IMG src="JimDilbert.jpg" align="left" border=0>

    <P>
      Hello, I'm Jim. I'm a software engineer with a bit of time on my
      hands and I've decided to use it to create a personal Web site.
      This isn't very spiffy yet, but stay tuned, because it's going to
      get lots better.
    </P>

  </BODY>
</HTML>
```

Figure 7-2 • The HTML behind the page

You can probably pick out the tags that identify and format each part. If you're so inclined, you can type this page into your HTML editor or text editor, substitute your image in place of JimDilbert.jpg and your text in place of Jim's, and in a few minutes you'll have your first Web page. Heck, why not do it right now? Follow these steps:

1. Open a text editor (such as Windows Notepad) or a Web authoring tool.
2. Type in the text shown in Figure 7-2, replacing "Jim" with your name. Or get creative and replace as much of the plain text as you want to. Just don't mess with the tags.
3. If you have a picture you'd like to use in place of Jim's (and it's already on your computer), change the "JimDilbert.jpg" to the name of your replacement image. Be sure to specify the location of the image as well, for example, "\myphotos\me.jpg." If you don't feel like bothering with this part right now, just leave out the line that starts with <IMG>.
4. Save your file. Choose File, Save As, and give your file a name that ends in .html. Pay attention to the location (aka directory); you're saving it so you can find it again!

Now let's look at it in a Web browser:

1. Fire up your Web browser (Internet Explorer or Netscape Navigator or your preference).
2. From the Text menu at the top of the browser, choose File, then Open, and then click the Browse button. Your particular browser might have slightly different wording, but the idea is the same.
3. Using the box that appeared when you clicked Browse, locate the file you just saved and click Open.

Voila! There it is. Magic.

Crash Course in HTML

Now that you know a bit about how HTML is used to make Web pages, it's time to go into a bit more detail. Although the type and order of tags that you'll use in an HTML document will vary depending on what you're trying to accomplish, there's a certain overall structure you need to follow.

HTML Document Structure

Every HTML page you create should start with the following tags. (Most authoring tools will automatically insert them for you when you start a new page.)

```
<HTML>
<HEAD>
</HEAD>
<BODY>
</BODY>
</HTML>
```

The opening and closing <HTML> </HTML> tags identify the content in between as HyperText Markup Language.

The <HEAD></HEAD> tags identify the heading section of the document. The heading area is used to store information about the document. You don't have to include a heading section if you don't have anything to put in it. Web browsers don't display anything between these two tags, but they may use information stored there to affect how later parts of the document are formatted.

NOTE: *You can add information in the <HEAD> section for search portals to use, but we'll talk more about that in Chapter 10.*

As you've probably guessed, the <BODY> </BODY> tags identify the main body of the HTML page. This is the meat of the document—the stuff that the browser will interpret and display. Most of the HTML you write will go between the opening and closing <BODY> tags.

Tags Can Have Attributes with Values

The effect a particular tag has can be further specified through the use of attributes, which is a fancy word for options. For example, if you want the background color of your document to be white, you can accomplish that by adding the attribute BGCOLOR to the <BODY> tag, like this:

```
<BODY bgcolor="White">
```

Notice that you also have to specify a value for that attribute, in this case "White", so that Web browsers know which background color to use. Attributes and values are only included in the opening tag of a pair, not the closing tag.

A tag can have more than one attribute, or no attributes at all. Although this might sound confusing at first, you'll quickly get the hang of it because it's largely based on common sense.

Consider the tag to insert an image into your document, for example. The tag itself is <IMG>. This alone doesn't tell the browser which image to use, whether or not to put a border around it, how to position it on the page, or what size to make it. At the very least, you're going to want to specify which image to display, and whether to position in the left, right, or center of the page. If you're following good HTML coding practices, you'll also want to specify the size (which will make it load more smoothly) and provide an alternate text description of the image. The text description makes it possible for people who can't view the images—either because they've set their browser not to load images or because they are visually impaired and are using special tools to view your site—to know what the image is about. So the final image tag, with attributes (and values), would end up looking like this:

```
<IMG src="\images\JimDilbert.jpg" align="left" height=210 width=202
 alt="Photo of Jim">
```

The order of the attributes doesn't matter, nor does whether you write them in uppercase (all capitals), lowercase (no capitals), or mixed case. The only place where case matters is the file name. Unix-based systems, which are widely used for Web hosting, consider "JimDilbert.jpg" and "jimdilbert.jpg" to be two different files. If you wish to follow standard conventions, write your tag name in uppercase, and the attributes and values in lowercase.

Some tags have no attributes at all associated with them. The <BR> tag is used to create a line break (or new line) in a document. It stands alone, with no attributes and no closing tag because none are needed.

TIP: *You don't have to remember every HTML tag, its attributes, and the possible values of those attributes. Most of the time you'll use the same ones again and again, and they will quickly become familiar to you. But to get you started, I've compiled a list of the HTML tags you're most likely to use, along with their attributes and purpose. You'll find it in the appendix.*

Commonly Used Text Tags

The primary method used to convey information on most Web pages is text. There are several simple ways you can control the display format of text.

Paragraphs and Line Breaks

The text tag you'll probably use most is <P>, which is used to start a new paragraph. <P> is one of those tags that doesn't require a closing tag, although </P> can be used if you wish.

The <P> tag causes the browser to skip a line before outputting the text, with the result that paragraphs are separated by blank space. It has one attribute: align, which can be set to left, right, or center. If you don't specify an alignment, the paragraph will align left. Here's a sample of the <P> tag in action:

```
<P align="center">This paragraph is centered.</P>
<P align="right">This paragraph is aligned right</P>
<P align="left">This one is aligned left.</P>
```

The top part of Figure 7-3 shows how the above would appear in a browser.

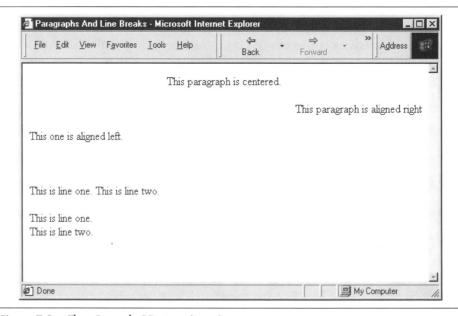

Figure 7-3 • The <P> and <BR> tags in action

To cause a line break—like pressing ENTER in a word processor—you have to enter a <BR> tag. Simply breaking text onto multiple lines like this

```
This is line one.
This is line two.
```

will have no effect, as demonstrated in Figure 7-3. To get the text on separate lines, use the line break tag like this:

```
This is line one. <BR>
This is line two.
```

The result is shown at the bottom of Figure 7-3. You don't actually have to put the lines on separate lines; they could be on the same line with the <BR> between them, and the effect would be the same.

Creating Headings

Heading tags are a quick and easy way to add organizational structure and headlines to your documents. There are six of them: <H1> through <H6>. <H1> is the largest and <H6> the smallest, as shown in Figure 7-4. Headings are rendered in bold text and remain separated from other text by a blank line.

Sometimes people use a particular heading tag because it produces text of the approximate size they are seeking, but this is really not the proper use of heading tags and may throw off text-based browsers used by handicapped site visitors. Heading tags should correspond to the structure of the document, with H1 being the title, H2 the first-level headlines, H3 second level, and so on. Control of text size and appearance is more properly accomplished through the use of the <FONT> tag.

Controlling Text Style and Appearance

The <FONT> tag lets you control the size, face, and color of specific words or phrases. The three most commonly used attributes are (surprise, surprise): size, face, and color. Let's start with size.

Font size can be specified as either a specific value (1–6) or an incremental value (+1 through +6 and –1 through –6). The default font size is 3. So if you do this

```
<FONT size="+2">This text is two sizes larger.</FONT>
```

you increase the font size two steps. Note that the <FONT> tag requires a closing </FONT> tag.

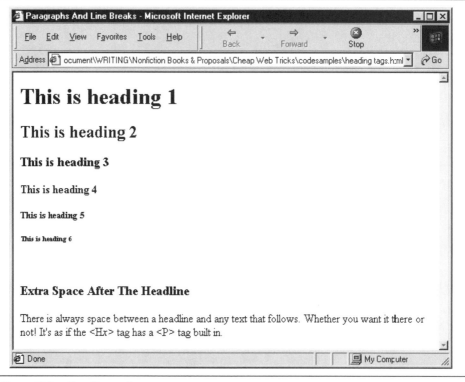

Figure 7-4 • Heading styles

The face attribute specifies which typeface to use. It looks like this:

```
<FONT face = "Arial">This text appears in the Arial Typeface</FONT>
```

The color attribute works similarly:

```
<FONT color = "Yellow">This text appears in yellow."</FONT>
```

The value for color can be specified using its name or its hexadecimal value (for example, #FFFF00 for yellow). If you use the hexadecimal value, make sure to stick a pound sign (#) at the beginning. Table 7-1 lists the colors of the rainbow and their hexadecimal values, plus the values for black and white.

These color values can be used with any tag that has a color attribute, not just the <FONT> tag. There are 140 color names available. A more complete list is included in the appendix of this book.

Name	Hex Value	Name	Hex Value	Name	Hex Value
Red	FF0000	Orange	FFA500	Yellow	FFFF00
Green	0080000	Blue	0000FF	Indigo	4B0082
Violet	EE82EE	Black	000000	White	FFFFFF

Table 7-1 • Colors and Their Hexadecimal Values

When a tag has multiple attributes, like the <FONT> tag does, you can combine them into one tag, like this:

```
<FONT face="Arial" color="black" size="+3">This text is in Arial,
the color black, and size +3</FONT>
```

Bold, Italic, and Underline

Sometimes the most efficient way to convey meaning is to bold, underline, or italicize words or phrases that you want to emphasize. This is easy to accomplish using <B> (bold), <I> (italic), and <U> (underline) tags. Be sure to insert a matching closing tag where you want the effect to stop. Here's an example:

```
Use a bold tag to make text really<B>stand out</B>. Italics
are useful for <I>adding emphasis</I>. Be frugal with
<U>underlines</U> though. Visitors may confuse underlined
words with links.
```

The result of the above HTML is shown in Figure 7-5.

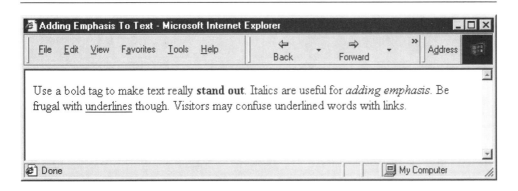

Figure 7-5 • Formatting words and phrases

Adding Images

Using only the HTML you've learned already, you could write decent Web pages with a well-formatted, neat appearance. But chances are that you have something spiffier in mind; something that uses graphical images.

If you're using a Web authoring tool, adding an image to your page is usually as simple as placing your mouse where you want the image to appear, and clicking the button for Insert Image. A box similar to the one shown in Figure 7-6 will pop up and ask you for the specifics, such as image name, whether you want a border around it, alignment, size, and alternate text description. Filling in the fields in this box will generate the tag and place it in your page. But even if you choose this point-and-click route to Web page design, you should know how image tags are constructed, so that you can look at the resulting HTML and understand what it means, as well as modify it to perform in the way you desire.

A basic image tag looks like this:

```
<IMG src="myimage.gif">
```

There's no closing tag. The src attribute identifies the file containing the image you want to display. We talked about image formats in Chapter 6,

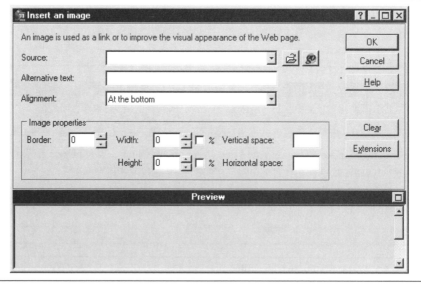

Figure 7-6 • Automagically creating image tags using ACE HTML 4

so you already know this could be myimage.gif, myimage.jpg, or myimage.png.

If you keep your Web site images and HTML pages in the same place (the same directory), simply specifying the file name will suffice. But if your images are stored somewhere else, perhaps in a subdirectory called "images," your src= tag has to reflect that, or Web browsers won't be able to find and display it. For example,

```
<IMG src="images/myimage.gif">
```

tells browsers to get the file myimage.gif from the images subdirectory.

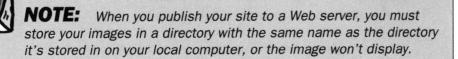

NOTE: *When you publish your site to a Web server, you must store your images in a directory with the same name as the directory it's stored in on your local computer, or the image won't display.*

The image tag has a few more commonly used attributes: align, border, and alt. Align lets you specify where you want an image to appear on the page—either at the left side, right side, or center. The border attribute lets you specify a border around the image with your choice of thickness. Use 0 for no border, as in:

```
<IMG src="myimage.gif" border="0">
```

The alt attribute is used to specify a textual alternative to the image. Chapter 6 explained why it is a good idea to use this attribute. Here it is in action, in an image tag that uses all of the attributes we've discussed:

```
<IMG src="myimage.gif" align="center" border="0" alt="photo of the author">
```

The above image tag places the image myimage.gif in the center of the page, with no border, and viewers using textual access will know what the image is because the alt attribute is included.

The Magic of Linking

One of the greatest features of the Web is the ability to connect documents together so that users can navigate between them with a single mouse click. They can be documents within a single Web site, companywide, or on the other side of the world.

Text Links

Linking to content outside the page is accomplished using a tag called an anchor. An anchor tag looks like this:

```
<A href="http://gocertify.com/">Click here to visit GoCertify.com</A>
```

In a Web browser, the above would appear as underlined text (in blue unless the default settings have been changed by the page designer or browser user), like this:

Click here to visit GoCertify.com

The blue underline is a clue to visitors that the text is a clickable link.

The attribute href stands for HyperText Reference, and its value tells the browser where to go when this link is accessed. Notice that, as with other attribute values, the href value is enclosed in quotes.

The anchor tag requires a closing tag </A>. Whatever lies between the opening tag and the closing tag is the "hot" area that visitors can click on to go to the specified link. Often it's text, but it can be an image instead.

Linking with an Image

The tag for an image link would look like this:

```
<A href="http://gocertify.com/"><IMG src="gocertifylogo.gif"></A>
```

In this case, clicking on the image would take the visitor to the GoCertify.com Web site. Remember that text between anchor tags is blue? Images between anchor tags will have a blue border around them by default, so visitors will know the image is connected to a link. If it's already obvious that the image is a link—say if it's clearly a navigation button—you can get rid of the border by adding a border attribute and setting it to 0, like this:

```
<A href="http://gocertify.com/" border="0"><IMG src="gocertifylogo.gif"></A>
```

Choose Your Target

By default, an <A href= > link will open the target document in the same browser window that the link is in. This means the current page disappears and the new page replaces it on the visitor's screen. For links that connect pages within your own Web site, this is exactly what you want to occur. But if you're referring people to a page on someone else's site, and you want to encourage the visitor to return to yours, it's a better idea to have the link open a new browser window. That way your site stays on the user's screen, too. Hopefully, when they're done inspecting the document you've sent them, they'll close the new browser window you opened for them, and the Web page where they started—yours—will still be on their screen. Although it may sound complicated, pulling it off is really simple. Just use the target attribute, like this:

```
<A href="http://gocertify.com/" target="outside">Click here to visit
GoCertify.com</A>
```

The above link will open the target in a new window named "outside." If you use target="outside" for other anchor links on your page, the links will open in that same window.

mailto Links

Documents and other Web sites aren't the only things you can link to. You can also use an anchor tag to create a link that users can click to send you an e-mail message. This is called a mailto link, and it looks like this:

```
<A href="mailto:webmaster@cheapwebtricks.com">click here to email me</A>
```

When visitors click on the "click here to email me" text, their e-mail program will open with the address webmaster@cheapwebtricks.com already filled out in the TO: field.

Creating Bulleted or Numbered Lists

Another easy thing you can do with HTML is create lists. Lists can be numbered (called ordered) or bulleted (called unordered). When you use an HTML list tag, the bullets or numbers are inserted automatically before each line item. Figure 7-7 shows each kind of list.

A list is started with either <UL> (for unordered list) or <OL> (for an ordered list). Both of these have closing tags, and by now you probably know exactly what they look like: </UL> and </OL>.

Between the list opening and closing tags are a series of list item <LI> tags. That tells the browser where to put the bullets or numbers. Closing

</LI> tags are optional. You can add them if you like, but it won't cause an error if you don't. So to create a list like the first (numbered) one in Figure 7-7, you'd write the following HTML:

```
<OL>
     <LI>Thing one.
     <LI>Thing two.
     <LI>Thing three.
</OL>
```

You can control the starting number, as well as the style of both bullets and numbers, by using attributes available for <OL> and <UL>. If you want to use them, check the HTML reference in the appendix for the exact syntax.

Using Tables as a Layout Tool

Now that you know how to create text, images, and links using HTML, you are well prepared to start pounding out great Web pages. You really don't have to know anything about our next HTML topic, which is tables, but I'm going to tell you about them anyway, and here's why.

When you think of a table, you probably picture something that provides a nicely organized view of data in rows and columns, like the one on color names and their hexadecimal values a few pages ago. You can use tables

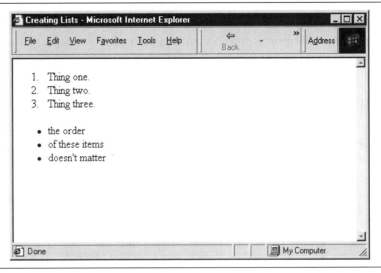

Figure 7-7 • Ordered and unordered lists

in Web pages to do the same thing, and that's what HTML table tags were originally intended for. But it turns out that where HTML tables really shine is in providing visual organization to a Web page. They make it vastly easier to line up multiple elements in a visually appealing way by making it possible to divvy up the screen into neat sections—in particular, columns.

Why would you want to do this? Let's say, for example, you've decided that you'd like to have your navigation buttons down the left side of the screen, running parallel to the main content. Getting the buttons to line up neatly and evenly while having your text come out in the right place is a real challenge. But if you use a table to divide your page into two columns—a small one for the navigation buttons and a larger one for the content—you can simply stack the buttons in the first column and put everything else in the second column. As a bonus, you don't have to worry about inadvertently messing up one column while working on the other.

NOTE: *Structural organization can also be accomplished using frames. Frames also allow you to carve up the screen into sections, and load a separate HTML page into each section. Not all browsers handle frames well, nor do all Web page creators. Although popular when they were first used, frames have fallen into disfavor. Still, some designers find them very useful. If you want to learn how to use frames, I suggest you visit the HTMLGoodies Frames Tutorial at htmlgoodies.com/tutors/fram.html.*

If you look closely at the Cheap Web Tricks home page, shown in Figure 7-8, you can see that it's designed with three columns: a smaller one on each side, and a large column with the majority of the content in the center. Organizing a page with so many components without using a table would be a real challenge, but with a table, it's easy.

Creating a Basic Table

Tables are made up of columns and rows, and unlike the tags discussed earlier in this chapter, tables require multiple tags in a particular order. The beginning and end of the table are identified by <TABLE> and </TABLE>. Between the table tags, rows are defined by <TR> and </TR>

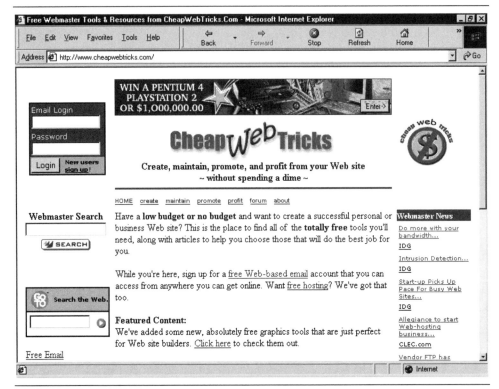

Figure 7-8 • Cheapwebtricks.com uses a table to format content.

tags. (TR stands for table row.) Within the rows, individual cells that contain data are defined, using <TD> and </TD>. (TD is short for table data.) Here's the HTML for a table with one row containing two data cells in it:

```
<TABLE>
    <TR>
        <TD>One</TD>
        <TD>Two</TD>
    </TR>
</TABLE>
```

And here's the table it creates:

One	Two

You could use this basic table to structure a two-column Web page like the one mentioned earlier with navigation elements in the first (left) column (between the first two <TD> tags) and the main contents in the second (right) column.

For a three-column template page, just add another set of <TD></TD> tags inside the table row <TR> </TR> tags. If you want more rows, repeat the whole <TR></TR> section, including the <TD> tags in between. Make sure you include the same number of cells in each row.

Table Attributes

You're already familiar with several of the main attributes that can be used with <TABLE>: align, border, and width. Figure 7-9 shows how these attributes affect the table.

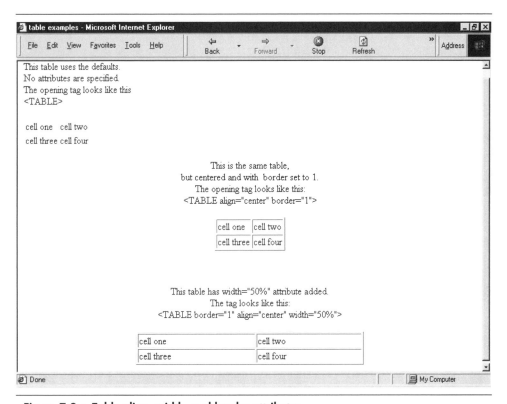

Figure 7-9 • Table align, width, and border attributes

Here's the HTML behind the first (top) table:

```
<TABLE>
  <TR>
    <TD>cell one</TD>
    <TD>cell two</TD>
  </TR>
  <TR>
    <TD>cell three</TD>
    <TD>cell four</TD>
  </TR>
</TABLE>
```

The HTML for the second (middle) table looks like this:

```
<TABLE align=center border=1>
  <TR>
    <TD>cell one</TD>
    <TD>cell two</TD>
  </TR>
  <TR>
    <TD>cell three</TD>
    <TD>cell four</TD>
  </TR>
</TABLE>
```

And the HTML for the third (bottom) table looks like this:

```
<TABLE align=center border=1 width="50%">
  <TR>
    <TD>cell one</TD>
    <TD>cell two</TD>
  </TR>
  <TR>
    <TD>cell three</TD>
    <TD>cell four</TD>
  </TR>
</TABLE>
```

Two other very useful <TABLE> attributes are cellspacing and cellpadding. These allow you to add a bit of white space into the table design so that the contents of different cells are as separated (or close together) as you wish. It's easy to confuse these two attributes, which accomplish this "spacing out" task in different ways.

The cellspacing attribute controls the width of the cell border. This means it controls the space between cells. The cellpadding attribute, on the other hand, controls the spacing between the contents of a cell and the edge of that cell. The next illustration makes the difference a bit clearer.

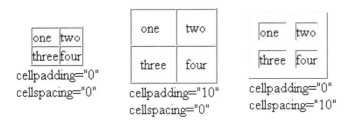

You can also affect the format of table rows and individual data cells. Attributes included in the <TR> tag affect only the cells in that row. Attributes added to a <TD> tag affect only that data cell.

The attributes that apply to rows are align and valign. Align works the same way as it does for the table, but at a row level. Use it to set the contents (cells) of a particular row to align at the left, right, or center. Valign stands for vertical alignment. Use the valign attribute to specify whether the cells in a row will align at the top, middle, or bottom of the row.

The cell (or <TD>) level has the most attributes. This includes the same align and valign attributes and values just discussed for rows, but when used inside a <TD> tag they affect only a single cell. If you're planning to use a two-column model to lay out your Web pages, this is where you set the width of each of those columns. Using a new attribute, bgcolor, you can also set the background color of the navigation column to be different from the background color of the main contents column.

Figure 7-10 shows a one-row table that makes use of the attributes we've discussed so far. This table, which would work well as a page layout template, has the following characteristics:

- It spans 100 percent of the screen.
- No border is displayed.
- It contains two columns, one that is narrow and one that is wide.
- The contents of the cells align at the top of each cell because the valign attribute has been used.
- The background color of the first column is set to a different color than the main column, making it easy to distinguish.
- The first column uses the align attribute to center its text.
- The cellpadding attribute has been used to keep the contents of the two columns from butting up against each other.

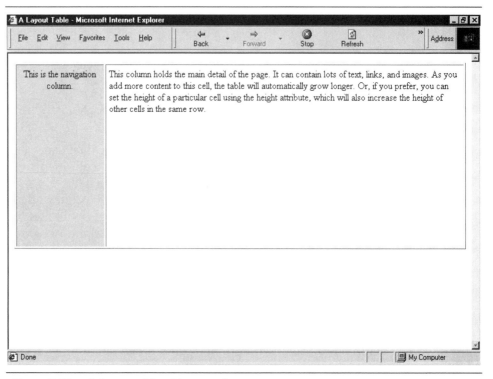

Figure 7-10 • A layout table with two columns

Figure 7-11 shows the HTML behind the table, as viewed in a text editor.

A basic table layout like the one in Figure 7-10 will carry you a long way toward a well-organized and well-designed site. It may take a bit of effort to get the hang of how they work, but once you have a firm grasp of HTML tables, you'll wonder how you ever designed a page without one.

```
tables.html - Notepad                              _ □ ×
File  Edit  Search  Help

<html>
<body>
<TABLE WIDTH="100%" BORDER="1" CELLPADDING="5" ALIGN="center">
  <TR ALIGN="left" VALIGN="top">
    <TD WIDTH="20%" ALIGN="center" BGCOLOR="Silver">This is the
navigation column.</TD>
    <TD WIDTH="80%" HEIGHT="300">
      This column holds the main detail of the page.
      It can contain lots of text, links, and images. As you add
more content to this
      cell, the table will automatically grow longer. Or, if you
prefer, you
      can set the height of a particular cell using the height
attribute, which will
      also increase the height of other cells in the same row.
    </TD>
  </TR>
</TABLE>
</body>
</html>
```

Figure 7-11 • The HTML that created Figure 7-10

8

Chapter Eight

Housekeeping for Webmasters

When you first create your Web site, chances are there will be just a few pages and graphics involved. But as time goes on, the number of files associated with a Web site has a way of snowballing. It's as if they self-propagate on your computer's hard drive when no one is looking. Before you know it, you've got a dozen (if not dozens) of pages and many megabytes of graphics, all interconnected, and remembering what's where and updating them all becomes a time-consuming process. Fortunately, there are several procedures you can follow that will make managing those files, and your site as a whole, as efficient as possible. I'll address those organization issues first. Then, at the end of the chapter, I'll throw some more webmaster terminology at you, so you can toss the jargon around with the best of them.

Organizing Your Files

Web sites with just a few pages and graphics can store everything in a single directory, but once the site gets bigger (and they always do), that directory becomes so stuffed with files that it's hard to find what you want. By organizing your files (and your Web site) into logical components starting on day one, you'll make it much easier to manage.

Start with a master directory for the site. Name it whatever you want. Something descriptive, such as the name of the site (with all spaces taken out) will work well. For example, the Cheap Web Tricks main directory is named cheapwebtricks. Within that directory, create a second directory for images. Name it images. Can you guess what's going to be kept there?

If the site will contain under a dozen pages, this simple structure will suffice. Keep all HTML pages in the main directory (cheapwebtricks in our example) and all graphics, pictures, or other images in the images directory. Remember to specify the path to the image when you insert one into an HTML document. An image tag would look like this:

```
<IMG src="\images\mypicture.gif">
```

Bigger sites will benefit from additional directories. The Cheap Web Tricks site has many pages for each of the main topics—Create, Maintain, Promote, and Profit—so a directory was created for each one.

The HTML pages for each section are stored in a subdirectory with a matching name. All the images are kept in a central images directory. As an extra bonus, visitors to the Web site are reminded which section of the site they are in by the URL. When a file in the create subdirectory is being viewed, the URL in the viewer's browser address bar starts with http://cheapwebtricks.com/create/.

Organizing Your HTML

As straightforward as HTML is, finding your way to a particular spot in a document containing 50 or more lines of code can be a challenge. It also takes a little work to remember what you put where on the page and to maintain a consistent design appearance across the site. Fortunately, there are a few easy steps you can take to simplify these tasks.

Writing Pretty Code

Chances are that no one but you will bother to look at the HTML behind your pages, so why should you care what it looks like? Because the same thing that makes it look nice makes it easier to maintain and troubleshoot. Besides, it's a simple matter of indentation.

Start each new page by placing the ever present <HTML> and <BODY> tags (<HEAD> too if you're using it) against the left margin of the page, like this:

```
<HTML>
<BODY>
</BODY>
</HTML>
```

Any tags inserted thereafter should be indented, with matching opening and closing tags vertically aligned. Any tag that is nested inside another tag (like <TR> is inside <TABLE>) is further indented, until you end up with something like so:

```
<HTML>
<BODY>
    <TABLE>
        <TR>
            <TD>
            </TD>
```

```
            </TR>
            <TR>
                <TD>
                </TD>
            </TR>
        </TABLE>
    </BODY>
</HTML>
```

This system makes it very easy to see where different tags on a page start and end. It also makes it easier to spot missing closing tags. The downside is that this can make for some long pages, which is why some HTML writers take a shortcut when the nesting gets deep. For example, the tags for a table could be done like this instead:

```
<TABLE>
    <TR>
        <TD>                    </TD>
    </TR>
    <TR>
        <TD>                    </TD>
    </TR>
</TABLE>
```

It's still easy to see the structure of the page, but it takes up less vertical space. When starting out, it's probably best to stick with the first method. Later, when you're an old hand at HTML, you can switch to a more compact format.

Adding Comments

There's a very useful HTML tag I haven't told you about yet: the comment tag. This is the place to put anything you want a Web browser to ignore. A comment tag is structured differently from other HTML tags. It starts with <!— and ends with —>, like this:

```
<!-- this is a comment the browser will ignore -->
```

Use it liberally to place notes to yourself in the HTML. Comments can help you find a particular section on the page, or explain why you did something a particular way, so that when you come back to it a month later you won't be baffled. You can make the comments as prominent or small as you wish. Here's another example:

```
<!--*********************************-->
<!--*        Change History            *-->
```

```
<!--********************************-->
<!--*  4/2/01 added forum to menu...*-->
<!--*  3/25/01 added  hot news  box.*-->
<!--********************************-->
```

The comment tag can also be used to temporarily remove a feature or section of the page. Instead of deleting the section and retyping it later, just enclose it in a comment tag and it will effectively disappear.

Don't put anything that will embarrass you in a comment. Site visitors can see comments, just as they can view the entire HTML of any page, by selecting View Content from the browser menu selections.

Creating and Using Templates

One of the simplest ways to accomplish a consistent look and feel for a Web site is to create and use one or more templates. A *template* is an HTML file that contains the elements that are the same on every page. This would probably include a layout table if you're using one, navigation buttons or links, and your chosen header and footer. This would also make it easier to maintain a consistent color scheme and stick with the same font selections throughout the site, which are also important elements of creating a coherent, well-designed Web presence.

JARGON ALERT: *A template is a form that shows which elements exist and their locations on the Web page. To produce a final page, the specific details, which are individual to the final page, are added.*

A header is a section at the top of the page that is the same on every page. It might include a logo, site name, an advertising banner, or other elements of the site builder's choice. A footer is similar, except that it goes at the bottom of the page, and often incorporates a copyright notice. By creating a header and footer and using them on every page, you can produce that consistent look and feel that signifies a well-designed site.

To create a template, start by designing the look and feel of your page. Sometimes this is best accomplished by actually creating the home page, so you can play around with the appearance until you achieve the effect you're after. Remember to make generous use of the comment tag. Use it to add explanations and notes that will make it easier for people who may work on the page later to figure out the planning you put into creating it.

Once the main page is acceptable, save it so you have an original copy. Then cut out the heart of it—that is, the part that will be different on every page—leaving only the common elements. Be sure to mark the "hole" with comment tags so that it can be easily located. Save this cannibalized version under a new name, such as template.html or empty.html.

Each time you begin a new page, start by loading the template, and immediately save it under the name of the new page. Why save it under a different name before you even make any changes? To assure that any changes you make will not overwrite the starting template.

If you start with the template, half the page is written already, and all you have to do is insert the detail. The Cheap Web Tricks site was created using templates. If you compare Figures 8-1 and 8-2, you'll notice that the perimeters of the pages are virtually identical; only the contents in the center differ.

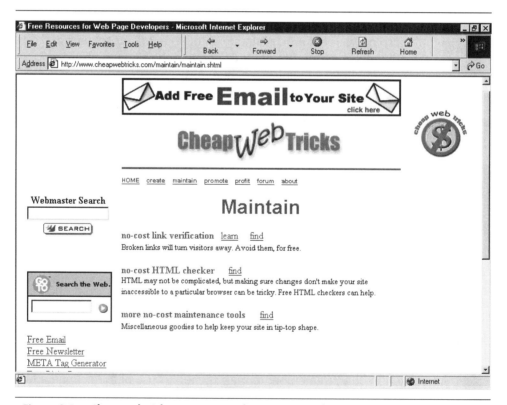

Figure 8-1 • Cheapwebtricks.com was made using a template.

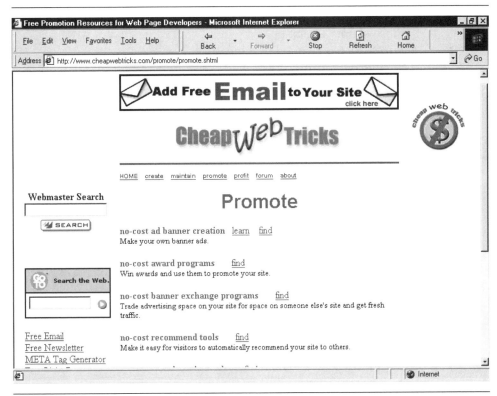

Figure 8-2 • This page has many of the same elements as Figure 8-1.

Take Notes

The day you start your Web site, start a file for notes relating to it. This is the place to record anything and everything you might need later, including:

- Details of the color scheme, including background color, link colors, text color, and special colors/shapes related to particular areas of your site.
- Plans for future expansion. You will have more ideas than you have time to implement. If you take a moment to jot them down, they won't get lost.
- Goals related to the site. Goals could include reaching a certain volume of visitors, sales targets, or achieving a particular measure of visibility, for example.

- Parts of the site that use scripts or other add-ons and how those scripts are set up.
- Publicity and promotional ideas.

Name this file something obvious, like notes.doc, and save it with your other Web site files.

Back It Up!

It would be a terrible shame, not to mention extremely inconvenient, if all of your hard work vanished one day in a matter of seconds. It can happen, and sooner or later, if you don't keep backup copies of your files, Murphy's Law ("anything that can go wrong will go wrong") guarantees that it will. Murphy's Law also guarantees that it will happen at the worst possible moment—the day the *Wall Street Journal* praises your Web site on its front page.

Okay, so maybe that last part is a slight exaggeration, but from time to time computer files do get destroyed, corrupted, or lost. If you have backups on hand, the setback will be minor; if not, hours and days of work can disappear.

Simple Backup Using Floppy Disks

The simplest way to back up your Web site files is to copy them to a floppy disk whenever you make significant changes. Ideally, you should store that disk somewhere other than by your computer so that if some catastrophe such as a fire takes out your entire workspace, the backup will be safely out of harm's way. But even if you just drop the disk into a desk drawer, you're way ahead of the person who didn't back up at all. If you've been saving all those AOL promo disks we all receive in the mail, you can use those and not even have to purchase extra disks.

NOTE: *You might be wondering if your Web hosting service will be backing up the site, making your efforts redundant. They may or they may not. Even if they are, getting the hosting company to successfully restore a file is an iffy and time-consuming proposition. It's safer to do it yourself.*

Building Archives

Although the most urgent reason for backing up your files is to protect against hardware failure, software emergencies, or accidental erasure (the oops factor) that could abruptly wipe out your hard work, it's also a valuable tool for creating an archive of past versions of your site. Archives make it possible to

- Restore earlier versions of a file or feature (not just the most recent version)
- Develop new pages based on earlier pages that are no longer part of the site
- Track how the site has developed and changed over time

Archiving is accomplished by saving old backup copies instead of writing over them. To make the archives usable, they must be organized and stored in a manner that makes it practical and possible to retrieve a particular file when you need it. Having to load and search through a hundred disks for a single file is hardly better than not having that file at all. All this really means is that you need to label each backup carefully and include a list of files it contains. There's plenty of software to simplify and automate this process. (I'll tell you where to get it in a minute.) You may never have a reason to access your archive, but keeping one doesn't add much work to a standard backup program, so it's well worth the effort.

Comprehensive Backup and Archiving Strategies

Periodically copying specific files to a floppy disk may be the simplest way to back up your data, but if your Web site is substantial, or if you have other data you wish to protect as well, you should consider implementing a more robust procedure. A complete backup strategy often includes several different types of backups, and is designed so that backing up data isn't too time consuming (or space consuming) and you are always assured of being able to retrieve a particular file. To accomplish these goals, three different flavors of backup are used in combination.

- **Complete**   As the name implies, a complete backup creates a duplicate of every file within the specified drive or directory. This is also called a full backup. It requires the most media (disks, tapes, CD-ROMs, or whatever you're using to store the backup files).

- **Incremental**   An incremental backup only copies files that have been changed since the last backup (whether complete or incremental). This is a form of partial backup. It is also the quickest type of backup, as there are fewer files to save.

- **Differential**   A differential backup copies all files that have been changed since the last complete backup.

How do you know which files were changed when? You don't have to; the computer operating system and/or backup software tracks that for you. Computer operating systems keep track of which files have been backed up using something called the *archive bit*. You don't need to concern yourself with exactly how an archive bit works, just know that every file has one and it specifies whether the file has been changed since it was last backed up. Backup software reads the status of that bit, and sometimes keeps a separate log file as well, to tell what needs to be backed up.

A typical backup strategy includes making a complete backup from time to time (on a regularly scheduled basis) and using a form of partial backup (either incremental or differential) on a more frequent basis, often daily, in between. The backup media (whatever you're storing the backups on) is labeled to identify date and type of backup, and kept in a safe and accessible place. Most backup software will help you set this up in any combination you prefer.

CD-ROM, Tape Drives, Zip, and Jaz

Although disks can be the quickest and easiest way to back up a few files, they simply don't hold very much data. Because Web sites often involve graphics, which take up a lot of storage space, the space limitation is a substantial drawback for webmasters. Fortunately, there are plenty of other options open to individuals who have more to back up.

Modern computers come equipped with a CD-ROM drive. Often this is a read-only drive (meaning that you can't write files to it), but an ever-increasing percentage of CD-ROM drives are writable as well. If yours is (the documentation that came with your computer should specify which kind you have), it can be a perfect place to store backup files. A CD-ROM typically holds about 650MB (megabytes) of data, which is

600 times as much data as a plain disk. If you use this method, be sure to purchase CD-RW disks, which can be written over and reused, not CD-R disks, which can only be written to once.

Another backup option is the tape drive. Few personal computers come with one, but you can have a tape drive installed for a few hundred dollars. A single tape will hold quite a bit of data—how much depends on the model of tape drive and other factors. This can be very convenient, as you can often insert a tape, set up the software that comes with the drive to perform backups when and how you want, and the backups will take place without your further involvement for days or weeks at a time. Tape backup does have several significant drawbacks. The tapes can be expensive, and if your computer goes down due to a hardware failure, you'll need another computer that has a tape drive in order to retrieve your files.

Zip drives and Jaz drives are specialized, proprietary hardware that allow quick backup of larger amounts of data onto sturdy disks that can be carried in a pocket. Zip disks hold up to 250MB, and Jaz disks can store 1GB to 2GB (gigabytes) per disk. Both are made by Iomega Corporation (**www.iomega.com**).

Remote Backup Services

Another backup possibility is brought to your desktop courtesy of the Internet. It's called remote automated backup, and here's how it works. Late at night while you're snoozing blissfully in bed, another computer connects to yours via the Internet, performs whichever backup process you've specified, and stores the results for you. By the time you sit down at your computer the next day, the job has been done for hours.

VirtualBackup (**virtualbackup.com**), shown in Figure 8-3, provides a free version of its remote backup service. The free version, called VBFree, provides up to 5MB of storage space. There are plenty of companies providing paid remote backup service. Prices vary quite a bit. If you use one of them, take advantage of the free trial most offer to be sure you find the system workable. You can find a list of these on Yahoo! by using the search words "remote backup."

Although there's a shortage of free remote backup services, there is a plentiful supply of companies that will provide free online file storage space. You could always use one of these to hold your backup files

Figure 8-3 • Virtual Backup offers remote automated backup services.

simply by copying the files to the free location. Sources of free online disk space include:

Free Online File Storage	Amount of Disk Space
FreeDiskSpace **freediskspace.com**	25MB of free storage. If you fill out their preferences survey, you get 300MB free.
FreeDrive **freedrive.com**	Up to 20MB storage.
i-drive **idrive.com**	50MB free personal storage.
Kturn **kturn.com**	125MB of free storage.

Automated Backup Software

As I've said all along, you can always back up files by copying them to a handy disk, and that's a great deal better than nothing. If you want to set up a more complete backup system, perhaps for all your files (not just your Web site), then special backup software is just the ticket. Backup software allows you to automate the task, so that all you have to do is provide fresh storage space when more is needed. It also gives greater control over finding and restoring files, sets that archive bit we talked about earlier, and often can be set to compress the backup files so that they take up less storage space.

If you're running Microsoft's Windows operating system, chances are that you already have backup software on your machine. Click the Start button, and look under Programs | Accessories | System Tools, where you should see something named Backup. Figure 8-4 shows what the opening screen of this program, named Microsoft Backup, looks like. It allows you to specify the files, directory, and drives you wish to back up,

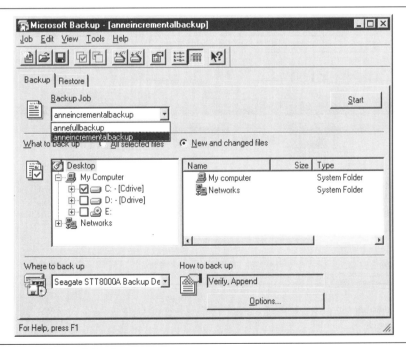

Figure 8-4 • Microsoft Backup

the type of backup (incremental or complete), and where to back them up to.

One of the easiest places to find free backup software is on c/net's download Web site (**download.cnet.com**). Simply select your operating system (PC, Mac, or Linux), and then choose Utilities, and then Backup. Figure 8-5 shows the backup utilities page for a Mac.

Practice Restoring a File

One of the important and often overlooked steps of implementing a backup system is testing the restore process. Don't wait until there's an emergency to try restoring a file. You may find out your backup system wasn't working properly, and then you'll be out of luck. To make sure that doesn't happen, choose and restore a file every once in a while to ensure the integrity of your backups.

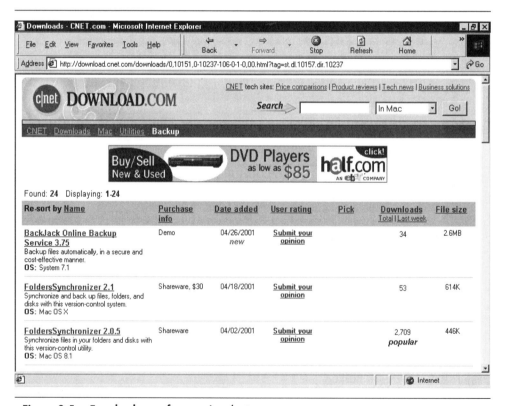

Figure 8-5 • Free backup software via c/net

Whichever backup procedure, hardware, and software you settle on, make it a part of your regular routine. Otherwise, it won't happen. Whenever you make changes to a file, save a copy of the original first. Be sure to save any open files every few minutes in case your computer loses power or locks up.

TIP: *There are only two kinds of computer users in the world: those who have lost data, and those who will.*

Going Beyond HTML

Although HTML supplies everything you need to build a solid Web presence, there are additional Web techniques and technologies you're sure to come across as you spend a greater amount of time online. Those that you'll most likely encounter are described here.

XML An acronym for eXtensible Markup Language, XML is thought by some to be the next generation language for creating Web documents. Like HTML, it centers around the use of tags to create structured documents, but with XML, developers can create and define their own tags instead of being limited to a predetermined set. If you want to learn more about XML, visit XML.com (**www.xml.com**).

Java and JavaScript Java is a full-blown programming language that is commonly used for developing applications on the Web. Programs written in Java are compiled into executable format before they can run. JavaScript, on the other hand, is a scripting language. Things written in JavaScript don't have to be compiled in advance. The more popular Web browsers support JavaScript, so Web page builders sometimes add a little JavaScript to spice up Web pages by adding dynamic content. Plenty of prewritten JavaScripts are available for free. You can find over 700 of them at JavaScripts.com (**javascript.internet.com**).

Cascading Style Sheets (CSS) Cascading style sheets are a way of specifying the characteristics, such as font, color, and alignment, that are associated with particular HTML elements. Styles are defined in one of three places: within the tag, in the <HEAD> section of the document, or in a separate file, called a style sheet, that is then linked to every page in the site. The idea is to separate the formatting of the page from its content so that each can be controlled separately. Although this seems like a great idea, in practice it results in different browsers displaying the pages differently.

Or at least it did as this was being written; the situation may have improved by the time you read this.

Server Side Includes (SSI)   Of all the things listed in this section, SSI is my favorite. SSI allows you to create a single file containing a common element (for example, a footer) and include it in other files using a tag line this:

```
<!--#include virtual="footer.html" -->
```

When a visitor calls up the page with an include statement in it, the Web server preprocesses that page, inserting the contents of the included file, before displaying it. The resulting page appears the same as if it were all one file. This is extremely useful because you can do things like create a single footer and a single header and include them on every page of your site. Then, if you want to change the header later, instead of editing each page individually, you just edit the file containing the header and it's changed everywhere.

To use SSI, your Web hosting service has to support it. Sometimes you'll have to name your files a special way, often as .shtml instead of .html, so the Web server will know to preprocess them. This is rather an advanced topic, so you might want to skip SSI for now, but if you end up building a large site with many pages, it's worth exploring further.

That ought to be enough jargon to hold you for now. If you run into a term you don't recognize, turn to the glossary at the end of this book for an explanation. If it isn't there, check your spelling. Okay, seriously, if it isn't in the glossary, try the Webopedia at **www.webopedia.com**.

9

Chapter Nine

Publishing Your Site

In order for anyone but yourself to see your site, you need to publish it to a Web server. At this point, you should already have a hosting service picked out. If not, please revisit Chapter 4 and find out how to select one.

If you create your site using online tools such as Homestead's SiteBuilder, you won't need to upload (transmit) the files to a server—they will already be there. But most people will be creating the Web pages offline, using a free HTML editor or authoring program. When you do it that way, the pages you create and any supporting files, such as images, need to be uploaded.

What You Need from Your Hosting Service

Pages can be uploaded using a stand-alone FTP program (see Chapter 5 for a list of free ones) or an authoring tool that has an FTP function built in. To use either one, you'll need to know three things:

- FTP address of your site
- User name
- Password

You'll have to input this information the first time you upload files. The FTP program will save the information so that you don't have to reenter it each time.

The FTP address of your site is usually the same as the URL of the site, but without the http:// at the beginning. The user name and password are those you were assigned (or that you chose) when you signed up for hosting service. If you have any trouble determining the proper information, send an e-mail to the tech support address of the hosting service and ask. Before doing that, you should look for a FAQ on the hosting site. Since publishing questions are among the most common questions that hosting services receive, your answer may be more quickly available online.

Connecting to a Web Server Using FTP

The first time you start an FTP program, whether it's a stand-alone application or a component of an authoring program, you'll see a

screen similar to the one shown in Figure 9-1. Start by clicking the New (or in some programs, Open) button to create a new connection.

The Profile Name box is simply the name you will use to identify this connection. This allows you to select from a list of other connections that are already included with the program, or that you might add at a later date. Most people enter the name of the site or the hosting service.

The Host Name/Address box is where you enter the FTP address of your site. If you have your own domain name, that's usually what goes in this box, but without the http:// at the beginning. If you have a subdomain account, as is provided by many free Web hosts, you may need to enter the hosting service's domain name (for example, Homestead.com) instead. In some cases, the FTP address will be different from either of these. Your hosting service should be able to tell you what yours is.

Host Type identifies the operating system of the machine that you will be connecting to. Most FTP programs can automatically detect this, so you won't have to set it yourself. If it's not automatically filled in, choose either Microsoft NT or Unix, depending on your choice of hosting service.

User ID and Password are the user name and password you selected or that were assigned to you by the hosting service when you opened your account. When you enter the password, the letters you type will be replaced by asterisks on the screen. This is a security measure to keep other people from peeking over your shoulder and learning your password.

If you want the program to remember your password so you don't have to type it in every time, click the Save Pwd box. Leave the Anonymous box blank. The Account and Comment boxes are unused as well.

Figure 9-1 • Connection screen from WS_FTP LE

Depending on which FTP program you use, the actual connection screen will vary a bit from the one shown in Figure 9-1. The basic information will be the same. Once you've filled in the blanks, click the OK (or Connect) button to log into your FTP server.

The FTP Program Interface

Once a connection is made, most FTP programs display two panes of information. Typically, files on the local computer are shown on the left, and those of the remote computer on the right. Figure 9-2 shows what this looks like in WS_FTP LE. The numbers in the illustration identify the elements of the screen, which are described next:

1. Address of the local directory that is being displayed.
2. Files and subdirectories in the local directory.
3. Buttons that perform actions on the local directory.
4. Buttons that transfer selected files from local to remote or vice versa.
5. Address of the remote directory that you are connected to.
6. Files and subdirectories in the remote directory.
7. Buttons that perform actions on the remote directory.
8. This is where you select the mode for file transfer. ASCII is for text files, HTML files, and scripts. Binary is for images. Auto tells the program to choose the mode. Not all programs offer the option to choose the transfer mode.
9. Log describing actions that have been taken during this session.
10. Program control and option buttons.

JARGON ALERT: *ASCII (pronounced "ask-key") is an acronym for American Standard Code for Information Interchange. It provides a uniform way for text characters (which people understand) to be translated and stored as numbers (the language of computers).*

You can navigate through both the local and remote directories by clicking your mouse on various parts of the screen. Begin by setting the local and remote start directories to the locations you will be using most often.

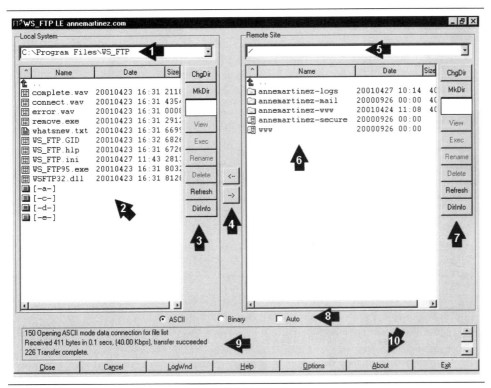

Figure 9-2 • The WS_FTP LE interface

When you start WS_FTP LE (or another FTP program) for the first time, the local directory that is displayed will be the place where you installed the FTP program. Change this to the directory that holds your Web site. To do so, click the up arrow that's on the top line of the local files screen, which will take you up a level in the directory structure. Keep going until you are at the top of the directory structure—or to the *root* of the drive. It may take one click, or two or three. The Local Files address will display C:\, and a bunch of file folders will be listed underneath, as demonstrated in Figure 9-3.

Next, find your way to the local file directory that contains your Web site files by clicking on the appropriate subdirectories in the local files pane. In the remote files pane, move into the directory that your hosting service has identified as the place to put your Web pages. This often

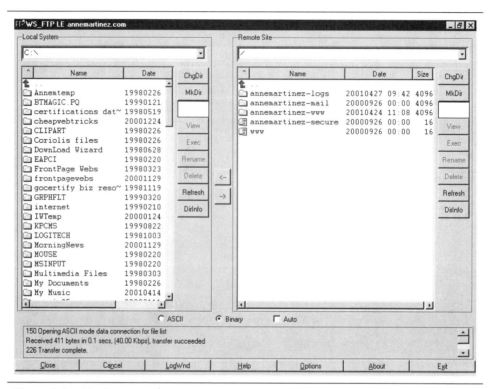

Figure 9-3 • Moving around using FTP

includes the letters "WWW." Figure 9-4 shows what your screen might look like after this step.

Many programs, including WS_FTP LE, allow you to set the current directories as defaults. This way, whenever you log into your Web site, the FTP program will automatically start in your preferred local and remote directories. In WS_FTP LE, this is accomplished by clicking the Options button (at the bottom of the screen) and then clicking the Save Window Locations button.

The first time you connect to your hosting service there will probably be one file in your remote WWW directory, and it will be named index.html. This file is put there by the hosting service when the directory is created. In Chapter 7, you learned that the main page of a Web site is usually named index.html. This is the page that is displayed whenever a visitor accesses the main URL of your site without specifying a particular page (for example, http://annemartinez.com). When you sign up for hosting service, the hosting company will put a temporary index.html into your directory. It usually includes some sort of "under construction" message,

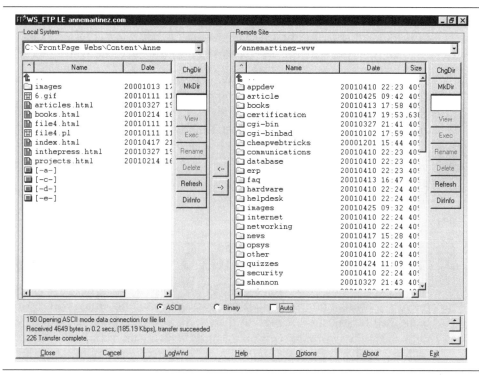

Figure 9-4 • The correct local and remote directories

and is what users who visit your site will see until you publish something else in its place.

> **TIP:**   *Until you get your site into satisfactory viewing condition, leave the temporary index.html file in place. You will still be able to access all the other pages you upload, but visitors will never know the pages are present, or see them in their unfinished state.*

Uploading Files

Once you've connected to the proper local and remote directories, publishing files to your Web site is a three-step process:

1.   In the local pane, highlight the files and directories you want to publish.

2. Choose the type of transfer (ASCII, Binary, or Automatic).
3. Click the button that starts the transfer. For WS_FTP LE, it's the arrow located between the two panes that points toward the right.

That's all there is to it. The files will be transferred from your local computer to the remote computer, and you (and visitors) will be able to see them on the Web. When you are finished transferring files, click Close (or Disconnect) to close the connection, and then exit the FTP program.

> **TIP:**   *Some FTP programs allow you to transfer files simply by dragging them from one pane to the other.*

Gotchas That Don't Have to Getcha

FTP programs have been around longer than the Web, and the protocol they use is stable and reliable. Any problems you encounter will most likely be due to user error rather than something the FTP program did wrong. Hey, we all make mistakes, and those mistakes happen while building Web sites too. If you think you've uploaded a file, but you can't view it in your browser, or the link from another page that's supposed to show the file doesn't work, there are several likely causes.

File Naming Error—Wrong Case   Check to make sure the file name you are typing into your browser and the name of the file on your Web server are identical. Case matters. It's a common mistake to name a file in mixed case, such as MyFile.html, and then try to access it with all lowercase (myfile.html). On a Windows machine, either of these would bring up the file, but on Unix machines, which are often used for hosting, the two are considered different names.

File Naming Error—Transposition   Another common naming error is to inadvertently switch two letters without noticing. It can happen when you name the file originally, or when you type the address into your Web browser. So scrutinize the name you're using to access the file and the name your FTP program says you've published to the Web server, and verify that they are identical.

Wrong Transfer Mode   If you view your Web page in a browser and the graphic that's supposed to appear on it appears as a distorted mess, you probably uploaded the image file under the wrong mode. Images should always be uploaded as binary; HTML files as text.

Wrong Address   If the file is in a subdirectory, and you don't specifically tell the browser to look there, it's not going to find it. Be sure to specify the full path to files that are contained in subdirectories. For example, if you've uploaded myfile.html to a subdirectory of your WWW directory called Create, then to view it in your browser, you'll have to type something like **http://mydomain.com/create/myfile.html**.

The Next Phase

At this point, you know what tools are needed to create a Web site, the steps to follow to develop an effective site design, how to use HTML to build pages, and how to publish them to a Web site. That's everything you need to know to build and publish a Web site.

But designing and building the site are only half the job. To be a success, a site needs a steady stream of visitors, or in the case of a for-profit venture, customers. It also needs features that go beyond the basic—features that promote community and interactivity and that bring visitors back again and again. If profits are in your future plans, the site needs a way to generate revenue. Potential revenue models were discussed in Chapter 2, but I haven't told you how to implement them yet.

All of that lies directly ahead. From here on, the focus of this book will change. Up to this point, we've concentrated on the fundamentals of creating and publishing a site. Now it's time to turn our attention to promotion and profit. Are you ready?

II

Part Two

Promoting Your Web Site

10

Chapter Ten

Building Traffic with Search Engines and Directories

What's the first thing you do when you want to find information about something on the Web? If you're like most Net users, you head straight for Yahoo!, Google, or another portal site, enter a few words related to what you're looking for, and click the Search button. Within a few seconds or minutes, a long list of Web sites matching your criteria pops up on your screen. You peruse the list, choose a likely site, and click the link that takes you there. It's a process that's repeated millions of times a day, by Web surfers in hundreds of countries around the world. And it's a process that you can take advantage of to funnel visitors to your little corner of the Net—your new Web site.

When you search your own computer's hard drive for something, the search program (for example, Find in Windows Explorer) reads through every directory and inspects each file to see if it meets the criteria you specified. A search portal such as Yahoo! doesn't work the same way. It can't, because the sheer size of the Web makes that impractical and impossible.

Your personal computer contains hundreds, or possibly thousands, of files. The Web consists of over a billion pages. Imagine the time and resources it would take to reach and search every one of them every time a user types in a query. So rather than searching every page that exists every time someone wants to find something, search portals use their own precompiled index of the Web instead.

The index is a giant database containing stripped-down information about each Web page that the search portal knows about. What's included in the index and how the information is organized is specific to each individual search portal, but at a minimum, it includes the name of the page or site, its URL, and a bit of text representing the page's content. Often part or all of the page's contents will be stored as well. This makes for a huge amount of data, but it's all stored within easy reach of the search software, and is accessed using painstakingly developed programs optimized for speed and accuracy. You can bet that the computers running the search software are a bit more powerful than the one on your desktop, too.

Your mission is to get your Web page (or pages) into these indexes, and to do it so that your site appears prominently when Web surfers go looking for content that is within your topic area. To make this happen, you need to understand how search engines work, how to get your

pages included in them, and what you can do to up the odds that your site will be among those listed near the top of the results page.

NOTE: *Getting your Web site prominently listed in search indexes is the most important element in promoting your site and building traffic.*

Search Engines vs. Directories

There are actually two kinds of search portals: search engines and directories. Often they are lumped together under the single heading "search engines," but understanding how they are different will help you maximize the results you get from each type.

How Search Engines Work

Search engines use automated software tools to create and automatically update their indexes. One of these tools is called a *spider*. When a search engine learns of a new Web page, the spider visits the page and follows the links it finds there to other pages within the same site. This is referred to as *crawling* the site.

JARGON ALERT: *A spider, crawler, or search bot is a program that automatically fetches Web pages and follows (crawls) the links on them to find additional pages.*

The information that a spider uncovers is added to the search engine's index. Sometimes human intervention is involved; other times the process is wholly automatic. From time to time the spider will revisit each page and record any changes that are found. There is often a time lag between when a spider visits a site and when the site appears in the index. Search engines often list multiple individual pages from a single Web site in their index. Figure 10-1 shows a results page from a search engine site.

JARGON ALERT: *The index used by a search engine or directory can also be referred to as its catalog.*

PART II

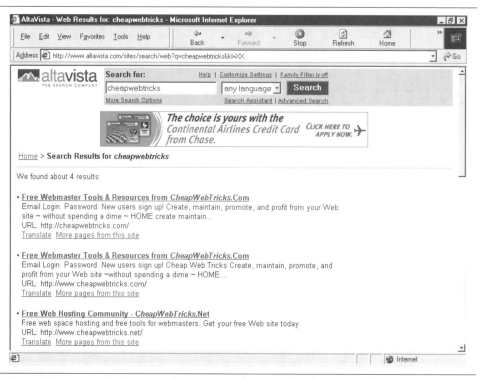

Figure 10-1 • Results from the AltaVista search engine for the entry "cheapwebtricks"

How Directories Work

Unlike a search engine, a *search directory* doesn't rely on spidering software to find and index Web pages. Instead, human beings do it. Often a brief description of the site, along with its URL and a few other particulars, is submitted by the site owner for inclusion. Or an editor at the search directory may become aware of a site she feels is useful and create an index entry for the site.

Directories organize their listings into categories to make them easy for Web surfers to find. A category (or categories) is initially selected by the person who submits the site, but has to be reviewed by someone at the search directory before receiving final approval. This assures that the most accurate and appropriate category is used.

As you've probably gathered, another difference between search engines and directories is that directories usually contain one listing for an entire Web site, rather than individual listings for each page. Figure 10-2 shows the results page from the Yahoo! search directory.

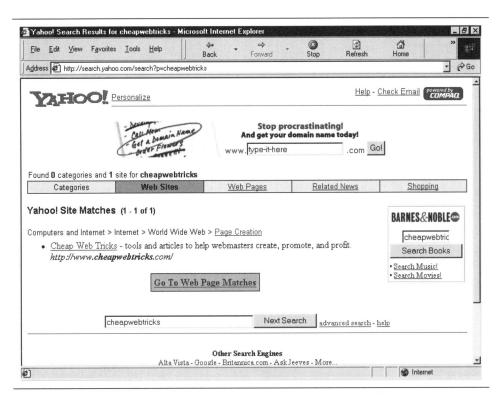

Figure 10-2 • **Search results from the Yahoo! directory are organized by category.**

Hybrid Search Portals and Shared Indexes

Like most other things on the planet Earth, search portals don't always fall strictly into one category or the other. Some search portals are hybrids, combining both a directory and a search engine component in an attempt to provide the best of both worlds. The directory component is human powered and returns single Web site descriptions, while the search engine component is spider powered and returns individual Web pages.

A hybrid site usually presents results from the directory as the primary search source, with a listing of individual pages as a backup. If you look at Figure 10-2 again, you'll notice that underneath the category results there's a link called Go To Web Page Matches. Click it and the page shown in Figure 10-3 comes up—listings of individual Web pages generated by a search engine.

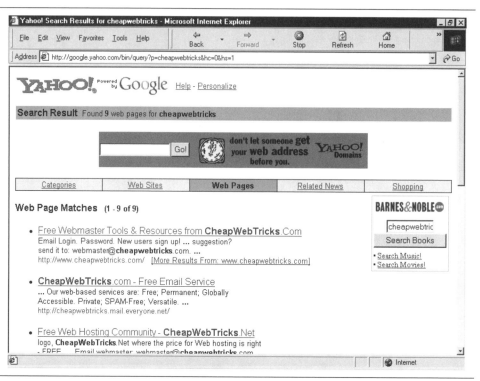

Figure 10-3 • Yahoo! backs up its directory with search engine results.

There's something else notable about Figure 10-3: that "Powered by Google" logo. Wait a minute, isn't Google a competing search portal? Yes and no. Both Yahoo! and Google are search portals, but Yahoo! is primarily a directory, while Google is a search engine. They've teamed up—allowing Yahoo! to provide additional results beyond what's contained in its own directory while keeping visitors on the Yahoo! site and adding another plentiful supply of searchers for Google's index. There's no doubt more to the deal than that, but only the two partners know the full details.

This isn't just good for Google and Yahoo!, it's good for Webmasters too. If you get your site in Google's index, it will appear in Yahoo! search results (though farther down the page), even if you're not included in the Yahoo! directory. There are other indexes that are shared, including those of LookSmart, Inktomi, and the Open Directory Project (ODP).

NOTE: *Some search sites, such as MetaCrawler (**metacrawler.com**), don't have their own index at all. These metasearch portals send a user query to a selection of popular search engines, and then organize and display the results. With this kind of search portal, you can't get your site added to the index, because there isn't one.*

Preparing Your Site

Okay, so you know all about what search engines and directories are and how they work, but how do you get your site listed in them? The short answer is by properly preparing and submitting your pages.

TIP: *Some Webmasters are so eager to get listed that they jump the gun and submit pages that haven't been properly prepared. This results in rejection by some search portals and poor placement in others. Don't fall into this trap. Take the time to set up your pages correctly and reap the reward of increased traffic to your site.*

As I said earlier, search portals don't always use the same methods to select and organize the material that goes into their indexes. Nor do they follow a set formula that determines where a particular listing will appear in the results. Some Webmasters take the extreme step of creating a custom page, called a *doorway*, for each and every search engine. Each doorway page is designed to meet all the known indexing/searching criteria for a particular search engine in order to achieve the highest possible placement.

JARGON ALERT: *A doorway page (also called jump, portal, gateway, or bridge page) is a page specially created to appeal to a particular search engine spider.*

You can do this if you want to, but in my opinion the investment of time and effort involved in individual doorway pages isn't worth the payout of nonguaranteed high placement in the results. Plus, search portals change their methods from time to time, leaving the owner of a dozen portal pages playing a perpetual game of catch-up.

Rather than create a dozen special pages, it's much more efficient to optimize the ones that already exist on your site. There are several basic steps you can take, which won't consume a huge amount of time, and will substantially increase the chances of achieving and maintaining decent visibility in search portals. And once they're done, they're done. There's no revising and updating involved (unless you want to).

The Power of Keywords

If you were allowed one word to describe what your site is about, what would it be? The answer is your first keyword. *Keywords* are words that are closely related to the content and purpose of your site. They are the words and phrases that someone in your target audience might type into a search box. Creating a list of them is the first step of optimizing for search engines.

Starting with that one word that perfectly describes your site's content and/or purpose, create a list of at least 10 keywords—15 or more is even better. These words are going to be used in several ways, so put some thought into choosing them. Organize the list so the most important keywords are at the top.

For example, keywords for the Cheap Web Tricks site include

free webmaster tools	search engine submission
frugal	HTML editor
hosting	freeware
message board	affiliate programs
chat	graphics tools
build traffic	making money
ISP	cgi scripts
internet access	directory
ad software	cheap web tricks
webring	cheapwebtricks
site tools	dynamite web site
hit counters	

Note that these are single words and phrases, not full sentences.

Why are keywords so important? They are one of the primary considerations, if not the single most important criteria, that search engines use to determine when to include a page in a set of search results. Although each search engine utilizes keywords in a distinct way, search engine experts agree that frequency and location of keywords is a critical factor. If your pages are a bit different from each other, consider making a separate keyword list for each one, or at least each major page.

Meta Tag Magic

The first thing you're going to do with your keyword list is use it to create meta tags. Meta tags are HTML tags that spiders read, but site visitors don't see (unless they choose to view the source code of your page). They go in the <HEAD> section of the page.

> **TIP:** *When creating a new page, make it a habit to add the meta tags first. That way you'll be certain not to forget them.*

Recall from Chapter 7 that an HTML tag has an attribute with a value. Meta tags follow this structure too. As far as preparing your pages for search engines, the two attributes that are most important are keywords and description. The keyword <META> tag looks like this:

```
<META name="keywords" content="word1, word2, word3">
```

The description <META> tag looks like this:

```
<META name="description" content="This is what this page is
about.">
```

Notice that the meta tag is one of the HTML tags that doesn't use a closing tag.

Many search engines use both of these tags to determine positioning in results pages. According to the underlying specification that defines how meta tags work, the entire tag (from < to >) can be up to 1024 characters long, including the quotes and spaces. In practice, few search engines are going to allow that much information, so don't feel that you need to inflate your tags to the full 1024 allowed. There are a few more considerations to keep in mind.

When creating a keyword tag, consider

- Keywords should all be lowercase and separated by commas.
- Phrases are allowed.
- The same word can be included more than once, but avoid repeating it more than three times or it may work against you.
- Include words you think people would use when searching for the material on your site.

When creating a description tag, consider

- The contents of the description tag often appear word for word as the site description on a results page, so make it an enticement for people to visit. This is one of the most critical places to sell your Web site, so it's worth repeated rewrites until it's the best you can make it.
- Include a few of the keywords, in a logical way.
- Avoid using hype, such as "We're number one!" or all capital letters.
- Be succinct and accurate. Aim for about 25 words.

The Title Tag

Another very important tag to use to prepare your site for search engines is the <TITLE> tag. This one also goes in the <HEAD> section. The <TITLE> tag specifies what will appear at the top of the browser window as a page's title, and search engines often use this as the title of the listing for a page. It looks like this:

```
<TITLE>my page title</TITLE>
```

Notice that it does require a closing tag. If you can work a keyword or two into this, do it.

Keyword Voyeurism

Want to see what terms people are really searching on? A few search engines allow you to spy on their users, and/or track the most popular search terms. The following screen shows the WebCrawler.com Search Ticker in action.

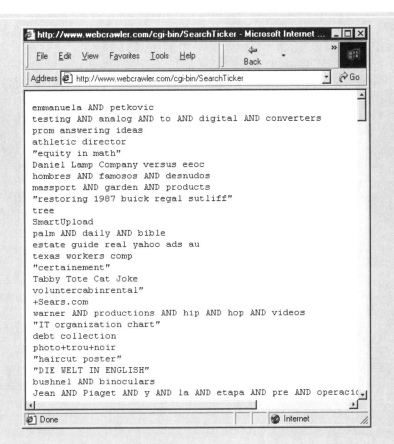

```
emmanuela AND petkovic
testing AND analog AND to AND digital AND converters
prom answering ideas
athletic director
"equity in math"
Daniel Lamp Company versus eeoc
hombres AND famosos AND desnudos
massport AND garden AND products
"restoring 1987 buick regal sutliff"
tree
SmartUpload
palm AND daily AND bible
estate guide real yahoo ads au
texas workers comp
"certainement"
Tabby Tote Cat Joke
voluntercabinrental"
+Sears.com
warner AND productions AND hip AND hop AND videos
"IT organization chart"
debt collection
photo+trou+noir
"haircut poster"
"DIE WELT IN ENGLISH"
bushnel AND binoculars
Jean AND Piaget AND y AND la AND etapa AND pre AND operacio
```

Other search tickers include:

- Ask Jeeves Take A Peek (**www.askjeeves.com/docs/peek/**)
- Excite Search Voyeur (**www.excite.com/search/voyeur/**)
- Lycos Weekly Top 50 (**50.lycos.com/**)
- metacrawler metaspy (**www.metaspy.com/spy/ filtered_a.html**)—excludes potentially offensive queries)
- metacrawler exposed (**www.metaspy.com/spy/unfiltered_a.html**)
- Search.com Snoop (**savvy.search.com/snoop**)
- WebCrawler Search Ticker (**www.webcrawler.com/cgi-bin/ SearchTicker**)
- WordTracker (**www.wordtracker.com/**)
- Yahoo Buzz (**buzz.yahoo.com/**)

PART II

Competitive Intelligence vs. Metajacking

As part of determining which keywords are best for your site, it's not a bad idea to check out competitors' pages to see what they have in place. To do this, you can go to the popular search engines, enter terms that you would expect to bring up your site if it was already listed, and see which sites come up on top. Then, go to those sites and view the source code behind the page (by selecting View | Source from your browser menu), and see what terms they are using. This is legitimate competitive intelligence. Wholesale copying of them isn't.

Swiping someone else's meta tags is called *metajacking*, and it isn't looked upon favorably. In fact, it can even land you in court. Including someone else's trademarked name or slogan in your meta tags can get you in trouble too—expensive legal trouble.

Once you've added the meta and title tags to your HTML page, it should look something like this:

```
<HTML>
<HEAD>
    <TITLE>my page title</TITLE>
    <META name="keywords" content="word1, word2, word3">
    <META name="description" content="This is what this
page is about.">
</HEAD>
<BODY>
    page contents go here
</BODY>
</HTML>
```

Free Meta Tag Tools

Even though it's not very difficult to create your own meta tags, there are plenty of free tools around to make the job even easier. These range from programs that will count keywords on your page to those that will produce meta tags for you. Here are two freebies you might want to try:

- The CheapWebTricks.com meta tag generator (**cheapwebtricks.com /products/meta_generator.shtml**), which is shown in Figure 10-4, automatically creates meta tags for your site based on information you provide.

- The Keyword Counter (**keywordcount.com**) counts the top keywords on any page on your site and compares them to another page (for example, a competitor's).

Additional Touches

There are a few more things you can do with those all-important keywords to improve search engine placement. First, make sure they appear more than once in the actual content of the page—the closer to the top, the better. Second, include them (as appropriate) in the alt="" attributes of your image tags. According to search engine experts, some spiders incorporate these into their calculations.

Finally, and perhaps most important of all, make sure your pages are well designed and provide meaningful content. If not, you won't get into directories built by editors in the first place, and the people who find your site via search engines won't come back a second (and third) time.

PART II

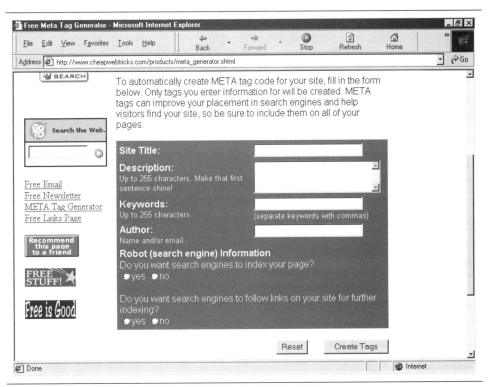

Figure 10-4 • Cheap Web Tricks free meta tag generator

Search Engine No-Nos

Given how important it is to convince search engines to drive traffic to your site, it can be tempting to try to trick search engines into giving you a higher listing than you might normally achieve. If you research search placement a bit further, you'll probably come across techniques that promise to do just that. By using them, you run the risk that search engines that figure out what you're attempting will ban you from their directory entirely. Here are search engine don'ts:

- Don't repeat keywords over and over.
- Don't "load" your page by putting keywords or other text in the same color as the background so that viewers won't see it but search engines will.
- Don't use keywords that you think are popular, but have nothing to do with your site (for example, "sex").
- Don't include competitors' names or slogans in your keywords if that's the only place they appear in your site.
- Don't insert comment tags just so you can stuff them with keywords.

NOTE: *Most search engines cannot successfully index sites that use frames. If you use them, create a <noframes> section on the main page. Put relevant content there. Only search engines and browsers that don't support frames will see it.*

Robot Exclusion

Every Webmaster wants every search robot to come and index every page of their Web site and place it in an index so more people will visit the site, right? Not always. Sometimes search portal spiders are not welcome on a site, a section of a site, or even just a single page. For example, someone with a personal Web site intended only for family and friends might want it kept out of search engines and directories. Or perhaps some temporary pages, which shouldn't be included in indexes, have been added to the site.

NOTE: *Compliance with the robots.txt or the robots meta tag is strictly up to the visiting spider program. Most legitimate spiders honor both.*

There are two ways you can discourage robots from indexing part or all of a site: the robots meta tag and the robots.txt file.

The Robots Meta tag

A robots meta tag, like other meta tags, goes in the <HEAD> section of an HTML document. When it's intended to discourage spidering it looks like this:

```
<META name="robots" content="noindex,nofollow">
```

"Noindex" tells the spider not to index the page. "Nofollow" tells it not to follow any links it finds on the page. You can use this tag to specify different things, for example,

```
<META name="robots" content="index,nofollow">
```

instructs spiders to index the page, but not follow any links that it contains. On the other hand,

```
<META name="robots" content="noindex,follow">
```

signifies that the page shouldn't be indexed, but it's okay to follow any links.

TIP: *The cheapwebtricks.com free meta tag generator will create a robots tag for you.*

Robots.txt

Webmasters can also control spidering of their site by adding a plain text file named robots.txt to the root directory of the site. That means the URL of robots.txt would be something like mydomain.com/robots.txt. If your site is a subdomain site, or is in a subdirectory, you can't use this method of excluding robots; you'll have to use the robots meta tag instead.

A robots.txt file can be created using any simple text editor, or with a special tool such as RoboGen (shown in Figure 10-5), which can be obtained from **www.rietta.com/robogen/**. A robots.txt file looks something like this:

```
User-agent: *
Disallow: /cgi-bin/
Disallow: /temp/
Disallow: /family/children.html
```

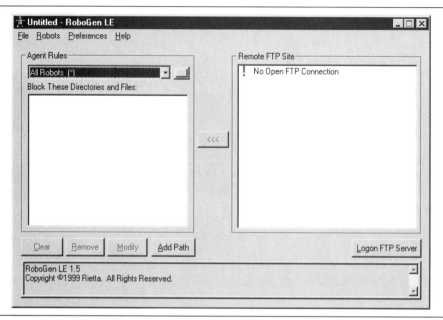

Figure 10-5 • RoboGen LE will build a robots.txt file for you.

The first line, "User-agent: *," indicates that the information that follows applies to all robots that visit the site. You can target a particular robot if you wish, but most likely you'll want all of them to follow the same instructions.

Each "Disallow" line specifies a directory or file that the spider should not visit. In the example, the entire contents of the cgi-bin and temp directories are off-limits—so is the file with the URL mydomain.com/family/children.html.

A robots.txt file intended to tell all spiders to go away without indexing any part of it would look like this:

```
User-agent: *
Disallow: /
```

Checklist for Search Engine Readiness

❑ Pages are in finished, viewable condition.

❑ Meta keywords and description tags have been added to every major page.

❑ Every page has a <TITLE> tag.

❑ Keywords appear near the top of each page.

❑ If desired, robots.txt or robot meta tags are in place.

Choosing Your Targets

Once your Web site is search engine ready, it's time to choose an array of search portals to invite in. Start with the major, don't-miss search sites, but don't overlook smaller, more focused search portals as well.

It's possible to use free search engine tools to submit your pages to a bunch of search portals at once. (I provide a list in "Automated Search Engine Submission," later in this chapter.) This can save hours of time, and I suggest you use them, but not for every search site. Some search sites either don't take automated submissions, or are so crucial that it's worth every minute it takes to submit to each one individually.

The submission process for most search engines requires you to provide a title and brief description of your site. Have these ready. For the description, use the meta tag description you crafted earlier.

Start with These Key Search Sites

Start your quest for search listings by compiling a list of your top targets. These are the biggest search portals—the ones that people think of first when they want to find something on the Web. This category also includes a few more portals that may not be at the forefront of the average Web surfer's list, but that have the power to send lots of users your way for various reasons. Submit to these sites by visiting each one individually and completing the process that's specific to the site.

Open Directory Project (dmoz.org)

Why It's a Must The Open Directory Project (ODP) is an ambitious attempt to create a massive and free directory of Internet resources, organized by category, and maintained by a network of volunteers. The key to the power of this resource is the free license associated with it. ODP grants free use of the directory data to virtually any site that wants to use it. Many search portals, including top names like AOL, Netscape, and HotBot, take advantage of this, incorporating ODP data into their systems. This means that if you get into the ODP database, you get into much more than a single search portal.

Submission Procedure   Drill down to the category that best fits your site. Click the Add URL link at the bottom of the page and complete the forms. Figure 10-6 shows the ODP site submission page.

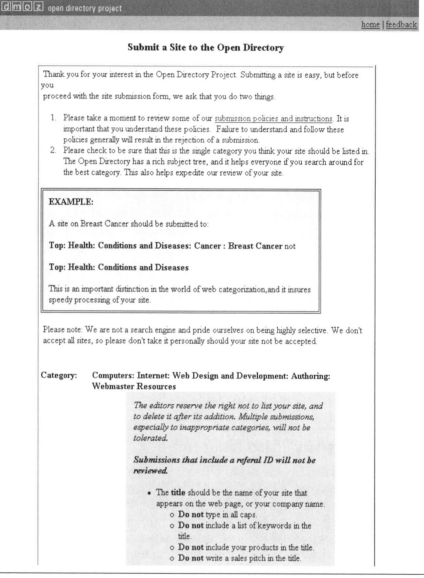

Figure 10-6 • Submitting a site to the Open Directory Project

- The **description** should be a brief summary of your site's purpose or products and services.
  - The description should be **in english** and in coherent **sentence form**.
  - **Do not** include superlatives or a sales pitch.
  - **Do not** submit your company history.
  - **Do not** submit a list of keywords.
  - **Do not** use unnecessary capitalization, or include HTML tags.

- **Submit to only ONE category**
  - Please check that your site does not have a sub-category dedicated to it already. If it does submit to that category, but **not** both.

  category description

⚠️Are you sure this is the most descriptive category for your site? If you are unsure, please take a little extra time in searching the directory and find the most appropriate category.

Site URL: http://

⚠️URL stands for Uniform Resource Locator, which means your site address. Example: http://dmoz.org

- Do not add mirror sites.
- Do not submit an URL that contains only the same or similar content as other sites you may have listed in the directory. Multiple submissions of the same or related sites may result in the exclusion and/or deletion of those and all affiliated sites.
- Do not disguise your submission and submit the same URL more than once. Example: http://www.dmoz.org and http://www.dmoz.org/index.html.
- Do not submit any site with an address that redirects to another address.
- The Open Directory has a policy against the inclusion of sites with illegal content. Examples of illegal material include child pornography; libel; material that infringes any intellectual property right; and material that specifically advocates, solicits or abets illegal activity (such as fraud or violence).
- Do not submit sites "under construction."
- Submit pornographic sites to the appropriate category under Adult.
- Submit non-English sites to the appropriate category under World.
- Don't submit sites consisting largely of affiliate links.

Title of Site:

⚠️Please supply a short and descriptive title.

- Always opt for the official name of the site.
- Do not use ALL CAPITAL letters.
- Exclude promotional language in the title.

Figure 10-6 • Submitting a site to the Open Directory Project (continued)

Site
Description:

⚠Keep the description of your site brief - no longer than 25-30 words. A well-
written, objective description will make listing your site easier.

- Do not use any HTML tags
- Write in complete sentences and/or descriptive phrases using proper
  grammar, punctuation and correct spelling.
  - Do not use ALLCAPS in your description.
  - Avoid capitalizing every word in a sentence.
  - Don't repeat the title of your site in the description.
- Avoid using promotional language and strings of key words and search
  terms. Words and phrases like "cool" and "best darn site" will be removed.

Your E-mail
Address:
(optional)

Submission Agreement

In exchange for ODP's consideration of the site I am submitting, I agree

- To be bound by the ODP's <u>Terms of Use</u>.
- To waive any claim related to the inclusion, placement, exclusion, or removal of this or any
  other site in the ODP Directory or to the title or description of any site appearing in the
  ODP Directory; and
- To grant Netscape Communications Corporation a non-exclusive, royalty-free license to
  use, publish, copy, edit, modify, or create derivative works from my submission.

I also acknowledge that Netscape and the ODP have unfettered editorial discretion to determine
the structure and content of the
directory and that, because a site's placement in the directory is subject to change or deletion at
any time, I may not rely on any aspect of a site's inclusion in the directory.

**I have read and understand the submissions guidelines, and
I'm ready to submit my site**

Submit

Figure 10-6 • Submitting a site to the Open Directory Project *(continued)*

Yahoo! (yahoo.com)

Why It's a Must   Yahoo! is typically one of the first search portals that a Web surfer turns to when looking for information. Yahoo! itself is a directory, but after displaying matches drawn from its own index, it provides additional listings of individual Web page results drawn from Google.

Submission Procedure   Drill down to the category that best fits your site. Click the Suggest A Site link at the bottom of the page and complete the forms. Commercial sites are required to use Yahoo!'s Business Express submission service, a for-fee service that's described later in this chapter.

About.com (about.com)

Why It's a Must   About.com has succeeded in making a name for itself as one of the best topically organized information resources on the Web. It combines editorial reviews and information with site listings, which means it has a higher proportion of quality links than many search engines. It also consists of a huge number of topic areas, all interconnected and driving traffic to each other (and potentially to you).

Submission Procedure   Go to About.com and find the category that is most closely related to your Web site. Each category has an editor (called a guide). This person is prominently named near the top of the page, along with a "contact guide" link. Click the contact link and send a personal note to the guide, asking to be added as a resource and explaining why your site merits inclusion.

Round Two

Once you've submitted to the top-tier search portals, it's time to move on to the next level. The search sites at this level are broad-based, general-interest sites that are popular or up-and-coming Web launching pads. You can apply to many of them by using automated submission tools. Of course, you can always do them individually, if you prefer to do so.

- AltaVista (**altavista.com**)
- DirectHit (**directhit.com**)
- Excite (**excite.com**)
- Google (**google.com**) *Especially important to submit to because of its partner arrangements with other search sites
- HotBot (**hotbot.com**)
- Lycos (**lycos.com**)

- NerdWorld (**nerdworld.com**)
- Northern Light (**northernlight.com**)
- WebCrawler (**webcrawler.com**)

TIP: *Directly submitting your site isn't the only thing that may cause it to appear in a search portal. Spidering software may follow links to your site from elsewhere and discover it that way.*

Getting on Specialized Sites

Once you've worked through the previous must-have lists, it's time to turn your attention to special-interest search engines and directories. Unlike general-interest search sites, specialized search sites target a specific topic or topic area. This means they can become a launching point for individuals seeking information on a particular industry or subject matter. There are hundreds of these specialized sites. They are much smaller than the portals you've already submitted to, but because of their focused nature, they can still be a significant source of visitors.

JARGON ALERT: *A search portal that focuses on a specific market is sometimes called a vortal, which is short for "vertical portal."*

Before you can submit to these search sites, you have to find those that are relevant to your audience. The Argus Clearinghouse (**clearinghouse.net**), which is shown in Figure 10-7, is a great place to start. It's a searchable index of search engines and directories, each of which has been visited and checked for quality. Another good spot is Yahoo!'s Search Engines and Directories category (**yahoo.com/Computers_and_Internet/Internet/World_Wide_Web/ Searching_the_Web/Search_Engines_and_Directories/**). A third resource is AllSearchEngines.com (**allsearchengines.com**), which, like Argus Clearinghouse, is a directory of search sites, but is a bit less selective of what gets included.

Automated Search Engine Submission

Submitting your pages to a dozen or more search sites, while not complicated, can be a time-consuming and tedious process. This means

Figure 10-7 • The Argus Clearinghouse is a searchable directory of search sites.

it's a job that's a good candidate for automation by computer. As mentioned earlier, certain top-tier search sites are worth visiting individually and hand submitting your pages. For the others, there are free submission tools that will take care of the clicking and typing for you. There are also paid submission tools, but for most people the free versions will readily suffice. Figure 10-8 shows the starting page of Submit Plus!, which offers both free and paid submission services.

Free site submission services include

Add Me! **addme.com**	Submit to 25 popular search directories.
Submit Plus! **submitplus.com**	Submit to up to 100 search engines for free.
Submit Corner **submitcorner.com/Tools/Submit/**	Submit to about 20 search sites with a few clicks.
SubmitShack aka Submit4Free **submitshack.com**	Easily submit to more than 50 search portals.

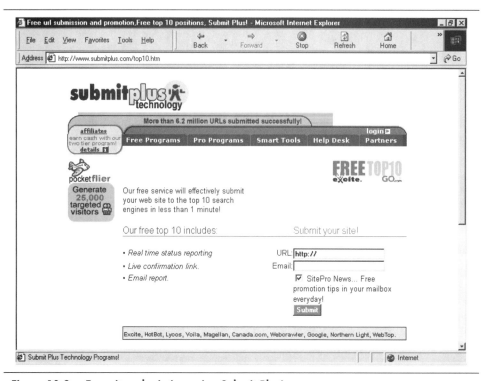

Figure 10-8 • Free site submission using Submit Plus!

You can find more on the Cheap Web Tricks site at **cheapwebtricks.com/ promote/**.

Free vs. Paid Listing

It used to be that getting a site included in a search index was always free to the site owner. This worked for the search sites because they could make up the bulk of their revenue through advertising and other sources. But advertising revenue on the Web hit a slump, and that forced many search portals to reexamine their revenue models. The result is that some of them now charge Webmasters for listings that used to be free. Others have added premium listings that give advantages to paid Web sites, but don't exclude nonpaying sites.

While it's tempting to categorically avoid those for-fee services, it's worth understanding what they are and how they work before you do that. For some sites, it just may make economic sense to participate in

one. And the for-pay search engine model seems to become more prevalent as time passes.

> **TIP:** *Keep records of the places and dates you submit pages. This will make it easier to check back later and will save you from inadvertently double submitting.*

Pay for Inclusion

"Pay-for-inclusion" search sites charge a fee to add your listing to their index. Sometimes this fee doesn't even ensure inclusion, just that your site will be reviewed for possible inclusion within a specified period of time. As penny-pinching and frugal as we are, we would love to sneer at this as ridiculous and unnecessary. However, we can't—commercially oriented sites should seriously consider paying for carefully chosen inclusion opportunities.

The most attractive thing about pay-for-inclusion services is that your site gets listed fast. With the free methods, there's no guarantee when or if your pages will be listed. Some search portals add new pages immediately. Others take weeks, or even months. For many frugal Webmasters, this is okay. There are other things you can do to promote your site in the meantime. But if waiting is not okay with you, the top pay-for-inclusion possibilities that you should consider are described next.

LookSmart (looksmart.com)

> **Cost:** $199 for review within two days; $99 for eight weeks. One-time charge.

As mentioned earlier, LookSmart is an index supplier to quite a few search portals (370+), including such top sites as Microsoft's MSN, Excite, AltaVista, iWon, Juno, and others. LookSmart claims to reach 83 percent of U.S. Internet users. This can be a relatively quick way to get a listing on many search portals. There may be a slight time lag between a site's acceptance into LookSmart and when it appears on partner sites.

Yahoo Business Express (add.yahoo.com/fast/add)

> **Cost:** $199; $600 for adult-oriented sites. One-time charge.

Yahoo! is arguably the most-used search site on the Web, largely because it was one of the first. The fee for Business Express guarantees that your site will be considered for inclusion within seven business days. If the site is rejected, there is an appeal process. Noncommercial sites are welcome to use this service too, though they are still allowed to use the free process if timing isn't urgent.

> **TIP:** *Paying Yahoo!'s Business Express fee does not ensure that your site will be included in Yahoo!, only that it will be considered within seven business days.*

Inktomi (positiontech.com/inktomi/)

Cost: $30/year first URL; $15/year 2–20th URL (price drops again at 21 URLs).

An underlying search technology provider, Inktomi is only recently entering public awareness. They provide indexing information to numerous search partners (125 per a recent count), including AOL, iWon, MSN, GoTo, and HotBot. Inktomi promises to include your page in its index, plus respider the site every 48 hours. This price keeps the URL in the index for a year.

Pay for Ranking/Click

The second approach that pay-to-play search engine sites take is to sell results placement to the highest bidder. This model is a bit more controversial. Site owners bid on individual search terms. The site owner that bids highest will be the first listing to appear in results that include the site's category, the next highest bidder's listing appears second, and so on. When a searcher clicks on a link, the owner of that site is charged the amount of his bid (for example, five cents).

It's important to note that this keyword bidding is for placement in the results, not advertising on the results page. It's also possible to purchase keyword-associated advertising, but that's a different matter.

Figure 10-9 shows the results page of GoTo.com, the best-known of the pay-for-placement/click approach. If you're interested in this method, you can find more such sites at **payperclicksearchengines.com**.

Frequently Asked Questions

Now you know the ins and outs of getting your site included in search portals, but chances are that you probably still have a few questions. The

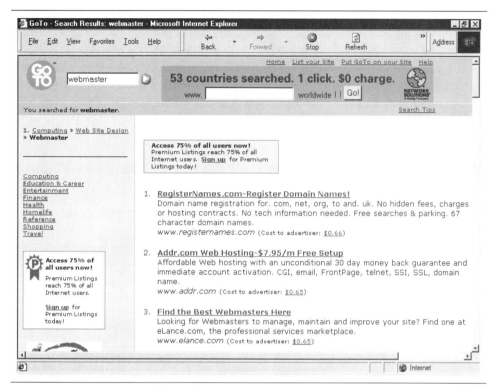

Figure 10-9 • GoTo.com sells results positioning to the highest bidder, who pays per user click.

following are some of the most frequently asked questions about getting listed on search portals. Heck, I'll even throw in the answers, for free.

How Long Will It Take for My Listing to Appear?

Your listing can appear within days, or it may take weeks, and in some cases months. (Yahoo! is a prime example of taking months.) Each search portal has its own methods and schedule. I suggest that if you submitted a site and it doesn't appear in the index after four weeks, resubmit it. *Don't* resubmit every day. That may just get the page permanently banned.

How Do I Tell if I'm in a Particular Search Engine?

Start by searching on your site's URL; if it comes up, you're in. That part is obvious, but what is less apparent is that even if your site doesn't come up with such a search, that doesn't necessarily mean you're not in the index.

Often, you can verify inclusion by typing a special command along with the URL that you wish to check into the search box. The exact command varies from portal to portal. Here are a few examples using cheapwebtricks.com as the domain being researched:

- url:cheapwebtricks.com (Yahoo!)
- domain:cheapwebtricks.com (HotBot)
- host:cheapwebtricks.com (AltaVista)
- site:cheapwebtricks.com (Google)

If none of those does the trick, try orginurl:cheapwebtricks.com/index.shtml.

You can also use free position checking software that will query several search sites and create a report on your presence (or absence) from each. Usually they will only report if you are included in the top 50 or so results, so don't count on them for the final word.

- Cybertack's Search Engine Position Ranking (**cybertack.com/position/position.cgi**)
- did-it detective (**did-it.com/search_engine/detective.cg**i)
- PositionAgent (**positionagent.com/**)
- RateMe (**autosubmit.com/rateme.html**)

Can Submission Services That Promise a Top 10 Ranking Really Deliver?

It's possible that under an obscure term, or for a term no one else is using (like your company name), the service could get you in the Top 10. But there's only so much room at the top, so everyone can't be there. For popular terms, it's unlikely anyone (with the exception of the search portal itself) should be guaranteeing anything. Regard all such claims with suspicion and get any guarantees in writing before spending dollar one. Ask for references and check them.

Does Anything Besides Keywords Influence Ranking in Search Engine Results?

Each search portal has its own method of ranking search results. They all look for keywords. Some also consider how many other links lead back

to a particular page. The logic is that a site linked to by lots of other pages is likely to contain better-quality material. Another factor that sometimes comes into play is how often searchers click on a particular link—sites that are clicked on more often in search results may receive a ranking boost. Keywords and meta tags are the elements you have the most control over, so start with those.

Where Can I Learn More About Search Engines?

You mean I haven't told you every possible thing you wanted to know? Sorry about that—I did try. But search engines and directories are a very interesting topic, and there's lots more you can read about them. I recommend Search Engine Watch (**searchenginewatch.com**) and SearchEngines.com (**searchengines.com**) as excellent resources on search portal technology, tips, and tricks.

PART II

11

Chapter Eleven

No-Cost Promotion Tips, Tricks, and Techniques

O nce you've built your site, made it search-engine friendly, and prepped and submitted it to search portals, you're well along the road to owning a successful Web site. Give yourself a well-earned pat on the back. If you want to take a break from all of this Webmaster stuff, now is the time. You've reached a point where the site should toodle along just fine on its own for a bit while you take a breather.

But if you're like many new Webmasters, chances are your enthusiasm is surging, and you're eager to charge ahead. That's good, because there's lots more you can do to draw visitors to your Web site. For many of us, it's kind of a personal challenge—how much traffic can we attract and how fast can we do it? Now is the time to find out.

Ad Swapping

One of the simplest ways to promote a site for free is to trade advertising opportunities with other sites. The most common way to go about this is to trade advertising banners or buttons, or simple text links. You post theirs, and they post yours, and it doesn't cost either party a dime.

Banner Advertising Networks

The quickest and easiest way to start swapping banners is to join an existing banner advertising network. There are lots of them to choose from, and virtually any Web site can join.

How Banner Ads Work

When you join a banner network, you're provided with a few lines of HTML to insert at the top of your Web page. The HTML causes banners belonging to other members of the network to appear on your site. The banner network records how many banners you display. Many networks also track how many times someone clicks on them.

JARGON ALERT: *A single display of an advertising banner is called an impression. A banner that has displayed 100 times has had 100 impressions.*

At the same time, you provide a banner that will advertise your site, and it will appear on other network member pages. This is usually not a one-for-one exchange; each network has its own ratio in effect. Commonly, for every two banners you display, yours will be displayed once. This allows the organization running the network to sell the remaining impressions to other advertisers, or to run its own advertisements.

Choosing a Banner Network

When you sign up for a banner network, you'll have to provide your site name and URL, your name and e-mail address, choose a password, and upload the banner you want displayed. (I'll tell you how to make a banner later in this chapter.) The password allows you to log into your account and check the statistics showing how many banners have been displayed on your site, and how many times your banner was shown. Figure 11-1 shows the sign-up page of a popular banner network. Figure 11-2 shows the statistics report from another network.

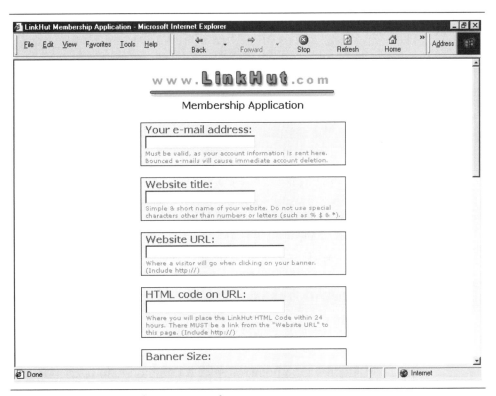

Figure 11-1 • Joining a banner network

PART II

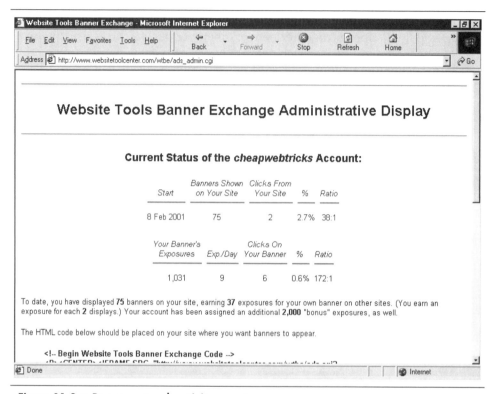

Figure 11-2 • Banner network activity report

When choosing a banner network, there are several factors to consider. First, look for one that is likely to get your banner in front of your target audience. This might mean joining a network that focuses on a special-interest group (for example, Webmasters), or choosing a network that lets you specify the types of sites your banner will appear on.

TIP: *Many banner networks run a referral bonus system. When someone joins the banner service through your Web page, you get extra credits toward the display of your banner. In some cases, you get ongoing credits for as long as the referred person remains a member.*

Next, consider the ratio being offered. A common ratio is 2:1 (for every two network banners shown on your site, one of your banners is displayed elsewhere), but 3:2 is not unusual. Resist any solicitations to purchase extra displays of your banner, at least until you discover how well your banner exchange is performing.

Many banner networks offer sign-on incentives in the form of extra displays of your banner. This is especially valuable to new sites because with fewer visitors to view network banners, a new Web site earns credits more slowly.

TIP: *Be very wary of networks that only give credit for banner clicks (not for impressions). This can be an extremely slow way to earn displays of your own banner.*

As far as controlling the banners that will appear on your page, while most banner networks assure you that no pornographic banners will be shown, beyond that there's usually little control over exactly what will appear. Usually this is no big deal, but it's something you should be aware of. A few banner networks allow members to target their own banners to a particular category of member sites, but this is a rare feature.

If the network sign-up page also includes a directory of member sites, use it to do a bit of browsing. By viewing current network members, you can learn what kinds of sites are included in the network, and get a feel for the types of ads that are displayed.

There are plenty of banner networks to choose from. Try a few different ones to see which works best for you. Table 11-1 contains a list to get you started. You can find more in the promote section of the Cheap Web Tricks site (**cheapwebtricks.com/promote/**).

JARGON ALERT: *When a Web page with a banner on it is displayed, the page requests the banner image from the server. This is called a request. If the visitor moves on before the banner finishes loading, the request does not become an impression and is usually not counted by ad tracking software.*

Banner swapping is the most prevalent form of free advertising networks, but a few networks offer the opportunity to swap other things, such as buttons or links.

Banner Network	Ratio	Description
MyComputer.com Banner Exchange **bannerexchange.mycomputer.com**	2:1	You can upload up to three banners and track their success rate individually.
linkHUT.com **linkhut.com**	3:2	Choose the types of banners that will display on your site, as well as the categories of sites your banner will appear on.
SmartClicks **looksmartclicks.com/promote/ smartclicks/**	2:1	Categorize your banner so it appears on appropriate member sites.
1for1 Banner Exchange **www.1for1.com**	2:1 most of the time, 1:1 five days per month	Upload and track an unlimited number of banners.
bCentral Banner Network **bcentral.com/services/bn**	Extensive statistics	Get added to bCentral's SurfPoint directory when you join. This network belongs to Microsoft Corporation.

Table 11-1 • Banner Networks

Webmaster to Webmaster Trades

While banner networks can result in broad exposure of your banner, sometimes more narrowly focused advertising can be more effective. That's where individual arrangements with other Webmasters can pay off.

As with any advertising option, the most important consideration for this kind of arrangement is this: Will the swap put your site in front of your target audience? If your site is all about exotic plants, an advertising trade with a site that's devoted to nutritional supplements probably isn't going to do much for you. A swap with an organic gardening site, on the other hand, could work well for both participants.

To find potential trading partners, your best bet is to brainstorm a list of categories of Web sites that might make good trading partners, and then use search portals to find sites that fit those categories. Once you're on a promising page, look for a "contact us" or "Webmaster" link, and use it to e-mail your proposal.

To avoid potential misunderstandings, be sure to clarify the exact terms of the trade: Will it be a banner, link, or button? Where will it be placed, and how long will it remain there? If your trading partner has a busier site, it may be fair to trade a more prominent ad on your site for a less prominent one on theirs. Keep it simple, but don't be afraid to

negotiate. Remember, there are other things you can trade besides banner advertisements; for example, links, reviews, or whatever creative possibility you can come up with.

How to Make an Advertising Banner

If you're going to join a banner network or swap ads with other Webmasters, you'll need at least one banner of your own. You can hire a graphic designer to create one for you, or (this is obviously my favorite route) make it yourself for free.

Free Ad Banner Generators

The quickest and least-expensive way to get a banner for your site is to use a free online ad banner generation program, like the one shown in Figure 11-3. There are a handful of them to choose from, and each one works a little bit differently and offers different capabilities. You'll probably want to try a few different programs to find the one you like best.

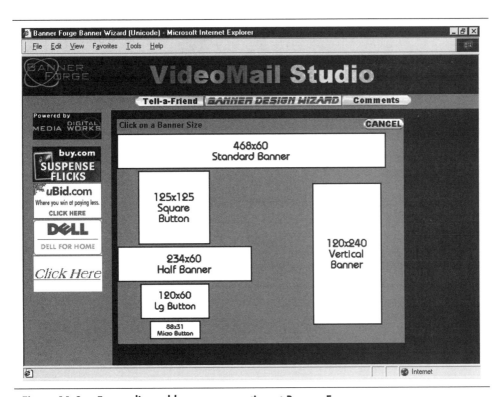

Figure 11-3 • **Free online ad banner generation at Banner Forge**

Here are my three favorite free banner generators:

- **Adobe Create a Banner (webservices.adobe.com/banner/)** Enter a line of text, choose type style, colors, animation effects, and more. Easy to use.
- **Banner Forge (bannerforge.com)** Start from scratch or use a template to simplify the process. Many options and sizes. Must sign up for free membership to use.
- **MediaBuilder 3D Text Maker (3dtextmaker.com)** Free animated banners you can create online. Striking special effects.

Standard Banner Ad Sizes

There was a time when banner ad makers rather randomly selected the size and shape of the ads that would appear on their site. This made it difficult for both buyers and sellers to compare, price, and position online advertising. Enter the Internet Advertising Bureau (IAB), an advertising industry trade association founded in 1996.

One of the IAB's efforts has been to create standardized banner sizes, and they've been very successful in doing that. A list of the most commonly used sizes follows. When creating your banners, try to adhere to these guidelines. The first number specifies the banner's width in pixels, the second is height.

Size (in pixels)	Type	Usual Page Placement
468 x 60	Full banner	Top, middle, or bottom of page. This is the most common type of Web page advertising.
234 x 60	Half banner	Top, middle, or bottom of page. Often used in combination with another half banner or the Web site's branding logo.
88 x 31	Micro button	Left or right page margin. Sometimes there's a row of these across the bottom.
120 x 60	Button	Left or right margin.
120 x 90	Button	Left or right margin.
125 x 125	Square button	Left or right margin.
120 x 240	Vertical banner	Left or right margin.
120 x 600	Skyscraper	Left or right margin. Often takes up the entire margin.
160 x 600	Wide skyscraper	Left or right margin. Often takes up the entire margin.

Creating Banners with a Graphics Program

The main drawback of free banner generators is that they can limit your ability to create exactly what you envision as a perfect banner for your site. If there's a particular design you really want, you may have to create it by hand using a graphics program. (If you don't have one yet, revisit Chapter 5 for suggestions.)

Every graphics program works differently, but the (very) basic steps are as follows:

1. Create a new image using one of the standard banner sizes.
2. Add a background color and/or texture.
3. Add any graphics or clip art (such as your logo).

PART II

4. Add the text.

5. Save the image in the format of the program you are using so it will be easy to edit later.

6. Save a second copy of the image in GIF or JPG format (usually GIF will be best). This will be the version used on the Web.

These programs can be a bit tricky to use, so many people find it easier to stick with the online freebies. If you want a quick start, surf on over to the Banner Warehouse (**stuff.uk.com/banners**), which has hundreds of text-free banner blanks that you can use as a starting point. All they ask in return is a link back to their site from yours.

Web Rings

There's another kind of free network you can join to promote your site—it's called a Web ring. Basically another way of trading free advertising, a Web ring connects a group of similarly themed sites by creating a network of links leading from one to another. Each participating site displays a special bit of HTML like that shown in Figure 11-4, which offers visitors a choice of Next, Previous, Random, or some other site in the ring.

JARGON ALERT: *A Web ring is a loosely affiliated group of sites that cover a common topic area. Each member site displays a Web ring logo and set of links that encourage visitors to visit other sites in the ring.*

To join a Web ring, you first have to find one that caters to your particular theme. The best place to do that is at Yahoo! WebRing (**dir.webring.yahoo.com**), which is shown in Figure 11-5. Another possibility is RingSurf (**ringsurf.com**). Both allow you to find existing rings or create your own. In terms of gaining added traffic to your Web site, the best choice is to join a ring that's already established.

Web rings do have a few drawbacks. The first, as you can see in Figure 11-4, is that you'll have to give up some space on your site for the Web ring display. Second, you have no control over which sites link to you and which you link to, which means you could end up connected to some real dogs (or shining stars). Viewers may tend to lump you in

Figure 11-4 • **This site participates in a half dozen Web rings.**

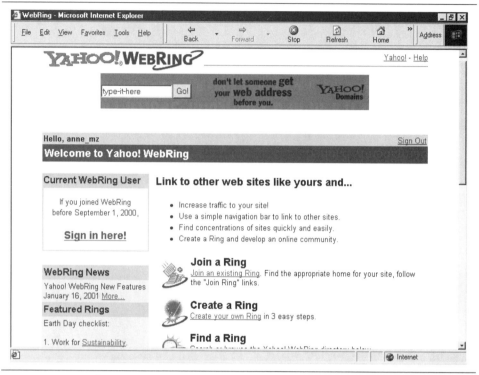

Figure 11-5 • Yahoo!'s WebRing directory

with other Web sites in your ring, as if you were all part of the same (good or bad) quality organization. Finally, especially for commercial Web sites, participating in a Web ring can sometimes be interpreted as an indication that the site is run by an amateur. Many Webmasters may not care about number three, but you should be aware of it nonetheless.

Award Programs

You started this chapter by giving yourself a pat on the back (or at least you should have) for the work you've done on your Web site; wouldn't it feel really good if other people started giving you them too? Besides feeding your ego, Web site awards can be used as a promotional tool for your Web site. And the best news of all is that if you've developed your site with care and attention to effective design, earning a few (or many!) accolades is relatively easy to accomplish.

Winning Awards

When Web award programs first appeared, there were only a few of them to choose from. Now there's a plentiful supply, even a surplus. Winning an award can bring you a bunch of promotional perks that can trigger a huge surge in traffic to your Web site. There are several ways the award granter accomplishes this, including:

- Descriptions and links of winning sites are posted on the award organization's Web site.
- Award winners are added to a searchable index of winning sites.
- E-mail containing links and descriptions of winning sites is sent to everyone on the award organization's mailing list.

NOTE: *Some award programs are not very discriminating— virtually all you have to do is send an e-mail about your site to receive the award. Such awards are of much less value than those that allow only superior sites to win.*

Some of the original award programs have become so popular, and as a result can drive so much traffic to winning sites, that you now have to pay to apply. But the competition is stiff, and there's no guarantee you'll win, so be a bit wary of the "pay to apply" awards. Besides, there are still plenty of free award programs that won't cost you a dime.

You can find a directory of selected free awards on **cheapwebtricks .com**. There's an award site Web ring too (**ringsurf.comnetring?ring= topawards;id=1;action=list**), and a master list of awards, with their associated logos, at **awardsites.com**.

Meanwhile, here are a few to get you started:

- Golden Web Awards (**goldenwebawards.com**)
- Project Cool Sightings (**projectcool.com/sightings**)
- USA Today Hot Site (**usatoday.com/life/cyber/ch.htm**)
- World Best Website Awards (**worldbestwebsites.com**)
- Yahoo! Picks of the Week (**www.yahoo.com/picks**)
- The Webby Awards (**webbyawards.com**)

TIP: *Think of awards as something you earn, not something you win.*

PART II

To increase the likelihood of award success, follow these five submission tips, and soon you'll own not just a Web site, but "an award winning Web site":

- Choose awards that have value to you, either because you would be proud to display the logo or you feel they have the power to bring you significant traffic.
- Read the criteria for the award before applying. This may list items that will cause your site to be automatically disqualified.
- Visit sites that have already won the award to see what they are like.
- If you are asked to provide a description of your site as part of the submission process, write it with care and attention to grammar and spelling.
- If you don't receive the award, try to determine why (sometimes it's only because there were so many submissions that day/week/ month), and reapply in a few weeks.

It's possible to mass submit to award programs using automated software. This is really only worthwhile if you like to collect awards without regard to where they come from or why, which some Webmasters do. It's kind of fun to see how many you can obtain. Figure 11-6 shows the list of awards that **award-it.com** will submit to automatically. For some reason, there aren't nearly as many free award submission services as there are free search engine submission services, so I can't provide an extensive list for you.

TIP: *To track your award submissions, download the free submission tracking worksheet from Website Awards (**websiteawards.xe.net/worksheet.htm**).*

Displaying Award Logos

If you garner one or two awards, you can display them on your home page with pride. If you collect three or more, you're going to need a separate awards page to display them. Each award comes with an associated graphic, and putting them all on your home page will slow its loading time beyond acceptable limits. Instead, create a special page to

Figure 11-6 • Award-it.com free automated award submission service

display them, and link to it from your home page with text like "Awards this site has won" or something similar. Figure 11-7 shows one site's awards page.

Offering Awards

The other side of awards is their power to draw people to your site, not in awe of its fabulous content and design, but in search of an award of their own. Each time you bestow an award on someone, they provide a link back to your site. This could potentially lead to a substantial amount of new traffic heading your way.

If you decide to launch an award program of your own:

- Develop a good-looking, fast-loading logo that includes your domain name. That way even people who don't click on the link will know where it came from.

Figure 11-7 • A bevy of awards for the HTML Guru Web site

- Pick an area of specialty related to your expertise to award. If your award is for "any excellent Web site," you will quickly be overwhelmed with submissions.
- Provide an area on your site that explains the award criteria and how to apply. Otherwise, you may be inundated with e-mails seeking that information.

Just creating an award program isn't going to bring you submissions and associated traffic; you're going to have to get the word out so people know it exists. Start by featuring it on your home page. Then go out and pick a few sites that are deserving of the award, and confer it on them, even though they haven't applied. Finally, seek out award sites such as those already mentioned, and ask them to include your award on their list.

Free-for-All (FFA) Links Pages

A *free-for-all links page* is just what the name implies: a form of organized chaos that allows Web site owners and others to submit a link back to their site, at no charge. Often, though not always, the links are organized into categories in a searchable directory. Figure 11-8 shows an FFA page run by the Cheap Web Tricks site.

> **JARGON ALERT:** *FFA is an acronym for free-for-all links page. FFA pages allow instant submissions of site names and URLs at no charge.*

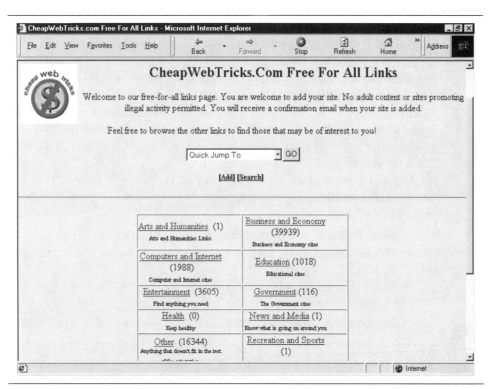

Figure 11-8 • The main FFA page at cheapwebtricks.com

NOTE: *FFA pages reside at the fuzzy edge of legitimate marketing techniques. Some people abuse them by sending tons of junk e-mail to any address they can collect, and this has given FFA systems a bad name. This doesn't mean that you shouldn't use FFA pages to your advantage, but be aware that they are somewhat controversial.*

Getting Listed

There are several ways FFA pages can be used as a promotional tool. The most obvious is actually the least effective: blasting your URL and link out to thousands of FFA pages so there are tons of links leading back to your site.

Why wouldn't it be great to obtain so many free links? Two reasons: First of all, FFA pages receive so many submissions that your URL will probably disappear within days, if not hours, pushed off the page by new submissions. Second, not very many people actually look at FFA pages when they're seeking information. Such pages are often a conglomeration of get-rich-quick schemes and other marketing come-ons. So your link may be in thousands of places, but few humans will see it.

On the upside, as I mentioned before, some search engines will boost a site's listing position if lots of other sites link to it. It's possible that getting your site included on thousands of FFA pages will help, though I'm a bit skeptical.

Still, if you want to give it a try, the price is right—absolutely zero. Don't even consider submitting to FFAs individually. Use one of these automated submission sites:

- **WorldSubmitter (worldsubmitter.com)**   Submits to over 2 million FFA link pages, plus classified ad sites, search engines, and message boards.
- **AutoLink Pro (autolinkpro.com)**   Submits to 8000 FFA pages for free.
- **SmallbizFFA (smallbizffa.net)**   Submits to about 7000+ FFA pages.

TIP: *Before submitting to FFA sites, set up an e-mail address especially for replies to your FFA submission. There will be lots them—confirmations that your URL has been added and various marketing offers. You can use an e-mail address at a free e-mail service, such as the one offered on **cheapwebtricks.com**, or through **hotmail.com**, **email.com**, or **yahoo.com**. This will keep your regular mailbox from becoming cluttered with FFA replies.*

An FFA Page of Your Own

The real FFA trick (at least as this was being written) is to host an FFA page of your own. As you might guess from the section on submitting to FFAs, this won't bring you a direct stream of visitors coming to submit to your FFA page because most FFA submission is automated. However, each person that submits provides a return e-mail address, and you can use that to get your marketing message out. For example, you could send each FFA submitter something like this:

```
Your Web site has been added to our Free-For-All links page
at http://cheapwebtricks.com (Resources for Frugal Webmasters).
Come visit our site and sign up for a free e-mail account.

Category: /Computers and Internet
Title: CheapWebTricks
URL: http://cheapwebtricks.com
Description:
Free Webmaster tools, tips, and resources.

Thank you for promoting your site with our site.

Best regards,

CheapWebTricks.com
```

It's true that quite a few FFA submitters will never see your reply because they never visit the mailbox used as a return address. But some of them will read your e-mail, and it might entice them to visit your site. If you put just a little effort into it, you could be sending out your marketing message hundreds or thousands of times a day via FFA responses.

JARGON ALERT: *An autoresponder is a program that automatically sends a premade e-mail message when a particular trigger event occurs. The trigger could be someone posting to your FFA page, or sending an e-mail to the autoresponder's e-mail address.*

How to Set Up an FFA Page

There are several different ways you can set up an FFA page on your site. The easiest is using a remotely hosted service. You just sign up and supply the requested information, and the page is generated

PART II

automatically and hosted by the FFA service. Figure 11-9 shows the sign-up page of an FFA service. Here are three for you to consider:

- EasyFFA (**easyffa.com**)
- FFA NET (**ffanet.com**)
- CGIForMe (**cgiforme.com**)

TIP: *Make sure any FFA service you sign up for allows you to specify the outgoing response message. Some do not, which takes away 90 percent of the value of the FFA to you.*

The second way to run an FFA page is to install your own software on your own server, which gives you complete control over the process. The catch is that you'll also bear the potential cost of the extra traffic to

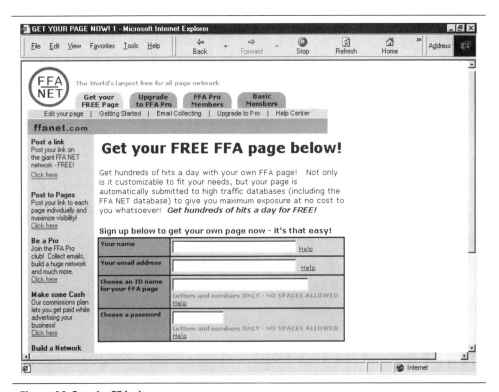

Figure 11-9 • An FFA sign-up page

your Web site, because the pages won't be remotely hosted. If you go over your allotted limit, you may have to pay a service charge.

If you want to install your own FFA, you'll need an FFA system, and your host will have to allow CGI scripts. Some hosting services allow users to install scripts, while others don't; so be sure to find out the rules at your service before you begin.

If your hosting service allows scripts, the next thing to do is pick one that you think will do the job. There are plenty of freebies to choose from. Two of my favorite resources for free scripts are Hotscripts (**hotscripts.com**) and The CGI Resource Index (**cgi-resources.com**).

Choose a script that comes with detailed installation instructions. Some script writers are willing to help you install their program for free or for a small fee. One FFA script I can recommend, because cheapwebtricks.com uses it, is Castle Links, which you can get at **castlecgi.castellum.net/scripts/CastleLinks/**. It creates the FFA system shown previously in Figure 11-8.

When you set up one of these scripts, you will need to specify two different response messages. One will be the message that is sent to FFA submitters by e-mail. This will be your marketing pitch. The second is a thank-you/confirmation page that will appear on screen when a user completes the submission process. Make the second one as succinct as possible—something like "thank you for submitting your link." It needs to be small because it's going to be displayed hundreds, if not thousands, of times a day. Each time it's displayed, a little bit of your traffic allowance (aka transfer amount) will be used up. By keeping the confirmation page small, you will avoid running into problems with exceeding your transfer allotment.

Once you have your site up and running, you need to get it listed with free FFA submission services. These are the same services that I mentioned as a way to autosubmit to FFA pages, only this time you will be the submittee instead of the submitter. Start by getting listed with just one of these services. You'll probably be amazed at the volume of traffic that inclusion in just a single FFA mass-submit list will generate. I suggest you start with WorldSubmitter (**worldsubmitter.com**). To be added to their directory, e-mail support@worldsubmitter.com with the URL of your FFA submission page.

Press Releases

Many of the methods that work for promoting traditional businesses also work for promoting an online presence. This includes that old standby, the press release. Press releases provide a way for you to get your news and announcements onto the desks of editors, who might choose to convey your information to their audience.

The key word in that previous sentence is "might." Press releases are a calculated gamble. Choose an appropriate topic, suitable targets, and write the release with care, and your chances of success rocket upwards. Dash off a hurried, boring press release, and you're wasting your time and that of the editors you send it to.

Press releases differ from advertisements because you are not paying anyone to run them. While this means your out-of-pocket cost is minimal, there are several other ramifications:

- You have no control over if, how, or when the material in the release is utilized.
- You have to craft the release carefully so that outlets will have a reason to pass the information on to their audiences.
- It carries more credibility than an advertisement.

Because press releases can be such a valuable promotional tool, many companies exist to help businesses make the most of them. However, frugal Webmasters are likely to prefer to undertake this task themselves, so I'll tell you how to do it. Promoting your Web site with press releases can be divided into two tasks: writing the release and distributing it. (You'll also want to track your results, but that's less critical.)

How to Write a Press Release

Before you start writing your first press release, take the time to read some others. You can find a bountiful supply on the Web, on almost any commercial company's Web site. Or you can go to a site that specifically carries press releases, such as Internet Wire (**internetwire.com**). Read these press releases with one question in mind:

Why should I care?

If the press release doesn't answer that question, it wasn't written with the reader in mind. The number one mistake made by amateur press release writers is to assume that other people are interested in their business. Unless you're already a highly visible corporation, charity, or individual that people like to keep up on, the automatic reaction to your press release is going to be "so what?" This is the main hurdle you have to overcome. The first step toward doing that is recognizing what is news, and what isn't.

Select an Appropriate Topic and Angle

The launch of a new Web site that sells computer professional training courses isn't very interesting news; in fact, to most reporters it isn't news at all. A Web site that connects IT professionals with discounted and convenient training with a few clicks of the mouse is more likely to snag a reporter's attention and column space.

The difference may be subtle, but it all comes down to the perspective of the reader. Is this something that's going to save readers time, or money, entertain them, or make their life easier somehow? Then that's what the release needs to convey. If not, then perhaps a press release isn't the right approach. Occasionally you can stray from this restriction a little—for example, if you've recently won a notable award or are sponsoring a special event—but even then, you need to quickly identify what the benefit of the reported item will be to the reader. Way back at the beginning of this book you defined your target audience(s). This is another place where you will put that information to work. Remember that the reporter and potential readers aren't necessarily computer experts, so make your pitch in layman's terms.

Standard Formatting

Press releases are a tried-and-true promotional tool—so much so that editors receive an inbox full of them every day. Although you want your release to stand out from the crowd, it shouldn't be notable because of formatting. There's a standard format for press releases, and adhering to it will show that you are approaching this professionally. Figure 11-10 shows a sample release in the proper format.

Note the following key features:

- It's on letterhead (not absolutely required).
- It has an attention-grabbing headline that conveys what the release is about.
- The subheadline further defines the subject, in just a few words.
- The date of the release and contact information are provided at the top.
- The first paragraph starts with a location, in all capital letters, followed by a dash.
- The first paragraph presents the reason for the release, in a nutshell.
- The next few paragraphs provide the details, and a quote.
- The last few paragraphs provide background information, including company details.

PART II

Leading·Web·Site·Primed·For·Expansion
Earthweb·transfers·ownership·of·GoCertify.com·to·site's·founder

April·24,·2001

For·more·information·contact:
John·Boffa
(202)·466-6977

WASHINGTON,·DC—Anne·Martinez,·author·of·the·best-selling·*Get·Certified·and·Get· Ahead*·series·of·books,·has·resumed·total·ownership·of·GoCertify.com,·an·Information· Technology·(IT)·certification·Web·site,·and·has·plans·for·expansion.

GoCertify.com·already·offers·exhaustive·information·on·more·than·500·IT· certifications,·plus·a·monthly·newsletter,·"Certification·Watch."·It·also·features·news,· articles,·and·a·discussion·area·for·professionals·interested·in·IT·certification.·As·a·free· service·to·IT·certification·candidates,·the·site·also·operates·a·"swapshop"—a·place·for· visitors·who·wish·to·exchange·used·certification·preparation·materials·including·books,· manuals,·hardware,·and·software.

Future·plans·include·expanded·training·resources,·and·new·partnerships·with·other· companies·in·the·certification·marketplace·that·will·bring·extra·services·and·value·to· GoCertify.com·visitors.·Several·one-of-a-kind·features·are·currently·under·development.

"Certification·is·more·important·today·than·it·has·ever·been·before,"·said·Anne· Martinez.·"I·am·thrilled·to·be·able·to·continue·providing·extensive·certification· information·resources·to·the·IT·community·through·GoCertify.com."

Founded·in·March·1998·by·Anne·Martinez,·GoCertify.com·has·continuously· served·as·a·resource·on·IT·certification.··From·February·1999·to·April·2001,·it·was·owned· by·Earthweb,·an·online·provider·of·career·development·resources·to·IT·professionals.

Anne·Martinez·also·owns·CheapWebTricks.com,·a·site·devoted·to·creating,· maintaining,·and·promoting·inexpensive·web·sites.·Both·sites·will·be·branded·under· Anventure.

##

Figure 11-10 • A properly formatted press release

As with most written communication, the headline is especially important. When documents are displayed in a list, often only the headline is listed. If that doesn't capture the reader's attention, the rest of the release will never be viewed. A better headline for this release might have been "Leading Certification Web Site Primed for Expansion." The simple addition of the word "certification" would make it less generic and be more likely to attract the attention of people who are interested in this topic.

Don't be disappointed if your first attempt at a press release is less than amazing. Plan to rework it a few times until it's as good as you can make it. Ask someone you trust to read it and make suggestions. Better yet, ask several someones.

Distributing Your Press Release

So now you've got a killer press release in hand—the kind that editors will call and thank you for (okay, maybe not that astounding, but good, right?). How are you going to get it in front of editors?

Do-It-Yourself Distribution

If you have a few specific target publications in mind, whether they are Web sites that cover your topic area or print publications, your best bet is to contact them yourself. Go to the publication's Web site (even most print publications will have one these days). Look for contact information for the editor who covers your subject area.

Sometimes it's not easy to identify the proper contact person. You might have to send a query to a more general e-mail address to get that information. If so, make your inquiry as personal as possible. Don't just say, "I have a press release, who should I send it to?" Instead, take the opportunity to introduce yourself and to create a connection. Mention that you have visited their Web site/read their publication and that you have a service/product that would be of value to their readers. This is almost like a mini-press release. With these preliminaries out of the way (keep them short), ask who would be the best person to receive a release describing your news.

TIP: *Get your news release out early in the day to increase the likelihood it will be looked at.*

PART II

For each potential outlet, create and update a list of the Web site or publication name, the contact person's name, title, and contact information. Each time you go through this process, add to it, and soon you'll have a substantial distribution list that you can reuse as the need arises. You can jump-start your list by sorting through existing compilations of media contacts. Here are some sources to start with:

- **Editor & Publisher Media Database (emedia1.mediainfo.com/ emedia/)** Huge searchable index of newspapers, magazines, radio, TV, and more.
- **Kidon Media Link (kidon.com/media-link)** Another gigantic searchable directory of international media links. Includes newspapers, magazines, television, radio, and news agencies.
- **News365 (news365.com)** Over 10,000 news media covering 300 topics.
- **RefDesk.com (refdesk.com)** Newspapers and news sites organized by geographic location.

TIP: *Don't limit yourself to contacting Web sites and print publications. Consider radio shows as well. There are plenty of Internet and traditional radio broadcasts that are hungry for guests.*

Distribution Services

There are some instances when you might want to consider using a distribution service. They can spread your press release far and wide in minimal time. However, with a few exceptions, they're not going to do it for free. Distribution of a single release can easily cost several hundred dollars or more.

The two biggest services are BusinessWire (**businesswire.com**) and PR Newswire (**prnewswire.com**). You can find these and many more through Yahoo! at **yahoo.com/Business_and_Economy/Business_to_Business/ News_and_Media/News_Services/Press_Releases/**.

Of course, I can't end this section without sharing the free distribution services too, or you might just toss this book in the trash. Since I don't want that to happen:

- **Comitatus Consulting Inc (comitatusgroup.com/pr/)** Free distribution to an extensive list of outlets. Will also archive your past releases for you, online (shown in Figure 11-11).
- **PRWeb (prweb.com)** Free posting of your press release to multiple, categorized databases.

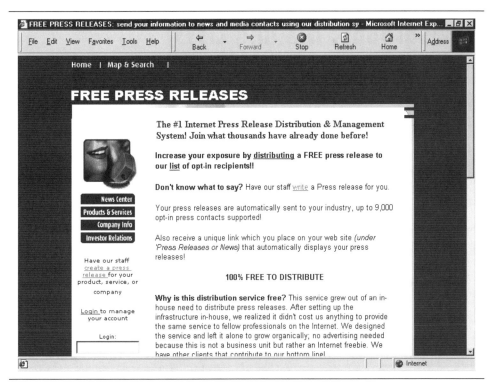

Figure 11-11 • Free press release distribution from Comitatus Consulting

- **WebWire (webwire.com)**   Free posting of your press release on the WebWire site and to participants of WebWire. For distribution beyond that, there's a fee.
- **freeprwire.com (www.freeprwire.com)**   Free posting to the freeprwire Web site.

TIP: *Post your press release on your Web site as well. Link to it from your "about us" page, or create a special newsroom section.*

Free distribution services are likely to be more cluttered and less effective than their for-fee counterparts, but are still worth a try.

Newsgroups, Mailing Lists, and Your Signature

Simply by adding a few lines to each outgoing e-mail message you send, you can turn your everyday correspondence into a promotional tool for your Web site. The extra lines look something like this:

```
Anne Martinez
webmaster@cheapwebtricks.com


-----------------------------------
Resources for the Frugal Webmaster:
http://cheapwebtricks.com
```

The little bit above is called a signature. Create one that promotes your Web site and insert it into every bit of correspondence you send out, even those e-mail jokes you forward to friends.

Creating an Automatic Signature

A successful signature should be short and to the point. And it must include a URL for readers to click on. Many e-mail programs will let you create a signature (or even more than one) and have it automatically inserted into each new e-mail message you create. To do this in Microsoft Outlook, follow these steps:

1. From the main menu, choose Tools | Options. A window like the one below will appear:

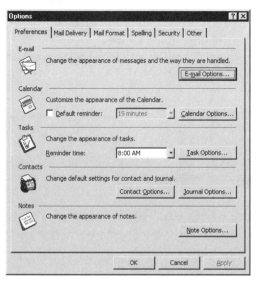

2. Click on the Mail Format tab. The window will now look like this:

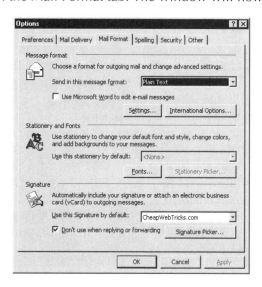

3. Click on the Signature Picker button. Then click New to create a new signature.

4. Enter a name for the signature and click Next. The Edit Signature window will appear, as below:

5. Type your signature lines exactly as you want them to appear, and click Finish.

6. Click OK, and the original Mail Format window will return, this time with your newly entered signature listed as the default signature. The next time you create a new e-mail, this signature will be automatically inserted.

PART II

Using Your Signature on Discussion Boards and Mailing Lists

Your signature can also be used on postings you make to more public places, specifically, to discussion boards or mailing lists. Postings to a discussion board (also known as a *forum*) are stored at a central online location. People who are interested in the topic area visit the site and browse or search through the postings.

Subscription mailing lists (also called *newsgroups*), on the other hand, distribute every message to all subscribers of the group, via e-mail. Like discussion boards, they are organized around a specific theme or topic area.

As you can imagine, a message posted to either of these venues has the potential to be read by many different people. The reach of a single message is expanded even further by the fact that most mailing lists and discussion boards maintain archives. Messages stay around for months, or in some cases, years.

People gravitate to the message boards and mailing lists that cover topics of interest to them. Find those that cater to your site's audience group, and you'll have a pool of potential visitors just waiting to be invited.

TIP: *Posting blatant advertisements to public discussions is frowned upon and may backfire on you. Make sure you post only meaningful responses or contributions, and keep your "advertisement" to a few lines of signature.*

Before you start spreading the good word about your resource, you'll need to find appropriate newsgroups and mailing lists. Here are two places that ought to keep you busy for a while:

- **Google's Usenet Archive (dejanews.com)**   Archive of thousands of newsgroups covering virtually every conceivable topic.
- **Yahoo! Groups (groups.yahoo.com/)**   Searchable directory of thousands of groups. Find some that suit your audience, or start your own.

Make Promoting Your Web Site a Habit

Promotion isn't a one-shot deal, and you need to keep it up over time. More than anything else, the key to successful do-it-yourself Web site promotion is to make it a habit. Methods like using a signature file and joining a banner exchange make this relatively easy to accomplish. It's also a good idea to schedule a particular day of the month to review your promotional efforts. Use the scheduled time to assess what you've accomplished so far, determine what works best, and reenergize your promotional efforts. Pretty soon you'll be able to answer those questions you asked at the beginning of this chapter: Just how many visitors can you bring to your Web site, and how fast can you do it? The answers may surprise you.

12

Chapter Twelve

Evaluating Your Progress

You've been diligently promoting your Web site using all the techniques you've learned, but is it working? Unlike a best-selling book, a Web site's appearance will remain the same no matter how many people paw through it. The pages won't get dog-eared or smudged with fingerprints, and there's no coffee spilled on the cover. So how can you tell if it's a hit?

Before I answer that question, it's important to recognize that the definition of success is going to vary depending on the purpose of the Web site. The goals of the women's hockey team Web site I've been using as an example are different from the goals of the Cheap Web Tricks site that supports this book, and the purpose of the PhoneEx Communications site mentioned in Chapter 2 is distinct from both of those. So if your goal is to create a Web site that enables family members to connect with each other and keep up on family news, and the family is using and loving the site, your goal is accomplished.

Many sites, however, will be seeking a larger audience. Otherwise, all these promotional activities wouldn't be worth the effort. Which brings us back to the question, how can you tell? There are three primary things I suggest you investigate:

- Quantity and composition of visitors to your site
- Presence and placement of your site in search portals and elsewhere on the Web
- Visitor feedback

You might argue that for a commercial site, sales are the one and only measure of success. However, this chapter is about assessing the success of your promotional efforts, not your sales strategies. Many other factors play into sales figures, not the least of which is the demand for the product itself. Before anyone can buy your products online, they have to know that the opportunity—in the form of your Web site—exists.

Determining your success in getting the word out, whether for a commercial, nonprofit, or personal Web site, is what this chapter is about. This is where you find out how to tell if your promotional efforts are paying off.

Web Site Traffic Statistics—A Gold Mine of Information

The place you're going to acquire the most information about your Web site visitors is from the site's traffic log. A line of data is recorded for each request the server receives. By analyzing this data, you can tell which are the most popular areas of your site, how many pages are displayed each day, and a whole lot more. At the most basic level, if the number of pages displayed each day rises, that's a pretty good sign that your promotional efforts are having a positive effect.

JARGON ALERT: *A log file stores information about files that have been retrieved from your Web site, including the location of the item requested (either an html page, image, or something else) and the source of the request.*

The log file is stored on your Web host, in a directory named something like www-logs. Old log files are saved, usually organized by date. If you look at the contents of a log file using a word processor or text editor, you'll see something like Figure 12-1. (Don't panic, you won't have to interpret it yourself.)

Although it's possible to access and download log files using FTP, that's really not necessary. You never need to directly view those pages of gobbledy-gook. A statistics package will do that for you, and it will organize the results into a much friendlier format, like the one shown in Figure 12-2.

You don't have to buy or install statistics software to get great reports like this. Most hosting services have done that for you and will provide you with directions on how to access it as part of your hosting package.

If Your Hosting Service Doesn't Provide Statistics

Some hosting services (usually free ones) don't provide their Webmasters with handy statistics information, and that used to be a significant drawback to choosing a free hosting service. But thanks to some industrious Web entrepreneurs, it's possible to sign up for a remote statistics service. And quite a few of them are available for free.

```
spc-isp-nitro-01-187.sprint.ca-·-·[15/May/2001:05:05:39·-0400]·"GET·/images/1.gif·HTTP/1.0"·200·1006·
"http://www.cheapwebtricks.com/create/freeaddonsdata1.shtml"·"Mozilla/4.0·(compatible;·MSIE·5.01;·Windows·98)"
spc-isp-nitro-01-187.sprint.ca-·-·[15/May/2001:05:05:42·-0400]·"GET·/images/2.gif·HTTP/1.0"·200·977·
"http://www.cheapwebtricks.com/create/freeaddonsdata1.shtml"·"Mozilla/4.0·(compatible;·MSIE·5.01;·Windows·98)"
217.11.167.74·-·-·[15/May/2001:05:05:55·-0400]·"POST·/cgi-bin/clinks/add.cgi?action=add·HTTP/1.0"·200·506·
"http://www.worldsubmitter.com/engines/ffa/sffa119.htm"·"Mozilla/4.0·(compatible;·MSIE·5.5;·Windows·98;·Win·9x·4.90)"
spc-isp-nitro-01-248.sprint.ca-·-·[15/May/2001:05:06:08·-0400]·"GET·/create/freeaddonsdata1.shtml·HTTP/1.0"·200·9783·"-"·
"Mozilla/3.01·(compatible;)"
spc-isp-nitro-01-248.sprint.ca-·-·[15/May/2001:05:08:24·-0400]·"GET·/create/freeaddonsdata2.shtml·HTTP/1.0"·200·8283·
"http://www.cheapwebtricks.com/create/freeaddonsdata1.shtml"·"Mozilla/4.0·(compatible;·MSIE·5.01;·Windows·98)"
spc-isp-nitro-01-248.sprint.ca-·-·[15/May/2001:05:08:24·-0400]·"GET·/images/3.gif·HTTP/1.0"·200·925·"-"·"Mozilla/3.01·
(compatible;)"
spc-isp-nitro-01-187.sprint.ca-·-·[15/May/2001:05:08:27·-0400]·"GET·/images/3.gif·HTTP/1.0"·200·925·
"http://www.cheapwebtricks.com/create/freeaddonsdata2.shtml"·"Mozilla/4.0·(compatible;·MSIE·5.01;·Windows·98)"
okc-65-28-133-6.mmcable.com·-·-·[15/May/2001:02:07:30·-0400]·"GET·/promote/promote.shtml·HTTP/1.1"·200·9266·
"http://www.cheapwebtricks.com/"·"Mozilla/4.0·(compatible;·MSIE·5.0;·Windows·98;·DigExt;·sureseeker.com)"
gatekeeper1-uk.bakernet.com·-·-·[15/May/2001:02:07:31·-0400]·"GET·/cgi-bin/getimage.cgi?unique?REGION=ffa_page·
HTTP/1.0"·302·245·"http://www.cheapwebtricks.com/cgi-bin/clinks/add.cgi?action=add"·"Mozilla/4.0·(compatible;·MSIE·5.0;·
Windows·95;·DigExt)"
okc-65-28-133-6.mmcable.com·-·-·[15/May/2001:02:07:38·-0400]·"GET·/promote/freesetoolsdata1.shtml·HTTP/1.1"·200·9577
"http://www.cheapwebtricks.com/promote/promote.shtml"·"Mozilla/4.0·(compatible;·MSIE·5.0;·Windows·98;·DigExt;·
sureseeker.com)"
okc-65-28-133-6.mmcable.com·-·-·[15/May/2001:02:07:39·-0400]·"GET·/images/1.gif·HTTP/1.1"·200·1006·
"http://www.cheapwebtricks.com/promote/freesetoolsdata1.shtml"·"Mozilla/4.0·(compatible;·MSIE·5.0;·Windows·98;·DigExt;·
sureseeker.com)"
```

Figure 12-1 • Raw log file data

TIP: *Remote statistics services can also be valuable to people with hosts that do provide statistics, but only at long intervals or in a minimally useful format.*

How can a computer that doesn't even host your Web site track your visitors? It has to do with the way Web pages are retrieved.

When a visitor types the URL of one of your Web pages into his Web browser, that browser requests the page from your hosting service. If it's a typical Web page, it includes a graphic or two as well as text. As the visiting browser loads the page and comes across an included graphic, it then requests the graphic from your host as well. If there's a third graphic, that triggers a third request, and so on, until the entire page and all of its components are loaded and viewable by the visitor.

Not all elements of a Web page have to be located on the local server. The visiting browser will request them from wherever the main HTML page tells it to. Most free statistics services take advantage of this. When you sign up, they provide you with a URL to a graphic that is called from their server. You include a link to that graphic on the page you want to track. Whenever that page is loaded, so is the graphic from that remote

PART II

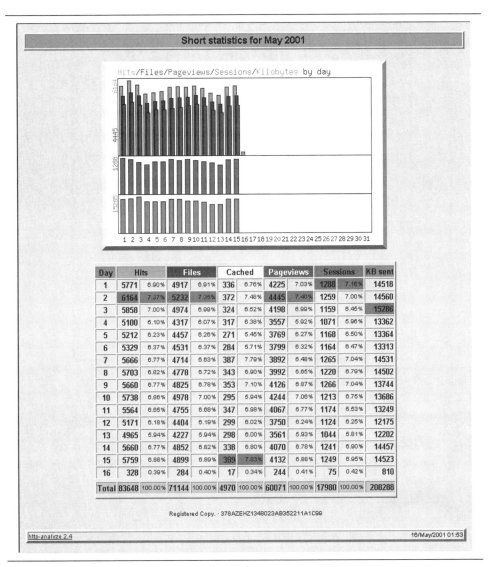

Short statistics for May 2001

Hits/Files/Pageviews/Sessions/Kilobytes by day

Day	Hits		Files		Cached		Pageviews		Sessions		KB sent
1	5771	6.90%	4917	6.91%	336	6.76%	4225	7.03%	1288	7.16%	14518
2	6164	7.37%	5232	7.35%	372	7.48%	4445	7.40%	1259	7.00%	14560
3	5858	7.00%	4974	6.99%	324	6.52%	4198	6.99%	1159	6.45%	15286
4	5100	6.10%	4317	6.07%	317	6.38%	3557	5.92%	1071	5.96%	13362
5	5212	6.23%	4457	6.26%	271	5.45%	3769	6.27%	1168	6.50%	13364
6	5329	6.37%	4531	6.37%	284	5.71%	3799	6.32%	1164	6.47%	13313
7	5666	6.77%	4714	6.63%	387	7.79%	3892	6.48%	1265	7.04%	14531
8	5703	6.82%	4778	6.72%	343	6.90%	3992	6.65%	1220	6.79%	14502
9	5660	6.77%	4825	6.78%	353	7.10%	4126	6.87%	1266	7.04%	13744
10	5738	6.86%	4978	7.00%	295	5.94%	4244	7.06%	1213	6.75%	13686
11	5564	6.65%	4755	6.68%	347	6.98%	4067	6.77%	1174	6.53%	13249
12	5171	6.18%	4404	6.19%	299	6.02%	3750	6.24%	1124	6.25%	12175
13	4965	5.94%	4227	5.94%	298	6.00%	3561	5.93%	1044	5.81%	12202
14	5660	6.77%	4852	6.82%	338	6.80%	4070	6.78%	1241	6.90%	14457
15	5759	6.88%	4899	6.89%	389	7.83%	4132	6.88%	1249	6.95%	14523
16	328	0.39%	284	0.40%	17	0.34%	244	0.41%	75	0.42%	810
Total	83648	100.00%	71144	100.00%	4970	100.00%	60071	100.00%	17980	100.00%	208288

http-analyze 2.4   16/May/2001 01:53

Figure 12-2 • Statistics you can actually read

server. When the visitor's browser requests the remote graphic, the information associated with that request is logged by the free statistics site. Then that information is used to create a statistics report for you. Some services use more sophisticated systems, often involving JavaScript, in order to provide a greater amount of tracking information. Figure 12-3 shows a selection of tracking graphics.

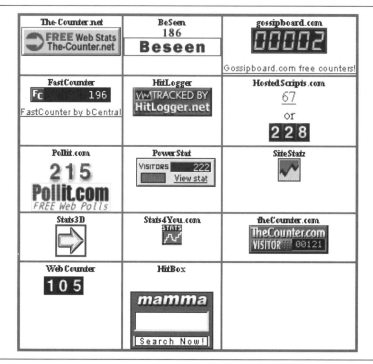

Figure 12-3 • A selection of traffic-tracking graphics

 JARGON ALERT: *A hit counter is a graphic that shows the number of times a page has been loaded. It automatically increments each time someone visits the page.*

Most of these free statistics services (JavaScript or graphics based) track on a per page basis; they only record information pertaining to the page that contains the special statistics code. Some offer sitewide tracking, as long as you include their code snippet on every page.

So, where can you find free statistics? There are lots of them around. Here's a list to get you started:

- **BeSeen (beseen.com/hitcounter/)** Total pageviews by the hour, day, and month. Can set starting number and choose counter style and colors.

- **FastCounter (bcentral.com/services/fc/)**   Simple, quick-loading counter. Receive stats via e-mail. Can set starting value. Choose from several different styles.
- **HitBox (hitbox.com)**   Pageviews and visitors by the hour, day, and month. Identifies busiest and slowest days. Their graphic is an ad for someone else.
- **HitLogger (hitlogger.net)**   Detailed statistics. Runs a "banner box" on your page with an ad. Can monitor multiple pages with one account. Log in to check your stats. Uses JavaScript.
- **Stats3D (www.stats3d.com)**   Site hits, hits per page, monthly hits, browsers, referrers, and more. Small graphic to put on your page.
- **Ultimate Counter (ultimatecounter.com)**   Over 500 digit styles to choose from. Counts hits only—no additional statistics.

NOTE: *Placing a publicly viewable hit counter on your Web site may not be such a good thing. Do you really want to advertise that the page has only been viewed 12 times? Some hit counters let you select a starting number, which helps alleviate this problem.*

Figure 12-4 shows a sample report from one of these free services. The statistics provided vary by service.

Free statistics services make their money by displaying advertising. Usually the only person who sees the ads is you, when you log in to view your statistics, or when a report containing them is e-mailed to you. A few services incorporate a third-party ad into the graphic you are required to display in order to track traffic, which means every visitor to the page carrying the graphic will see it.

If your Web host does provide log files, but their statistics package isn't very impressive, and you don't want to use a free system that requires you to add special code to each page to be tracked, consider getting and installing a statistics package of your own. It's possible to download raw log files to your personal computer, and use software installed there to analyze it. You can find a list of log analyzer vendors on Yahoo! at **dir.yahoo.com/Business_and_Economy/Business_to_ Business/Communications_and_Networking/Internet_and_World_ Wide_Web/Software/World_Wide_Web/Log_Analysis_Tools/**.

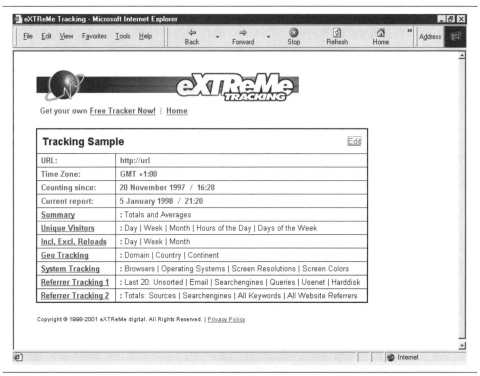

Figure 12-4 • Sample free statistics report from eXTReMe Tracking

Reading and Utilizing Statistics Reports

The report shown in Figure 12-2 is only one of the many that can be generated by a statistics program. The exact reports vary depending on which statistics package program you're using, but common reports include most popular pages/sections of the site, visitor browser type, unique visitors per day (or other period), error listings, countries that your visitors are from, and if you're lucky, a referrer report. Many statistics reports are largely self-explanatory, but we're going to look at a couple in detail, as they are especially useful.

Most Viewed Pages Report

Let's look at Figure 12-5 first. Besides the "nice to know" factor, how might you utilize the information this report provides? Why would you care which pages or sections of your site are most popular? Primarily so that you can tell which areas of your site are worth expanding, and which are not.

Total Transfers by Items/URLs (Overview)

Total hits		Files	Pageview	Bytes sent		Size	URL
55881	58.00%	55881	55881	52323958	24.53%	0	/cgi-bin/clinks/
13782	15.48%	8812	0	77918255	36.53%	0	All images
2257	2.70%	2257	0	39993800	18.75%	0	/cgi-bin/getimage.cgi/
1104	1.32%	1104	1104	21035580	9.85%	0	/
1088	1.30%	1088	1088	10935735	5.13%	0	/create/
410	0.49%	410	410	3735755	1.75%	0	/promote/
172	0.21%	172	172	1483011	0.70%	0	/profit/
141	0.17%	141	141	1153972	0.54%	0	/maintain/
85	0.10%	85	85	755188	0.35%	0	/products/
55	0.07%	55	55	30855	0.01%	0	/ffa/
53	0.06%	53	53	588328	0.28%	0	/cgi-bin/
20	0.02%	20	20	188177	0.09%	0	/stats/www2001/
19	0.02%	19	19	10427	0.00%	0	/cgi-bin/anyboard.cgi/anyboard/f
13	0.02%	13	13	155742	0.08%	0	/anyboard/forums/general/
12	0.01%	12	12	70055	0.03%	0	/cp/rac/
8	0.01%	8	8	23305	0.01%	0	/cgi-bin/mojo/
4	0.00%	4	0	115	0.00%	0	/cgi-sys/
4	0.00%	4	4	15455	0.01%	0	/stats/
3	0.00%	3	3	65087	0.03%	0	//
2	0.00%	2	2	12345	0.01%	0	/anyboard/forums/general/posts/
42	0.05%	0	0	214805	0.10%		Partial Content (Code 205)
5	0.01%	0	0	1448	0.00%		Moved Permanently (Code 301)
7334	8.77%	0	0	1800998	0.84%		Moved Temporarily (Code 302)
2	0.00%	0	0	512	0.00%		Bad Request (Code 400)
12	0.01%	0	0	1958	0.00%		Unauthorized (Code 401)
3	0.00%	0	0	554	0.00%		Forbidden (Code 403)
105	0.13%	0	0	742465	0.35%		Not Found (Code 404)
83548	100.00%	71144	50071	213285144	100.00%		

Figure 12-5 • A report showing which pages and sections of the site are most popular

For example, if you create a site on stamp collecting, and you see from your statistics report that your "Stamps from Malaysia" page is getting more views than any other, you might consider providing even more information and resources related to that special area. On the other hand, if the "Stamps from the USA" page gets little to no traffic, you might devote less effort to updating that one.

Here's another example. Let's say your Web site was created to sell Widgets, but no Widget orders have arrived. A check of your statistics reveals that plenty of people are viewing the Widget order page. This could mean that your Widget order form isn't working, or that you need to revise that order page because something on it (price, delivery options, ordering options, or something else) is stopping interested people from making that buy decision. Without the statistics, you'd never know if the potential customers were reaching your site, or the right page of your site, in the first place.

Page Not Found Report

Figure 12-6 is a Page Not Found report. It identifies files that visitors attempted to access on your site, only to receive a 404 (Page Not Found) error informing them that the file doesn't exist.

JARGON ALERT: *A 404 error, or "Page Not Found" message, is generated by a Web server when a visitor tries to access a file that doesn't exist.*

Page Not Found errors can occur for several reasons:

- The user has clicked on a broken link within your site. This could be a link containing a typo, or a page that once existed but doesn't any more.
- The user has followed a bad link from another site to yours. As above, that link could contain a typo, or link to a page you've since removed.
- The user typed in a URL incorrectly, or it doesn't exist anymore.

```
Code 404 Not Found Requests

Hits Sessions    Bytes sent | URL
----------------------------------------------------------------------------------------------
   63        0      441985 | /favicon.ico
    8        3       55699 | /faq_site2.ihtml
    5        0       36235 | /+global_article[counter].document_url+
    5        0       36346 | /+global_article[counter].access_registration+
    4        2       29108 | /regs.ihtml
    2        0       14590 | /create/favicon.ico
    2        0       14513 | /+global_article[counter].url+
    1        0        7249 | /cgi-bin/clinks/s.com/cgi-bin/getimage.cgi/unique
    1        0        7244 | /'"+global_article[counter].url+"'
    1        0        7350 | /create/gif/line.gif
    1        0        7251 | /promote/gif/line.gif
    1        0        7247 | /promote/favicon.ico
    1        0        7287 | /'"+global_article[counter].access_registration+"'
    1        1        7282 | /robotsxx.txt
    1        0        5324 | /edit.ihtml
    1        0        7334 | /profit/gif/line.gif
    1        0        7291 | /maintain/gif/line.gif
    1        0        7291 | /products/gif/labo.gif
    1        0        7252 | /'"+global_article[counter].document_url+"'
    1        0        7291 | /products/gif/line.gif
    1        0        5657 | /temple.css
    1        0        7271 | /com_brand
    1        0        7357 | /gif/line.gif
----------------------------------------------------------------------------------------------
  105        6      742465
==============================================================================================
```

Figure 12-6 • Page Not Found report

If a Page Not Found report shows a particular URL with just one error, you can pretty much ignore it. But if something consistently appears—that is, more than one person has gotten the error—then it's time to investigate; 404 errors can drive visitors away.

Often the cause of the error will be obvious—for example, you transposed letters in a linked file name—and you can quickly remedy the bad link. Always check the case: Myfile.html and myfile.html are not the same file to Unix Web servers. If you've removed a file and now it's appearing on your Page Not Found report, consider putting it back. Or, if you think the bad link is coming from another page within your own site, track it down and remove it.

TIP: *When you redesign part or all of your site, strive to use the same page names as before unless you have a very good reason not to. Changing them ever so slightly (for example, from mypage.htm to mypage.html) will break every link that connects to the old URL, including links in personal bookmark files, search portals, and on other Web sites. This is very annoying to regular visitors and will negate many of the promotional efforts previously undertaken.*

Sometimes there's nothing you can do to correct a bad link that is coming from somewhere outside your site. In these instances, consider placing a temporary page at the bad URL (so that URL will no longer be bad) that leads visitors to the page they are really seeking.

You can transfer visitors to a new page automatically by placing a meta refresh tag in the <HEAD> section that looks like this:

```
<META HTTP-EQUIV="Refresh" CONTENT="5; URL=http://newurl.html">
```

The number 5 indicates how many seconds to wait before displaying the page specified in the URL= section. For an instant transfer, set it to 0. Leave at a higher number if the page that has the refresh tag also includes text you want the visitor to have a chance to read. For example, there might be some text explaining that the old page has moved.

Referrer Reports

When a visitor comes to your site by following a link from another location (either a search engine or another Web page), that starting point is called a *referrer*. The identity of the referrer is often included among information that the visiting browser uses to request the page on your

The Mysterious Favicon.ico

If you look again at the Page Not Found report in Figure 12-6, you'll see that a file named favicon.ico tops the list. In fact, it often tops Page Not Found reports, to the bewilderment of many a Webmaster. But its presence is really good news; it means people are bookmarking pages on the site.

Whenever a visitor using Microsoft's Internet Explorer (IE) bookmarks a Web page, the page is added to the visitor's favorites list. A tiny image, called an *icon*, is placed alongside the name of the site, like this:

What's On Now

Windows Media Showcase

Real.com Radio Tuner

Where does that image come from? When adding a favorite URL, IE requests a file named favicon.ico from the remote server. If it finds none (usually the case), it adds the site to the visitor's bookmark list with the default IE logo beside it. The request for favicon.ico is recorded in the server logs as not found, even though it's not really an error and no error message is ever seen by the visitor. So every call for favicon.ico means someone has bookmarked a page on the site.

Webmasters can cause a custom icon to appear instead of the default IE logo, as the Real Networks site does in the above illustration. All you have to do is use an icon editor to create an icon, name it favicon.ico, and place it on the Web server in the same directory as the pages users might bookmark. When IE looks for favicon.ico, it will find your file and use the icon it contains instead of the default.

If you want to create your own favicon.ico, you'll need an icon editor. There's a free one online at **favicon.com**. The site also has a downloadable version.

site, and thus is recorded in the log file. By looking at referrer logs, you can see where many (though not all) of your visitors are coming from. Figure 12-7 shows a referrer report from the Cheap Web Tricks site.

A referrer report can tell you many things, such as

- How much of your traffic is coming from which search portals, which lets you gauge the success of your efforts at getting included in such sites.
- If there are one or two sites providing you with lots of traffic, and who they are.

- How successful a link swap with another Webmaster is, if you've made one.
- If someone has posted an article or mention of your site somewhere, with a link.
- If anyone has followed a link to your URL that you've posted in a message to a forum.

Let's look at the report in Figure 12-7 to see which of the above questions it can answer. Before we start, there are two things to keep in mind about this sample report. First, it shows only the top 30 referrers.

No.	Hits		Files		Pageviews		Sessions		KB sent	Referrer Host
1	63568	69.48%	63566	81.86%	63566	96.69%	18432	93.65%	57237	http://www.worldsubmitter.com/
2	26528	29.00%	12882	16.59%	1247	1.90%	519	2.64%	139126	http://www.cheapwebtricks.com/
3	233	0.25%	226	0.29%	215	0.33%	173	0.88%	2339	http://www.google.com/
4	141	0.15%	141	0.18%	141	0.21%	128	0.65%	2986	http://search.yahoo.com/
5	140	0.15%	131	0.17%	35	0.05%	9	0.05%	922	http://www.cheapwebtricks.net/
6	118	0.13%	32	0.04%	16	0.02%	4	0.02%	499	http://cheapwebtricks.mail.everyone.net/
7	104	0.11%	102	0.13%	102	0.16%	84	0.43%	1075	http://google.yahoo.com/
8	94	0.10%	90	0.12%	19	0.03%	6	0.03%	606	http://cheapwebtricks.net/
9	86	0.09%	31	0.04%	1	0.00%	4	0.02%	307	http://partners.everyone.net/
10	79	0.09%	79	0.10%	79	0.12%	64	0.33%	1623	http://search.msn.com/
11	75	0.08%	75	0.10%	75	0.11%	65	0.33%	1587	http://dir.yahoo.com/
12	39	0.04%	27	0.03%	3	0.00%	1	0.01%	95	http://search.sandybay.com/
13	31	0.03%	31	0.04%	0	0.00%	6	0.03%	219	http://www.anventure.com/
14	27	0.03%	27	0.03%	27	0.04%	21	0.11%	554	http://auto.search.msn.com/
15	26	0.03%	26	0.03%	26	0.04%	25	0.13%	551	http://www.looksmart.com/
16	11	0.01%	11	0.01%	11	0.02%	10	0.05%	233	http://search.excite.com/
17	9	0.01%	9	0.01%	9	0.01%	9	0.05%	154	http://srd.yahoo.com/
18	9	0.01%	9	0.01%	9	0.01%	7	0.04%	191	http://www.altavista.com/
19	8	0.01%	8	0.01%	8	0.01%	7	0.04%	169	http://sitereview.org/
20	8	0.01%	8	0.01%	8	0.01%	8	0.04%	170	http://uk.dir.yahoo.com/
21	7	0.01%	7	0.01%	7	0.01%	7	0.04%	149	http://boards.entrepreneur.com/
22	6	0.01%	6	0.01%	6	0.01%	3	0.02%	128	http://64.4.20.250/
23	6	0.01%	6	0.01%	6	0.01%	3	0.02%	127	http://www.clickthru.net/
24	5	0.01%	5	0.01%	5	0.01%	4	0.02%	106	http://rr.looksmart.com/
25	5	0.01%	5	0.01%	5	0.01%	5	0.03%	106	http://www.netfactual.com/
26	4	0.00%	4	0.01%	4	0.01%	3	0.02%	60	[unknown origin]
27	4	0.00%	4	0.01%	4	0.01%	4	0.02%	85	http://www.gocertify.com/
28	4	0.00%	4	0.01%	4	0.01%	2	0.01%	55	http://216.33.240.250/
29	4	0.00%	0	0.00%	0	0.00%	0	0.00%	0	http://216.33.236.250/
30	4	0.00%	1	0.00%	1	0.00%	0	0.00%	10	http://website.lineone.net/

Figure 12-7 • A referrer report shows how visitors reach your site.

There's another report that includes sites that send even a single visitor. Second, the referrer host is shown, not the full referrer URL. So this report doesn't tell you exactly which page the visitors are linking from (the more detailed report does), but rather groups things by domain.

As you look at the report's detail, the first thing that jumps out is the top referrer—www.worldsubmitter.com. Do you remember who that is? That's the FFA submission engine that includes cheapwebtricks.com in its database. When WorldSubmitter.com posts something to the FFA page, it does so through automated software. So any view from WorldSubmitter.com isn't a view by human eyes. To get a more accurate "eyeball count" for this site, we have to disregard the WorldSubmitter hits. Without checking the referrer report, we wouldn't know how much they were inflating the traffic count.

The number two referrer is cheapwebtricks.com. Wait a minute, isn't that the site this report is about? Yes, it is, and that line shows that people are moving about within the site. Every time a visitor that's viewing a Cheap Web Tricks page clicks on a link to another page within the site, it's added to this total. This line shows that people don't just look at one page and leave; they travel around within the pages of the site. That means they're finding content of interest to them.

Next in line is www.google.com, followed by search.yahoo.com. These show traffic sent directly from Google and Yahoo!. If you scan down the page, you'll see several more variations on these domains, plus entries from Excite, MSN, LookSmart, and AltaVista. All reflect traffic from those search portals. This means our efforts to get a decent listing position in search portals are paying off.

Other items of note: board.entrepreneur.com is listed. It so happens we responded to a posting there a few days before this report was created, and included the Cheap Web Tricks URL. Apparently, it's paying off. It's also tempting to follow a few of the referrers that are unfamiliar and see what their link to Cheap Web Tricks looks like.

TIP: *Occasionally, when you go to a page that supposedly links to you, there's no sign of that link. This can happen when the link has been removed, or the page containing the link was renamed or moved to another part of the site.*

User Agents and Spider Spotting

Another snippet of information sent by visiting browsers is their own name. This little tidbit is called the *user agent.* Many statistics packages create a User Agent report (alternatively titled Browsers). Figure 12-8 shows a relatively unsophisticated example of this kind of report.

Internet Explorer and Netscape, the most common browsers, both incorporate the word "Mozilla" into their user agent name. Figure 12-8 shows lots of visits by Mozilla user agents. It also reveals that quite a few search spiders have visited the site, including Inktomi, Google, and Northern Light. How can you tell? Check the User Agent (or Browser) report against a list of known search engine user agents. Table 12-1 lists some common search portals and their user agents.

Some statistics packages will automate this spider spotting process for you by creating a spider report. But if not, now you know how to identify them yourself.

Keeping Statistics in Perspective

As you can probably tell, it's possible to spend quite a bit of time reading, interpreting, and generally fooling around with site traffic

PART II

```
Access Statistics for cheapwebtricks.com (May 2001) - Microsoft Internet Explorer

 File  Edit  View  Favorites  Tools  Help   ← - → - ⊗ ⊘ ⌂ | ⊘ ⊗ ⊗ | ⊗- ⊛ ⊗ - ⊗ ⊗ »| Links »| Address

Total Transfers by Browser Type (Overview)

        Total hits    Files Pageview        Bytes sent | Browser Type
     ------------------------------------------------------------------------------
     100550  98.56%  84865   71563   252729264  96.05% | Mozilla/4.*
        471   0.46%    357     111     2942191   1.12% | Mozilla/3.*
        169   0.17%    169     169     1427937   0.54% | Googlebot/2.*
        162   0.16%    156     130      413720   0.16% | Mozilla/5.*
        145   0.14%    128     128     1137299   0.43% | NetMechanic V2.*
        143   0.14%    126     126     1255958   0.48% | WFARC
        116   0.11%    115     115     1057396   0.40% | FAST-WebCrawler/2.*
         49   0.05%     49      49      462445   0.18% | LinkWalker
         46   0.05%     46      46      167987   0.06% | ia_archiver
         22   0.02%     21      21      212731   0.08% | Zeus 52602
         21   0.02%     16      16      124426   0.05% | Mozilla/2.*
         12   0.01%     12      12      121651   0.05% | lwp-trivial/1.*
         12   0.01%     12      12      121703   0.05% | LWP::Simple/5.*
         12   0.01%     12      12      132275   0.05% | Slurp/si (slurp@inktomi.com; http://www.inktomi.com/slurp.html)
          9   0.01%      5       1       49872   0.02% | CacheabilityEngine/1.*
          9   0.01%      8       3       59263   0.03% | Zeus ThemeSite Viewer Webster Pro V2.*
          8   0.01%      8       8      172983   0.07% | Slurp.so/1.*
          8   0.01%      8       2       43224   0.02% | Mozilla (X11; I; Linux 2.0.32 i586)
          7   0.01%      4       0       29001   0.01% | Dual Proxy
          6   0.01%      6       1       32346   0.01% | Opera/5.*
          5   0.00%      5       5       44453   0.02% | ArchitextSpider
          4   0.00%      4       4       44169   0.02% | cosmos/0.*
          4   0.00%      2       2       36466   0.01% | DIIbot/1.*
          4   0.00%      4       4       22963   0.01% | JennyBot/0.*
          3   0.00%      3       3        1704   0.00% | CGI
          3   0.00%      3       3       55087   0.02% | True_Robot/1.*
          2   0.00%      1       1       28919   0.01% | PlantyNet_WebRobot_V1.*
          2   0.00%      2       2       22019   0.01% | Jack
          2   0.00%      1       1       21656   0.01% | Marvin/1.*
          2   0.00%      2       2       43184   0.02% | The_Intraformant
          2   0.00%      0       0           0   0.00% | Gulliver/1.*
          2   0.00%      2       2       22010   0.01% | psbot/0.*
          1   0.00%      1       1       21637   0.01% | www.eshandylogo.de
          1   0.00%      1       0       12537   0.00% | MIIxpc/4.*
          1   0.00%      0       0           0   0.00% | oBot ((compatible,Win32)
          1   0.00%      1       1       10072   0.00% | PBrowse 1.*
          1   0.00%      1       1         406   0.00% | BaiDuSpider
          1   0.00%      1       1         406   0.00% | KIT-Fireball/2.*
                                                                          Internet
```

Figure 12-8 • A User Agent (aka Browser) report

Search Portal	User Agent(s)
AltaVista	Scooter, Mercator
Excite, WebCrawler	Architext
Fast/AlltheWeb	FAST-WebCrawler
Google	googlebot
Inktomi, HotBot	slurp
Northern Light	gulliver
Lycos	Lycos_Spider (T-Rex)

Table 12-1 • Search Portals and Their User Agents

statistics. In fact, it's easy to go overboard in this area. Given how valuable they can be to judging the success of promotional efforts, every site should have some form of traffic statistics, even if it's just a basic hit counter. The more thorough the statistics (as long as you're not spending a fortune on them), the better.

At the same time, don't let an obsession with what these reports say eat up your precious Web development time. As I said in the beginning of this chapter, statistics are only one measure of a site's success.

NOTE: *A referrer report won't tell you where every single visitor comes from. If someone types the URL directly into the browser, there's no referrer to record. Plus, some browsers don't include referrer information with requests.*

The Language of Web Site Statistics (Or, a Hit Is Not a Pageview)

When talking about Web site traffic, people tend to throw numbers around without really knowing what they mean (or hoping that you don't). For example, how many times have you heard someone brag about the huge amount of hits their Web site is getting? I'll tell you right now that the number of hits is meaningless.

Each time a page is loaded, a hit is recorded in the server log file. Each time a graphic is loaded, that generates another hit. So a page containing five graphics generates six hits every time it's loaded (one for the page plus one for each graphic). If that same page incorporates 10 graphics, it generates 11 hits. A call to a program (such as ad serving software or special scripts you might have installed) generates a hit too. Taken together, these factors mean that hits mean nothing.

Sometimes people say hit when they mean pageview. A *pageview* is the display of a single page, including any graphics it might incorporate. This is a much more meaningful measure of what's happening at a site.

Another commonly used metric is *session,* or *unique visitor*. This is an attempt to measure unique hosts accessing your site during a predefined time period (often a day). If the same visitor comes to your site three times in one day, that would be counted as one session (or one unique visitor). This type of statistic isn't entirely reliable for a number of reasons. For one thing, it's really measuring which computers access your site; so three different people using the same computer would be counted as one visitor, and one person who used two different computers would count as two. There are other issues that affect accuracy as well. But a sessions statistic can still give you a general idea of the number of unique visitors to your site during the specified time period.

Besides providing you with an accurate picture of your site's popularity, meaningful statistics will also make your site more attractive to potential advertisers.

Finding Sites That Link to You

We already discussed how referrer reports can identify sites that link to yours. But that's not the only source of such information. You can also use search portals to find them. This is accomplished by using the standard search function at the portal, but incorporating specific keywords and formatting, like this:

Search for:	Help	Customize Settings	Family Filter is off
link:cheapwebtricks.com - host:cheapwebtricks.com	any language ▾ Search
	Search Assistant	Advanced Search

The exact keywords and syntax vary, but the next few sections show how to do it at several popular search sites. For the purpose of illustration, cheapwebtricks.com is used as the target domain in these examples.

Finding Links Using AltaVista or Excite

Type this into the Search box:

```
link:cheapwebtricks.com - host:cheapwebtricks.com
```

The "link:" specifies the domain to look for links to. The "- host" section says exclude results from the cheapwebtricks.com domain. This is to spare you from having to wade through links that are within your own pages.

Finding Links Using Google

Type this into the Search box:

```
link:cheapwebtricks.com
```

This doesn't exclude links from your own pages, but there's no apparent way to do so.

Finding Links Using HotBot

In the Results For box type

```
http://cheapwebtricks.com
```

In the Look For box, select Links to This URL.

Finding Links Using LinkPopularity.com

You can search several portals at once to use the free online tool **LinkPopularity.com**. This site, shown in Figure 12-9, will query multiple search portals for links to your domain and report the results to you. You can then click on the name of an individual search engine to view the actual list of sites found.

NOTE: *Remember, you use the instructions above to check for other sites that link to yours, not to determine whether your site is included in any search portal index. A 0 result only means links to you weren't found, not that your site isn't in the index.*

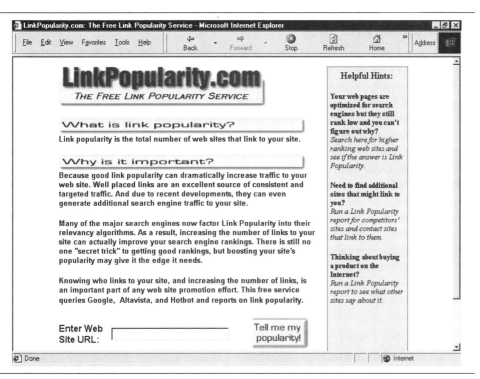

Figure 12-9 • LinkPopularity.com

Determining Your Position in Search Portals

If you have referrer reports, they will reveal whether people are actually arriving at your pages via search portals. But perhaps you don't have access to those reports. Or even if you do, they aren't going to tell you how high on the results page your pages appear.

To get a simple yes/no answer as to whether your site is included in the index of a particular search engine, follow the instructions in the section "How Do I Tell If I'm in a Particular Search Engine?" in Chapter 10. This is a good starting point. If you want to check your position in the results of an actual search, it gets a bit tougher.

The Manual Method

The low-tech way to check search portal positioning is simply to go to each major search site and pretend you're a member of your site's target audience. Type in the search terms that you imagine others would use if they were looking for the content on your site. This should include the keywords you identified as part of creating your meta tags. Does your page come up, or someone else's?

Given the huge amount of competition that's out there, your site's chances of popping up in the number one results position are slim. But if it's anywhere within the first page or two, you've done very well. Try several different combinations of keywords. If your site doesn't appear at all, add your site's name and see if that helps. If there's still no sign of it, you need to revisit your search engine readiness, and/or resubmit your pages to the index.

Automatic Position Checkers

Because search engine position is such a hot topic among Web site owners, several companies have come out with software that promises to check your position in multiple search engines with one click, and provide a summary report. Usually the free service is offered by someone selling search engine services.

- **did-it Detective (did-it.com/search_engine/detective.shtml)** Checks your position in top search engines every month and sends you a report. Interestingly, they have a disclaimer on their page saying that results aren't relevant for pages they have optimized.
- **PositionAgent (positionagent.com)** Checks one key phrase for free. If you want multiple phrases tracked over time, you must subscribe ($60/year).
- **Cybertack (www.cybertack.com/position/position.cgi)** Checks ten search engines for free.

TIP: *The same input produces different results on each of these position checkers, so keep that in mind when you use them.*

Obtaining Visitor Feedback

The third way to assess your Web site efforts is by soliciting feedback from site visitors. This can take the form of a simple "Tell us how we're doing" link that sends you an e-mail. (If you don't recall how to create a mailto: link, revisit Chapter 7 for a quick review.) Or it can be something more sophisticated, such as an online survey or simple poll question. Another possibility is to create a feedback session in a discussion area you have added to your site. I'll explain how to create a discussion area or add a poll question in Chapter 17.

Unfortunately, such efforts are often met with dead silence. If you really want visitor feedback, consider offering something in return. For example, everyone that provides suggestions or comments within a two-week period could be entered in a drawing for a free prize. An incentive like this will dramatically increase your response rate. If you give away anything of substantial value, seek a lawyer's advice first, to avoid potential legal problems.

The combination of the three elements we've discussed—Web site statistics, link popularity, and visitor feedback—will give you a good picture of who is using your site and how. This is empowering information. Use it to improve your site and assess the effectiveness of your promotional efforts. Use it to drive your efforts to turn your Web site into a dynamite success.

PART II

III

Part Three

Making a Profit

13

Chapter Thirteen

Making Money with Affiliate Programs

For many Webmasters, the driving purpose for creating a Web site is to build a profitable online venture. For others, profit isn't the primary motive, but a secondary goal is to make the site at the very least self-supporting, or better yet, to financially support a hobby related to the site's content. Affiliate programs offer a way for companies and individuals with no products or services of their own to work toward either of these goals.

JARGON ALERT: *An affiliate program is a sales relationship in which a merchant pays a Web site owner to sell and/or market the merchant's products. The site owner usually does so by posting banners, buttons, or links.*

How Affiliate Programs Work

The process of becoming an affiliate is amazingly simple: Choose a program, sign up for it online, get accepted (or not), add the links to your site, and then track and tweak the relationship over time. Occasionally you'll encounter a variation in this procedure. For example, a program might require you to sign and fax an agreement rather than simply sign up online.

There are several different approaches to finding and selecting affiliate programs for your site. We'll get into that later in this chapter, but before you start shopping around or signing up, it's important to understand how such programs are structured.

Payment Terms

Affiliate programs come in many different flavors, but one of the first issues most people care about is how much the program will pay for which activities. Although every merchant defines its own payment structure, the categories described in the following sections are most commonly used.

Commission (Pay per Sale)

One of the most common arrangements, a straight commission agreement, provides the affiliate a payment for each sale generated as a result of

links from the affiliate's Web site. This can be a set amount, but more often it's a percentage of the sales total.

Usually the commission is tied to the particular sale, but occasionally commissions continue to be earned on anything the customer buys within the next six months to a year. Commissions earned on an ongoing basis are called *residual commissions.*

Commission rates vary widely, but those using a percentage often fall in the 10 percent to 20 percent range. A few offer as high as 50 percent. Sites that generate a substantial amount of sales can sometimes negotiate a rate increase beyond the initial offer. In the case of a set rate, the amounts are all over the place—starting with $1 and rising to $100 or more for big-ticket items.

A pay-per-sale rate can sound highly attractive, but keep in mind that for every person who makes a purchase, many who view the links or ads will not. That means you could display a commission affiliate link thousands of times and get absolutely nothing in return. On the other hand, if your target audience is buying the affiliate's products, this can be the highest paying of the alternatives.

Click-Through (Pay per Click)

The second most common affiliate arrangement, pay per click, is just as the name implies: You earn a fee each time someone clicks on an affiliate link at your site and is transferred to the merchant's Web page. Usually the payment is tiny—one cent is not uncommon; ten cents is at the high end. Most offer two or three cents. Take it from me—this is a very slow way to earn money. It's still better than nothing, but just barely.

NOTE: *Some unscrupulous people sign up for a pay-per-click affiliate program and then click their own ads, have their friends do so, or generate false clicks in some other way. This is a bad idea, and you will surely be detected, as such activity is easy to identify.*

Lead Generation (Pay per Lead)

The lead-generation model pays you a set amount for each lead that comes from your Web site. You're probably already wondering just what constitutes a lead. The answer varies from merchant to merchant, but usually involves a potential customer completing an online form that indicates interest in a product or service. Once that form is completed, you get paid whether or not they eventually buy anything. Per-lead payments usually run two dollars or less, occasionally a little higher.

Bounty (Pay per Customer)

When a merchant pays you a one-time set fee for each new customer you send who makes a purchase, it's called a *bounty*. Bounty rates usually range from $10 to $20 per new customer.

> **TIP:** *Always read the fine print, especially about rate changes. Can the affiliate rate be changed (usually, yes), and if so, will you be notified first?*

Combination Incentives

In an attempt to create an attractive deal for affiliates while maximizing their own bottom line, merchants sometimes create hybrid plans that borrow from several of the above categories, for example, ten dollars per sale and one dollar per lead, or three cents per click and 25 percent of sale.

> **NOTE:** *The exclusion of pay per display from this discussion isn't an oversight. Affiliate programs simply don't use this arrangement.*

Multitier Programs

Occasionally an affiliate program will reward you for bringing new affiliates into the network. They do this by providing you with a percentage of that affiliate's earnings, in addition to any earnings you generate through direct sales. Programs that do this are called *2-tier.* The percentage often runs in the 5 percent to 10 percent range, though it can be much lower (as low as 1 percent) as well. Some programs pay you for an additional level—i.e., a percentage of what the people referred by the people you refer earn.

Payment Threshold and Frequency

It's very inefficient for merchants to cut a check for ten cents (or even five dollars) to hundreds of affiliates every month. To keep this from happening, they institute a minimum payment amount, called a *threshold.* Until you reach that threshold, you don't get a check. If you never reach it, you never get a check. Threshold amounts are often set at $50 or higher,

so be sure to check on whether the threshold amount for any program you join is reachable.

The other way merchants trim their disbursement workload is to make payments only once a quarter. A few stretch it farther than that. Once again, be sure to read the fine print of the affiliate agreement so that you know what to expect.

Tracking Methods

In order to connect sales, clicks, or leads to the affiliate that generated them, merchants employ a tracking system. There are several different methods in use, and each has its benefits and drawbacks. Before joining an affiliate program, find out what kind of tracking they use and determine whether it is satisfactory.

Embedded Affiliate ID

The most common type of tracking system is to embed a unique affiliate ID into referral links. It can be a letter/number combo like HK1234X or something less cryptic, such as the referring site name. As the visitor travels around the site, the merchant's tracking software continues to associate this ID with the visitor. A link with an embedded affiliate ID typically looks something like this:

```
http://www.bigstore.com/index.html&from=HK1234X
```

The big drawback to this method is that it doesn't allow for human nature. Few people make a purchase decision immediately; they like to think about it awhile, maybe shop around a bit. So let's say the visitor bookmarks the product page and goes off to ruminate over his desire for a purple widget. When he decides he can't do without one, and clicks that bookmark to return, he will go right to the product page instead of following a link from your site. And you will get no credit for the sale. There isn't anything you can do to keep this from happening.

Cookies

To counteract the huge flaw in the embedded affiliate ID method, some merchants serve up a tiny file (called a *cookie*) to each visitor's browser when the visitor follows a link that contains an embedded affiliate ID. This file records which affiliate was responsible for the referral and is saved to the visitor's hard drive. If the visitor returns later to make a purchase, the merchant site retrieves the affiliate ID stored in the cookie, and you receive proper credit.

JARGON ALERT: *A cookie is a small bit of data that is passed from a Web server to a visiting browser and stored on the visitor's hard drive. If the person returns to the same Web site in the future, the bit of data will be automatically transmitted back to the Web server. Cookies are often used to track affiliate sales, automate logins by remembering user names, or personalize a Web page. Only the server that sent the cookie can read it back again; a Web server can't access a cookie left by another Web server.*

This method isn't without its downside either. It's possible to adjust browser settings so that cookies aren't accepted. If someone who follows your referral link has cookies disabled, you're back to the plain old embedded link scenario: If they don't purchase immediately, you don't get credit. In addition, some Web surfers regularly clear out cookies, at which time yours will be sent to the trash can too.

The good news is that most people leave their cookie settings alone. And even if some cookies are lost or not accepted, a tracking system that uses cookies is still a leap forward from relying solely on a link with an embedded ID.

TIP: *Browser cookies don't last forever. They have a preset expiration date, kind of like the sell-by date on real cookies. Each affiliate merchant determines how long a cookie will remain valid. Many will last a month, six months is less common, and only the rare few never expire.*

Unique Web Address

Sometimes merchants provide each affiliate with a unique URL to link to. Since no one else will have any reason to connect to that URL, the merchant knows that all visitors to that page came from a particular affiliate. Such a URL might look something like this

```
http://bigstore.com/cheapwebtricks
```

or this:

```
http://cheapwebtricks.bigstore.com
```

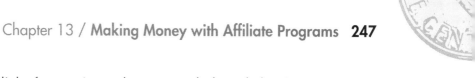

This unique link often persists as the user travels through the site, courtesy of a special program running on the merchant's server. Anytime visitors bookmark a product page, they are bookmarking a page with your custom URL in it, which means you will get credit if they return later and make a purchase.

Reporting

Every affiliate program you join should have a clearly specified reporting facility in place. At a minimum, it should report sales you've made. Better yet, reports will be available to show you how many people followed your links versus how many made purchases. The GoTo.net affiliate report shown in Figure 13-1 reveals the number of times the linking graphic was displayed as well as the number of times it was actually clicked.

Ideally, affiliate reports would reflect real-time, up-to-the minute transactions, but that's rare. Usually they will be a day or week behind. If updates are less frequent than that, be wary, because it will take longer to notice and rectify any problems that occur.

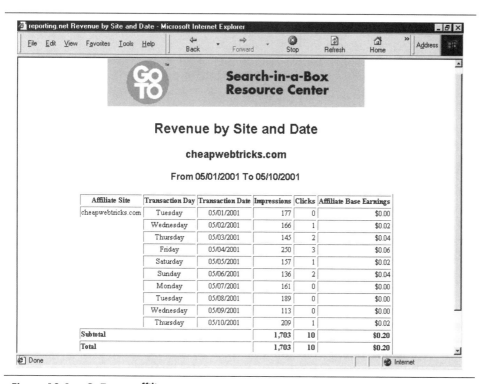

Affiliate Site	Transaction Day	Transaction Date	Impressions	Clicks	Affiliate Base Earnings
cheapwebtricks.com	Tuesday	05/01/2001	177	0	$0.00
	Wednesday	05/02/2001	166	1	$0.02
	Thursday	05/03/2001	145	2	$0.04
	Friday	05/04/2001	250	3	$0.06
	Saturday	05/05/2001	157	1	$0.02
	Sunday	05/06/2001	136	2	$0.04
	Monday	05/07/2001	161	0	$0.00
	Tuesday	05/08/2001	189	0	$0.00
	Wednesday	05/09/2001	113	0	$0.00
	Thursday	05/10/2001	209	1	$0.02
Subtotal			1,703	10	$0.20
Total			1,703	10	$0.20

Figure 13-1 • GoTo.net affiliate report

PART III

Selecting Affiliate Programs

Now that you understand the various ways affiliate programs can work, it's time to start selecting a few that will generate revenue for your site. Although it can be tempting to sign up for the first offer that you encounter, resist the urge. There are literally hundreds of programs to choose from, and by being a bit picky you'll end up with better results.

The Wrong Approach to Affiliate Marketing

A few—okay a lot—of wannabe Internet entrepreneurs go out and sign up for every affiliate program that will accept them and then slap up a page that contains nothing but an extensive array of affiliate links and banners. Figure 13-2 shows one such page. I can tell you four things about it:

- Nobody intentionally visits this page more than once.
- The site is almost certainly not making any money (see the first point).
- The page conveys an image of the Web site owner as an amateur huckster.
- The Webmaster would be more successful by creating a useful Web site and adding affiliate links to it than by using this shotgun approach.

Any amount of time you spend on this kind of approach is wasted time.

The Right Approach to Affiliate Marketing

For affiliate partnerships to have a chance to work for you, relationships need to be chosen with care. The first step is to identify programs that provide something your site's audience is likely to want.

You could evaluate each program you encounter to determine whether it would serve your visitors, but an even more effective approach is to turn the process around and start by answering the question "What would my audience want or need?" Then go in search of affiliate merchants that could make those things available. This is likely to bring you an array of products and service ideas well suited for selling via your site.

Finding Affiliate Merchants

Affiliate marketing has become so popular that it's very easy to find merchants. There are several master directories that list, describe, and

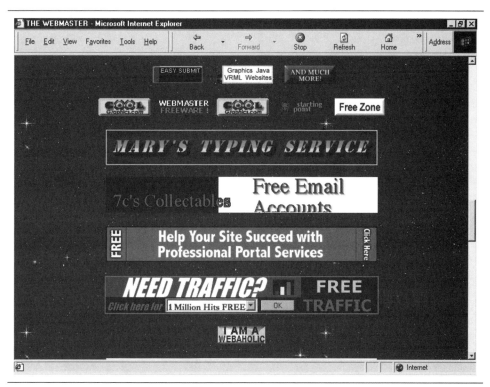

Figure 13-2 • How not to be an affiliate

rate affiliate programs. In addition to these independent lists, a large percentage of merchants who run an affiliate network do so through one of a handful of affiliate service networks. The networks provide centralized servicing of a collection of programs, making it easy for Webmasters to find, join, and track results.

One successful affiliate network is Commission Junction. This network provides one-stop shopping for Webmasters and, equally important, one-stop payment. At Commission Junction, all the pennies, nickels, and hopefully, dollars that you earn from any participating program are collected in a single account. Plus, you can search for merchants by keyword, category, payment terms, or other criteria. Figure 13-3 shows a few of the more than 100 merchants in the financial services category, along with the terms they offer. Applying for any of these programs is as simple as clicking the word "join."

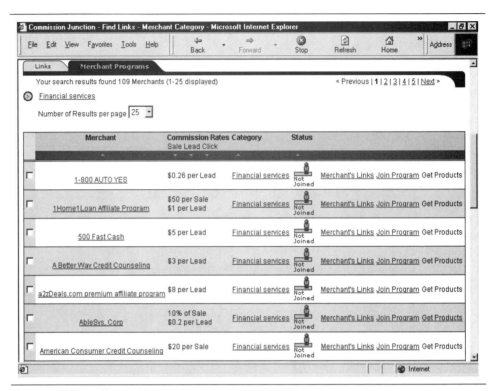

Figure 13-3 • Affiliate choices at Commission Junction

Here's the rundown on the major affiliate networks:

- **BeFree (befree.com)**   Signed its first merchant, Barnes and Noble books, in 1997, and now has over 350 participating merchants. Reporting is through the companion reporting.net Web site, which in my experience is often slow or not working at all. Does not aggregate payments from multiple merchants.
- **ClickTrade (clicktrade.com)**   Part of Microsoft's bCentral. Over 7000 merchants. Aggregates payments from multiple merchants, making it possible to reach payment thresholds sooner.
- **Commission Junction (cj.com)**   Over 1500 merchants, ranging from very small to well-known brands. Aggregates payments from multiple merchants into one account.
- **LinkShare (linkshare.com)**   The pioneer of affiliate networks, LinkShare launched in 1996 and is still thriving today. Over 400 merchants use this system.

- **Sponsorships.net (sponsorships.net)**   A newer affiliate network owned by iBoost, this network pays monthly, and offers both banner and text links. Most programs are pay per lead.

TIP: *Before joining an affiliate network or program, try to find a help e-mail address and send a message to see if someone (a real person, not an autoresponder) replies. In the event of a dispute, you're going to want to be able to contact them. A few are notoriously hard to reach, and it's best to know this up front.*

You may find you want or need to join more than one network. If there's a particular product you want to sell, that product's vendor may be running its affiliate program through one of the networks, and you'll have to join that network to participate.

A few merchants (fewer each week) don't operate through a third-party affiliate network, but run their own program in-house instead. If you limit yourself to affiliate network offerings, you can miss out on some good opportunities. Amazon.com is a prime example. One of the most successful affiliate programs ever, Amazon.com probably sells books that have something to do with your Web site's topic. But if you want to become an Amazon affiliate, you'll have to sign up directly through them. They're not in any of the networks (at least as this was being written).

So how do you find independent programs like this? Besides going to merchants you know and trust and looking for an "affiliates" link somewhere on the site, you can utilize the services of an affiliate directory Web site. These don't offer direct sign-ups, but collect, organize, and report on affiliate programs across the Web. Here are a few sites to get you started:

- **AffiliateFind (affiliatefind.com)**   Programs organized by payment type, product category, or searchable keyword. Shown in Figure 13-4.
- **Affiliate Match (affiliatematch.com)**   Organized by category.
- **AssociatePrograms.com (associateprograms.com)**   Searchable directory of affiliate programs. Many are rated by site visitors.
- **QuickClick (quickclick.com)**   Thorough reviews and comments on a wide variety of affiliate programs.

PART III

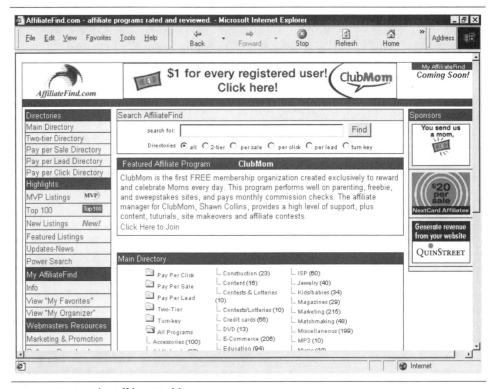

Figure 13-4 • The AffiliateFind home page

Storefront-in-a-Can

A few affiliate programs offer substantially more than links, banners, and buttons; they provide entire virtual storefronts. This allows you to create a store that has your site's look and feel but the contents of a much larger merchant's catalog. Figure 13-5 shows a NextDayPC.com affiliate store as it appears on the affiliate site GoCertify.com. (To get your own, go to **resellersonly.com**.)

JARGON ALERT: *Cobranding is the process of creating a page, site, or service that carries the brand identity (such as logos, company names, and/or color scheme) of more than one company.*

The virtual storefront is especially nice because it allows you to link the buying experience with your Web site and build brand loyalty for

Figure 13-5 • Why stop at a link when you can have an entire store?

your own venture instead of someone else's. When simple links are used, buyers are transferred to the merchant's site and do all their searching and shopping there. They then associate the purchase with the merchant instead of with you, the affiliate. When they're ready to purchase again, they're likely to go directly to the merchant site, not yours.

But if you have a cobranded storefront, visitors do their shopping without ever leaving your site (at least psychologically). Even though the store pages are drawn from another location, the brand identity of your site is always present. When the visitor is ready to purchase again, hopefully they will return to your store, instead of going directly to the merchant's site and bypassing yours.

Choosing Affiliate Programs

As I said in the beginning, there is a virtually endless supply of affiliate merchants to choose from. They range from well-respected, widely recognized brands such as AT&T to unknown widget sellers who set up shop last week. So how do you decide which are worthwhile?

Step one was described earlier: Choose products and services that are suited to your site's audience. Step two is to begin browsing through associate networks and directories in search of candidate programs. The second-to-last step before actually signing up for a program is to run through the affiliate assessment checklist.

- ❏ Is the product or service something your site visitors will want?
- ❏ Is the merchant a reputable company?
- ❏ What is the payment structure and rate?
- ❏ How often do they pay?
- ❏ What is the payment threshold?
- ❏ How do they track referrals?
- ❏ If cookies are used, what is the duration of the cookie?
- ❏ Is online reporting available, and how often is it updated?
- ❏ Have people complained about this program?

To answer the final checklist question, are there any complaints, you're going to have to do a bit of online research. You won't have to look much farther than **affiliateprogramsthatsuck.com**. Here you'll find a fair amount of ranting, along with notices of programs that have reportedly folded without paying affiliates, or committed other offenses. Another place to check is **blacklist.com**, which spreads the bad word on affiliate programs, Internet Service Providers, and other Web businesses. A few of the affiliate directory sites mentioned above include user ratings or other comments on the benefits and drawbacks of individual programs.

The final step before signing up is to read the affiliate agreement. Every program has one. If the program you're considering doesn't, run far and run fast. Look over the fine print for anything especially objectionable. Usually it will just be the standard legal mumbo jumbo that says you won't post their links on porn pages, and so on; but to be safe, read it. Then, if the program has met all your criteria, go ahead and take the plunge. This isn't a commitment like marriage, and if it doesn't work, it's easy to break off. All you have to do is drop the program and stop using their links.

NOTE: *If you have more than a few affiliate programs, you'll need the ability to automatically rotate banners. Chapter 15 describes how to do this.*

Running Your Own Affiliate Program

If joining an affiliate program can generate income, will starting your own earn even more? If you have products or services of your own to sell, it's certainly worth a serous look-see.

It's easier than ever to start and run an affiliate program, but still requires a significant investment of time, effort, and even money. In order to be able to sign up affiliates and track sales, you'll either need to sign up with an affiliate network (which can charge $5000 or more in start-up fees) or obtain and install affiliate tracking software of your own. The latter is probably the less expensive option as far as cash outlay.

You'll also need to recruit and retain qualified affiliates, and plan on communicating with them regularly. The bigger your network grows, the more time this will take. Plus, those affiliates will need a steady supply of affiliate links and banners, which someone is going to have to generate. And there's the small matter of commission checks—these will have to be calculated, created, and mailed at regular, timely intervals.

As you can see, starting and running an affiliate program requires a substantial commitment. If you don't take the time to do it properly, you'll end up with a network of people mad at you and bad-mouthing your Web site rather than an outsourced sales force. For many merchants, the payoffs make the process worthwhile. If you want to explore the possibility of launching an affiliate program of your own, I suggest the following Web sites as helpful resources:

- **Affiliate Handbook (affiliatehandbook.com)** A combination directory and primary source of affiliate program information. Includes recent affiliate news and case studies.
- **Affiliate Marketing (affiliatemarketing.co.uk)** Packed with primers, information, and resources for affiliate program managers.
- **ClickZ's affiliate marketing column (clickz.com/column/ am.html)** Articles and information for new and experienced affiliate program managers.

PART III

After You Sign Up

Once you sign up, you're only halfway there. To draw in the largest amount of income even from well-chosen affiliate programs, you need to promote them appropriately and vigorously.

The first step is simply to place the links on your Web pages, but according to affiliate marketing experts, if you stop there, you're not optimizing your opportunity to earn income. If you just leave the same banner on page after page of your Web site, the click-through rate for that banner will drop over time. That's because repeat visitors have already seen (and possibly clicked on) it. Most affiliate merchants offer a variety of banners, so be sure to change to a fresh one periodically.

If you have a newsletter or mailing list, use it to pitch your affiliate products. If you don't have one, Chapter 18 will tell you how to set one up. This can be a successful way to reach people who will read e-mail, but just don't click on banner ads.

Marketing experts also suggest that affiliates use the time-tested method of providing personal endorsements. If you can say anything personal and positive about the products you're marketing, do so. One technique is to write an article about something closely related, and pitch the product or service within that. Don't slather on the praise if you don't believe in the product; your insincerity will quickly show through.

Many merchants maintain an affiliate center on their Web site. They will provide you with tips and techniques to help you maximize your profits (and not coincidentally, theirs too). Take advantage of these resources, and don't be afraid to try new techniques and experiment a bit.

Don't be afraid to drop a program that doesn't work. Give it a reasonable try—a few weeks at least—but if the income just isn't there, drop the program and carefully choose another one that may perform better.

TIP: *Continue your efforts to increase traffic to your Web site. The more visitors you have, the larger your pool of potential customers will become.*

Realistic Expectations

While some people are wildly successful with their affiliate efforts, many more, by far, are disappointed in the resulting income. It seems that affiliate programs work better for the merchant than for its affiliates. But there are Webmasters who make a decent amount of money from their affiliate efforts.

To become a successful affiliate, it's important to have realistic expectations up front. If you think you're just going to throw up a

banner ad and watch the cash come rolling in, think again. Affiliate success relies on choosing the right affiliate program and products, marketing them to the correct audience, and modifying your approach based on the results you receive.

The most successful affiliates have a passion for their subject matter and everything connected with it, including related products. Become an expert in your subject area and share that expertise with your visitors. Use that expertise to choose specific affiliate products and services, and market them on the most relevant pages of your Web site. Even though you won't get rich overnight, with care and attention, affiliate marketing can make your Web site not just an enjoyable and useful pastime, but a profitable venture as well.

PART III

14

Chapter Fourteen

Selling Products or Services Through Your Web Site

If you have goods or services to sell, a Web site can be a great way to expand your customer base nationally or internationally—reaching as far as you want to. A Web-based store has significantly lower startup and operational costs than a traditional storefront, which makes it especially appealing to entrepreneurs.

If you want to run a full-blown online storefront offering your own products and services, and accept credit cards, you're going to have to open your wallet to get it up and running. If your online sales plans are less expansive, you can get started selling with little or no cash outlay.

Selling products and services online consists of four activities: providing product information, taking orders, processing payment, and fulfilling the orders. The first two can be done primarily online, the third, online or off. The fourth activity, fulfillment, isn't provided by your Web site, so it's not covered in this book, but don't overlook the fact that you need to have a plan in place for packing and shipping orders. As part of fulfillment, you'll also need to plan for typical customer service issues, such as how you will handle customers who are not satisfied and how you will replace faulty items. All four elements must be in place and working in harmony for your sales plan to pay off.

The Big Picture Alternatives

There are three ways you can get an online store up and running on your site:

- Acquire and install the necessary software and services on your own Web server. This requires a significant amount of research and effort, but is doable, even for free. You can also get someone else to install the software on your server for you, at surprisingly affordable rates (often $50 or less).
- Sign up for Web site hosting with a hosting service that offers built-in e-commerce. The entire transaction will take place on your Web site. No free Web hosts offer such services.
- Sign up with a (usually for a fee, sometimes free) service that provides e-commerce services to other Web sites. Users will most likely link to another site to complete the transaction.

Just because huge companies like Amazon.com take orders online, process credit cards immediately, and otherwise take advantage of electronic transaction possibilities, that doesn't mean that you have to do the same. They've got plenty of resources (that is, money) behind their efforts, and operate on a much larger scale than the average frugal Webmaster. Ideally, you want to provide the same convenience for your customers, but without the resource commitment. The reality is likely to fall a bit short of that mark, but there's a lot you can do to make buying online an easy and comfortable experience for your customers, without laying out a chunk of up-front cash. In other words, a Mercedes might be your ideal method of travel, but a Ford Escort will still get you from point A to point B. It's up to you to choose which one you want and can afford.

Anatomy of an Online Purchase

Although the ambience is different, the actual steps involved in making an online purchase are in many ways similar to the traditional experience of shopping in a retail store. It works like this:

1. Customer enters store (visits Web site) and browses through merchandise.
2. Customer adds desired merchandise to shopping cart.
3. When finished shopping, customer proceeds to checkout.
4. At checkout, order amount is totaled, shipping and applicable taxes are added, and the total is presented to the customer for payment.
5. The customer completes an online form that collects the necessary payment and delivery information. The information is encrypted and stored in a secure location for the merchant to retrieve, or sent to the merchant by e-mail. In some cases the customer might print out and fax, mail, or phone in the order.
6. The transaction is processed. This can occur through any of the methods described in the "Payment Methods" section of this chapter.
7. The merchandise or service is delivered to the customer.

Displaying Your Wares

Before anyone purchases a product or service from you, they'll want to know exactly what they're buying and how much it will cost. You need to get your products online in a format that customers can easily browse and you can easily manage.

A Product or Two

If you have only one or two products or services to sell, your task is much simpler than if you have a lot of items. You won't need to invest in special shopping software, or install and run it. If you have only a few items, you can simply create a Web page for each one or put them all on one page, as shown in Figure 14-1. You can process orders through one of the methods described in the "Ways to Take Orders" section.

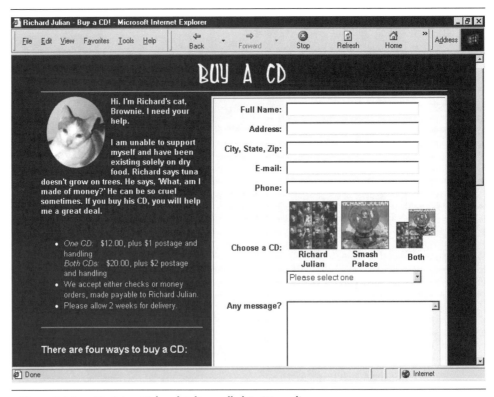

Figure 14-1 • Musician Richard Julian sells his CDs online.

A Whole Catalog

If you have more than a couple of products or services on offer, maintaining an individual Web page for each can quickly get cumbersome. The solution is to use an online catalog system, similar to the one shown in Figure 14-2.

NOTE: *Setting up a multiproduct catalog isn't as easy as some promotional blurbs would have you believe, but it is within reach of the determined do-it-yourselfer.*

Catalog software allows you to enter specific item information, such as product description, item number, pricing, and an image of the product. Items can often be organized into categories so that like items will appear near one another. The catalog software then uses that information to

Figure 14-2 • GoCertify.com's store uses a catalog to display merchandise.

generate individual product pages. To update the catalog, simply update the product information. Often, catalog software includes a shopping cart component. This allows customers to add items to their shopping cart as they browse, so multi-item ordering is simplified. When catalog and shopping cart features are included, the program is often called shopping cart software.

JARGON ALERT: *A Web site shopping cart system works just like a standard grocery store shopping cart, except that when customers take things out, no one has to reshelve them. As visitors travel through the store, they can place items they wish to purchase in the cart. When they are finished shopping, they can pay for all the items in one transaction, just as they would in a traditional store.*

Sources of free catalog and/or shopping cart software include

- **1StopCommerce (1stopecommerce.com)** Free shopping cart software. Comes configured to work with this vendor's payment system, but you can alter it as you wish.
- **Commerce.cgi (commerce-cgi.com)** Shopping cart system (scripts) with browser-based store manager for managing your inventory. Works with several different credit card processing services.
- **PerlShop (arpanet.com/PerlShop/perlshop.html)** Complete shopping cart script. Can be set up to process credit card transactions online.
- **RediCart (itransact.com/redicart/index.html)** Consists of three Perl scripts. Works with ITransact's order processing system or can be modified to work with another system.
- **VIPCart.com (vipcart.com/cgi-bin/info.pl?sub=info)** Remotely hosted shopping cart system. Free, but runs banners on the pages.

TIP: *Beware of shopping cart systems that rely on JavaScript. Although relatively simple to install, they always use browser cookies, which many Web surfers disable. With cookies disabled, the system won't work.*

When selecting a script or service, ask the following questions:

- Will it run on your Web server?
- Does it work with all of the popular Web browsers?
- Does it require any additional software in order to function?
- Will it work for the kinds of products/services you offer?
- Can you use it at any hosting company, or do you have to use a particular host?
- What technical support is available to help you get it up and running?

Expect to do a fair amount of tweaking to get the service to work smoothly.

> **TIP:** *Some credit card services may require you to sell a minimum amount of goods or pay a hefty service fee. Others may limit the amount of goods you are allowed to sell, so be sure to read the fine print.*

Ways to Take Orders

Your visitor has browsed through your offerings (whether one service or a dozen products) and selected the item(s) she wishes to purchase. Now you need to record the order and collect the information needed to process it. There are several different ways you can do this.

Orders by Phone, Fax, or Mail

When selling items online, you should provide a facility for online ordering if at all possible. But sometimes, for one reason or another, online ordering just isn't in the cards. The old standbys of phone, fax, and mail-in ordering can be offered as alternatives.

There's another reason you should offer offline ordering—some people just don't want to order things over the Internet. They don't trust it (even though it's very safe). Or they want to speak to an actual person before plunking down their money.

When going the offline route, it's best to create an order form that can simply be printed and then faxed or mailed in. If the customer is ordering by phone, the form will speed the process and reduce the likelihood of mistakes.

If you are using a shopping cart or catalog program, the customer can simply print out the final screen that includes item numbers and pricing, and that will serve as an order form. If you're not using a shopping cart system, you can create a Web page that contains a blank order form, such as you would find in a magazine. Figure 14-3 shows an example. The customer can print it and fill it in manually. Include your full mailing address on the form. Even if the order won't be mailed in, the address provides reassurance that your business actually exists and isn't a front for a scam.

For phone and fax orders, provide a toll-free number whenever possible. Online orders can come in any time day or night, and having

Figure 14-3 • A standard order form placed online

your bedside phone ring at 3:00 a.m. won't be a positive or productive experience.

If you don't have a fax line, or you don't want to make it available for this purpose, consider using a free fax service such as e-Fax (**efax.com**) or OneBox (**onebox.com**). e-Fax will provide you with a fax number (usually not in your own area code). Faxes that are received are immediately forwarded to you by e-mail. You need special software to read the faxes, which is also free. As with many freebies, you'll have to tolerate a bit of advertising along the way, but that's what makes the service free. You can't send faxes using this service, unless you upgrade to a paid version. OneBox offers similar services, with a few variations.

Orders by E-Mail

E-mail ordering offers a step up from the offline ordering choices. Although e-mail ordering can be as simple as providing a "mailto:" link in your HTML page, it's very little work to create an online order form that can be sent to any e-mail address you specify with a single click. Figure 14-4 shows what such a form might look like.

Once again, if you're using a shopping cart system, you will probably be able to select e-mail ordering as an option when you configure the software, and the system will take care of creating the form for you. The rest of us will need two things: a Web page with an HTML form on it, and a form-mailing program that will take the contents of that form and e-mail it to you. Many hosting services provide a free form-mailing script, but if yours doesn't, fear not; there are plenty of freebies you can use, even if you can't install scripts on your server. So if you don't have a form-mail program installed, and don't want to (or aren't allowed to) install your own, use someone else's:

- **Freedback (freedback.com)** Add a form to your site and have the results mailed back to you—no cgi and no experience needed. Everything is done online. Thank-you page carries an ad from the provider.
- **Response-O-Matic (response-o-matic.com)** Create your form online and have the results mailed to you. The action points to the Response-O-Matic Web site script, so there are no scripts to install. Thank-you page carries an ad.
- **FormSite.com (formsite.com)** Another completely remotely hosted forms service. Free version limits you to 100 form submissions a month.

Finally ready to build that new website? Is you current site in desperate need of attention?

Fill out the form below to receive a free custom quote within 24 hours.

(Hey! Something for free - you've got nothing to lose!)

E-mail: info@shoestringsites.com
Phone: (212) 613-6307

Name:

Phone:

E-mail:

Which of the following are you most interested in?
New site design

Would you like a free custom quote?
Yes please!

How did you hear of Shoestring Sites?
The Internet

Your message:

Submit Query   Reset

Figure 14-4 • Users can order a free Web site consultation with this form.

A Brief Introduction to HTML Forms

Webmasters who like to get elbow deep in their HTML code and do it themselves will need to know how. In the earlier section covering offline ordering, I suggested that you create a Web page that looks like an order form, which can be done simply by applying the HTML you already know to create a page that appears in the desired format. Making a form that can be sent by e-mail is a bit different: It requires using a new HTML tag named, appropriately enough, <FORM>. You'll also need the

URL of the script (form mailer) that sends the contents of the form to you via e-mail once the user finishes filling it in and clicks the Submit button.

NOTE: *You can also add forms to your site and process them using free tools mentioned in the previous section. But even if you go the remotely hosted route, it will help to understand how HTML forms are constructed.*

The form tags are used like this:

```
<FORM ACTION="http://mydomain.com/cgi-bin/formmail.cgi"
METHOD="POST">
</FORM>
```

As you can see, the opening <FORM> tag has several attributes: ACTION and METHOD. The ACTION attribute specifies the URL of the script that takes the contents of the form and does something with it after the user clicks the Submit button. In our case, that will be the form-mailing script that you've installed on your server or are using from somewhere else. The METHOD attribute is always either GET or POST. For form-mailing purposes, you will always use POST (*which must be in all caps*). Taken together, these attributes tell the server to POST the form contents to the form-mailing script, which will then send it on to you via e-mail.

Form tags alone won't make a working form. You need to add more elements between them, like this:

```
<FORM ACTION="http://mydomain.com/cgi-bin/avformmail.cgi"
METHOD="POST">
<INPUT TYPE="text" NAME="name" SIZE="40"><BR>
<INPUT TYPE="submit">
<INPUT TYPE="reset">
</FORM>
```

Now you have a very simple working form that looks like this:

The first <INPUT TYPE> tag creates a text field, called name, that is 40 characters long. The second displays a button that users can click to

PART III

submit the form (to the form-mailing script) after filling it in, and the third displays a button users can click to reset the form to blank fields if they want to start over. If a Joe Schmo filled in this form, and clicked Submit, you would receive an e-mail that would read

name Joe Schmo

A text field is good for inputting things like names or phone numbers that fit on one line, but sometimes you might want users to select items from a list, or provide several lines of comments. Fortunately, you have a nice toolbox of input types to choose from, including radio buttons, check boxes, drop-down lists, and text areas.

Radio buttons look like this:

    ◯ Choice 1
    ◯ Choice 2
    ◯ Choice 3

The <INPUT TYPE> tags that create them look like this:

```
<INPUT TYPE="radio" NAME="favorite" VALUE="choice1">
Choice 1<BR>
<INPUT TYPE="radio" NAME="favorite" VALUE="choice2">
Choice 2<BR>
<INPUT TYPE="radio" NAME="favorite" VALUE="choice3">
Choice 3<BR>
```

TYPE specifies that these are radio buttons. NAME indicates that these buttons belong to a group named favorite. VALUE is the name assigned to the specific button. Only one radio button can be selected from a group; for example, favorite can have only one value when the form is completed—choice1, choice2, or choice3.

Check boxes look like this:

    ☐ Choice 1
    ☐ Choice 2
    ☐ Choice 3

The <INPUT TYPE> tags that create them look like this:

```
<INPUT TYPE="checkbox" NAME="favorite" VALUE="choice1">
Choice 1<BR>
<INPUT TYPE="checkbox" NAME="favorite" VALUE="choice2">
Choice 2<BR>
<INPUT TYPE="checkbox" NAME="favorite" VALUE="choice3">
Choice 3<BR>
```

These work very much like radio buttons with two key exceptions. First, the check box is square instead of round. Second, more than one can be chosen.

A drop-down box looks like this:

The HTML that creates it looks like this:

```
<SELECT NAME="my_choice">
<OPTION>choice 1
<OPTION>choice 2
<OPTION>choice 3
</SELECT>
```

<SELECT> is a special tag for creating drop-down boxes. It has an attribute, NAME, that serves the same purpose as it does for other form fields. The <OPTION> tag specifies the items that will appear in the drop-down list. Note that <SELECT> requires a closing tag </SELECT>.

A text area box looks like this:

The HTML line that creates it looks like this:

```
<TEXTAREA NAME="comments" ROWS=6 COLS=60></TEXTAREA>
```

ROWS specifies how many lines tall the box should be; COLS (columns) specifies how many characters wide.

You can put these form elements together to create a form that collects

TIP: *Forms can contain other HTML elements in addition to form fields, including formatted text, color, links, and images.*

the information you're after. Remember to put the Submit and Reset buttons at the bottom. Here's an example of an order form for widgets:

Widget Order Form

Widget Model:
○ Standard ○ Deluxe ○ Super Deluxe

Customer Information:
Name:
Address:
City: State: Zip:
Phone Number:

Payment Method:
Check ▾

[Continue] [Reset]

And here is the HTML behind it:

```
<FORM ACTION="http://mydomain.com/cgi-bin/avformmail.cgi"
METHOD="post">
<H1>Widget Order Form</H1>
Widget Model:<BR>
<INPUT TYPE="radio" NAME="model" VALUE="choice1"> Standard
<INPUT TYPE="radio" NAME="model" VALUE="choice2"> Deluxe
<INPUT TYPE="radio" NAME="model" VALUE="choice3"> Super
Deluxe
<P>
Customer Information:<BR>
Name: <INPUT NAME="name" SIZE="40"><BR>
Address: <INPUT NAME="address" SIZE="40"><BR>
City: <INPUT NAME="city" SIZE="15">
State: <INPUT NAME="state" SIZE="2">
Zip: <INPUT NAME="zip" SIZE="10"><BR>
Phone Number: <INPUT NAME="city" SIZE="15">
```

```
<P>
Payment Method:<BR>
<SELECT NAME="payment_method">
<OPTION>Check
<OPTION>Credit Card
<OPTION>Paypal
</SELECT>
<P>
<INPUT TYPE="submit" value="Continue">
<INPUT TYPE="reset" value="Reset">
</FORM>
```

Now that you know how to create HTML forms yourself, that's probably the way you'll want to do it. You'll need a form-mailing script. Your Web host probably has one already installed. Check the tech support area for instructions on how to use it. If you want to install your own, flip ahead to Chapter 17, where you'll find a list of script repositories.

> **NOTE:** *This information on forms should be enough to get you going. If you want to learn even more about forms and what they can do, visit an online tutorial such as the one at **mastercgi.com/ howtoinfo/formtutorial.shtml**.*

Secure Order Forms

If you are collecting credit card information, you should use a secure order form instead of a plain old HTML form. What's the difference? A secure order form uses a special set of rules for sending data back and forth between the user's browser and the Web server. Data traveling either direction is encrypted so that in the extremely unlikely event that it was intercepted on the way, it would be unreadable. Purchasers can look for two signs that tell them the secure connection is being used:

- An image of a lock, or other similar symbol, appears in the lower-right corner of their browser.
- The URL of the form will start with https:// instead of http://.

Figure 14-5 shows an order page that is utilizing a secure connection. Note that the URL starts with https://, and there's a lock in the lower-right corner of the browser screen.

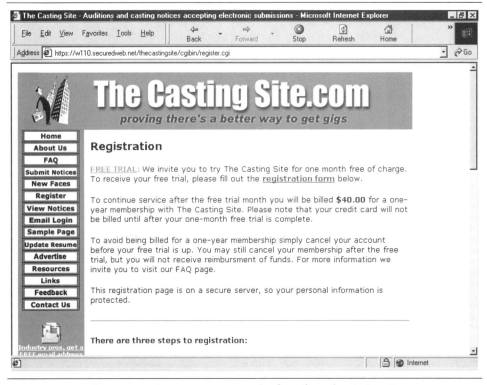

Figure 14-5 • The Casting Site uses a secure order form for subscription sign-ups.

JARGON ALERT: *SSL stands for Secure Sockets Layer. This is the protocol, or set of rules, that Web server software and browsers use to make secure connections work.*

Even though the chance of credit card information being intercepted between the form and the Web server is extremely remote, secure order forms are a must if you are collecting credit card information. Users expect them, and often won't buy over a connection that isn't clearly secure. So why isn't every connection made secure by default? Because encrypting and unencrypting takes time and server power. For nonsensitive information, it simply isn't worth the overhead.

Using a Secure Server

I could go on for pages, or even a whole book, on the nitty-gritty details of how secure connections and SSL actually work, but I won't, because what most Webmasters really care about is how to use them. So I'll only tell you what you need to know.

For a secure connection to be possible, the server that's being accessed must be running SSL software. Many hosting services include it in their packages. Free hosting services do so much less often. The form itself is exactly the same as for a nonsecure connection, but the way you call it is different. Instead of loading the form with

```
http://mydomain/myform.html
```

a URL such as

```
https://secureservername/mydomain/myform.html
```

is used instead. The exact format (and secureservername) will be specified by the hosting service. This routes communications through the secure server and causes the encrypting to take place. Make sure the ACTION that the form uses refers to the secure server too, like this:

```
<FORM ACTION="https://mydomain/cgi-bin/formmail.cgi" METHOD="POST">
```

> **TIP:** *If you decide not to employ a secure connection, you can always collect order information, except credit card details, using a regular (nonsecure) form, and then call the buyer for the credit card information.*

Using Someone Else's Secure Server

SSL software isn't something you can install yourself. If your hosting service doesn't have SSL installed or wants to charge more for it than you want to pay, it's possible to use a service. When users reach the point where they are about to enter the sensitive (credit card) information, they are transferred to the secure server of the service, and the transaction is completed there. This service is rarely offered as a stand-alone product, but is usually packaged with online credit card processing services, which are covered shortly.

PART III

NOTE: *An SSL connection only protects the link from the browser to the server. It doesn't afford any special protection once the data is on the server, or control what happens to it after that.*

Payment Methods

Once an order is placed, it's time to collect payment from the customer. In a traditional store, buyers typically have their choice of cash, check, charge, or debit card. On the Internet things are a bit different.

First of all, cash is out. No one's invented a computer component yet that allows you to insert cold hard cash into a slot on your machine and have it emerge from a slot on the seller's machine. But something else, called *cybercash*, or *digital cash*, is in. You might not know it, but you can also accept checks online. The next few sections describe your alternatives.

Low-Tech Payments

Checks and money orders can be sent by traditional mail, which you can simply deposit in your bank account. This costs nothing more than a stamp, but you'll potentially face bounced checks, which can rack up charges very quickly. Plus, you are totally missing out on the power of the Internet to provide the ability to purchase things instantly, which Web surfers expect these days. If you seriously want to sell online, consider accepting either credit card payments or, as a second choice, cybercash.

Accepting Credit Cards

Credit cards are increasingly central to accepting payments for goods and services sold over the Web. You can't expect to sell a substantial quantity of your wares online (though you can certainly market them) without accepting credit cards as a form of payment. While some buyers might feel anxious about using their credit card online, many more feel it is a form of insurance: if you turn out to be a fraud, they can dispute the charge and get their money back. Credit cards are also the simplest way for buyers to purchase something online, and you want to make it as simple for them as possible.

Online credit card payments don't have to be processed instantaneously. You can collect credit card information using a secure order form, and process it later, offline, if you wish.

Credit card processing is a two-step process. First the card is verified and approved to assure that it actually exists, hasn't expired, and isn't stolen. Then the customer's account is debited and the money is deposited in the seller's account. Both of these functions can be performed by a single vendor, such as a bank, or they can be done by separate companies.

TIP: *Always authorize the credit card before fulfilling an order. The card might be declined, expired, or simply bogus.*

The Easy Way

The quickest and easiest way to start accepting credit cards online is to sign up with a vendor that will accept and process them for you. They provide an ordering link for your customers to use, collect and process the credit card information, and send you a check. You don't have to set up a special bank account. While you won't have to lay out any money up front, they will take a fee, sometimes a substantial one, for their services.

- **CCNow (ccnow.com)**   Includes shopping cart service, toll-free order number. Pays 1.5 percent interest on balance in your account. Charges a 9 percent commission. No startup fees. Shown in Figure 14-6.
- **iBill (ibill.com)**   Works for services and/or products. Credit card base commission is 15 percent. Drops a little as sales revenues grow. Also processes online checks.
- **DigiBuy (digibuy.com)**   For "publishers of software, shareware, electronic art, information (such as an e-book), and data." Order processing fee is 13.9 percent. Will process faxed or phoned-in orders too. Setup fee for minimum service level is $29.99 for the first product, $9.99 per product after that. Obviously, this is only feasible for a few products.

The Other Way

To accept credit card payments yourself, online or off, you'll need a special kind of bank account that's set up to receive them. This kind of account is called a *merchant account.* Merchant accounts usually have a per-transaction charge (called a *discount rate*), plus an application fee, and sometimes a setup fee too. They also take longer to set up, so if you're in a real hurry, you'd better use the easy way described above.

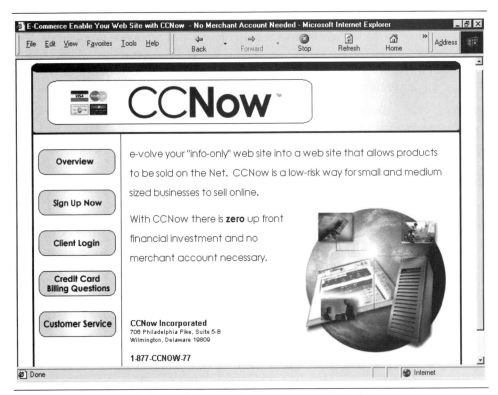

Figure 14-6 • CCNow helps Web site merchants accept credit card payments.

You'll also need either an online credit card processor or an offline manual system. If you're using an online processor, you can send the transaction off to the service when it occurs, and the money (less their commission) will be deposited in your account, usually a day or two later.

If you have a membership service, or subscription-based product where you will bill people on a regular basis, find out if your software/service will do this automatically, or if you'll have to hand process it yourself each month.

Some companies offer both services. Or you can look for the best deal on each one separately. You'll want to shop around for the best deals. You can find a slew of choices through the Yahoo! site. Just search using the phrase "merchant account" or go directly to **dir.yahoo.com/ Business_and_Economy/Business_to_Business/Financial_Services/ Transaction_Clearing/Credit_Card_Merchant_Services/**. Check with your local bank and see what they have to offer as well.

JARGON ALERT: *A reserve is an amount a credit card processing service will hold back to cover potential problems, such as customer chargebacks.*

Accepting Checks Online

Not everyone wants to or is able to use a credit card to buy things online. You can provide an alternative for these customers by accepting payment via check. All they have to do is provide the information from a physical check, including check number, bank name and address, and the routing number at the bottom of the check, and state that they authorize the amount. The information is used to create a physical check (technically called a *bank draft*), which can be deposited into your bank account. This is legal and acceptable practice, as long as you do one of the following:

- Receive written authorization from the customer by fax or mail, *or*
- Tape-record the authorization with the customer's knowledge, *or*
- Mail out written notice to the customer before depositing the check in your bank account. Notice must be in the mail prior to making the deposit.

NOTE: *Most online check systems work only for U.S. checking accounts and funds.*

Do-It-Yourself

You can set up a secure form to collect the check information, and then use a check printing program to produce the actual check. Or, stepping down a level, you can have customers phone or fax in the check information. Then you can use check printing software to actually produce the check. You'll need blank check stock, which you can get at any office supply store. You can't just write the checks by hand, because the routing information has to be printed using special characters and digits so it can be read by bank check-processing machines. In case you're wondering, the signature line contains the phrase "Signature Not Required."

PART III

Sources of check printing software include

Check Printing Software	URL	Cost
CheX Bank Draft software	ww.compu-sult.com/chex/	$24.95
ChekFaxx	checkfaxx.com	Standard Edition $99
ChecksNet Professional	checksnet.com/prices.htm	$59.77 if downloaded
DraftCreator	advancemeants.com/draft/	$79

Online Check Processing Services
The second alternative is to sign up with an online check processing service that will collect the information and process it for you. Some of the credit card processing services will handle checks for you as well. Try these check-specific vendors too:

- OnLine Check Systems (**onlinecheck.com**) is shown in Figure 14-7.
- PayByCheck (**www.paybycheck.com**).

You can also find more on the ever-handy Yahoo! Web site at **dir.yahoo.com/Business_and_Economy/Business_to_Business/ Financial_Services/Transaction_Clearing/Check_Services/**.

NOTE: *Check processing services don't guarantee that a check is good. It can still be returned as NSF (not sufficient funds) and leave you empty handed.*

Digital Cash
The last payment method on our list is digital cash, which is also called cybercash. This is enjoying a growth in use among smaller online entrepreneurs because it is free for the vendor to set up, and provides a way for customers to pay for things immediately, online. The digital cash vendor charges a small fee for each transaction.

The downside is, for this to work, the customer has to have an account set up with the same digital cash vendor as the merchant, or set one up at the time of the order. The account is funded with a check, credit card, or link to the customer's bank account. Most buyers don't have such an account, at least as this is being written. But digital cash transactions are growing in popularity, and several digital cash vendors are becoming

Figure 14-7 • Online check processing services will handle customer checks for you.

well known enough that people recognize and trust their name. So it's worth considering as a payment form.

To use digital cash, you'll have to sign up with one or more vendors. Each has its own payment process, but usually it involves clicking on the vendor's link, which takes the buyer to the digital cash Web site, where the transaction is conducted using a secure server. Frugal Webmasters commonly use one of the following digital cash services:

- **PayPal (paypal.com)** Perhaps the best known and most widely used. In operation since November 2000. Shown in Figure 14-8.
- **Amazon Honor System (amazon.com/honorsystem/)** Offers visitors an opportunity to pay whatever they wish out of the kindness of their heart. Amazon.com gets 15 percent of the total payment per transaction plus 15 cents.

PART III

Figure 14-8 • The PayPal home page

Remember the Red Tape

This book is about the Webmaster end of things, not your local tax laws, but I want to remind you that setting up a business that you run from home or office is likely to be subject to local tax and business regulations. Although this red tape can be a hassle, it's better to know up front than to get an ugly surprise a year down the line.

Check local and state regulations before you start selling. You may need to get a business license or register your business name. Depending on the type of products and services you sell and to whom, you may need to collect sales tax. You can usually get this information from your local chamber of commerce, or through your state's government Web page.

A Matter of Trust

The technical details of how to sell items through your Web site are only one aspect of joining the e-commerce world. Buyers are often a reluctant lot, and even more so online where they can't see or touch the merchandise, or the merchant. They wonder if their financial information will be safe, if the product will be as promised, and whether they will have anyone to turn to if it's not.

To counteract these not unreasonable fears, it's important to demonstrate that you're a vendor worthy of their trust, and to provide all the information a buyer might possibly need to make a decision to purchase.

Don't Hide Behind Your Web Site!

How can you show potential customers that you're an honest, reliable merchant? The most basic and powerful step is to make it easy for them to contact you. As obvious as this sounds, many, many Web sites don't do this. Perhaps it's intentional, or maybe due to fear that placing contact information online will result in dirty phone calls in the middle of the night. Who knows? But it drives a wedge directly between the merchant and the customer. You can't hide from your customers and expect them to trust you.

Put your contact information in a prominent place, such as behind a "contact us" link that appears on every page. Consider plastering your phone number (use one that can ring in the middle of the night without disturbing anyone) on every page. Make sure you offer several ways for people to get in touch—phone, e-mail, and street address.

You may get some spam, or a few catalogs you didn't order. Maybe you'll even get an obscene phone call or two, though that's highly unlikely. But you also have a much greater chance of getting actual, paying customers.

Make Sure Your System Operates Correctly and Fast

Don't take anyone else's word for it that your online sales system is functioning properly. Periodically run a test transaction through the site yourself. This is the only way you can be assured that the system is working in an acceptable fashion.

Give a Guarantee

Consider offering a money-back guarantee. This helps convince potential customers that you are a reputable merchant who stands behind the products or services offered. Better to give a disgruntled customer or two their money back than to have them bad-mouthing you to everyone they meet. For similar reasons, have a product return process in place and make sure it's easy to find on your Web site. If you are a member of the Better Business Bureau, be sure to convey that prominently on your site.

Provide All the Necessary Information (and Then Some)

Strive to give buyers every possible bit of information they might need to make a purchase decision. That might include sizing information, shipping costs and procedures, color choices, and of course, pricing and discounts.

Send a Confirmation

Your order-taking process should include a confirmation system. Especially when ordering online, people want to know that their order was received and that all of the information they intended to include is correct.

The E-Commerce Challenge

As you can see, the world of e-commerce can be fairly simple if you have just a few products or services to offer, but quickly grows more complex. And the technical end of things is only one part of the picture. If you are planning to sell goods or services online, and you're not currently selling those same things offline, you are basically launching a new business. That means you not only have to learn the Web end of it, but you also have to learn the ins and outs of running a going concern from day to day. This can be quite a challenge, and also very rewarding. Setting up shop on the Web is a whole lot more affordable than renting a spot in the local shopping mall, and your potential market spans the globe. I wish you the best of fortunes.

15

Chapter Fifteen

Selling Advertising on Your Web Site

One of the revenue models introduced in the beginning of this book is selling advertising on your Web pages. Some Webmasters use this service to produce an impressive stream of income, while others are just seeking to cover the costs of running the site. Whichever is your goal, if you want to jump into the online advertising business, this chapter will tell you everything you need to know.

Despite the appearance of advertising banners on virtually every online site a Web surfer visits, Internet advertising still claims only a tiny share of the advertising budgets of most companies. According to a February 2001 Morgan Stanley Dean Witter report on Internet direct marketing and advertising services, the top six U.S. advertisers spend less than 1 percent of their budget on the Web. The same study finds that the companies that do the most online advertising are dotcoms. But this doesn't mean you should forget about advertising as a source of revenue, because it keeps many Web sites afloat and has for years.

To sell advertising on your site, you'll need to understand how your site rates as an advertising outlet. You'll also need to know the formats and flavors of advertising that are bought and sold, and the terminology of the Internet advertising marketplace. And, you'll need a way to deliver and track advertising that you sell.

Your Site as an Advertising Venue

In order to sell advertising on your Web site, the site must provide an audience that advertisers want to reach. The main factors that determine the attraction your audience has for potential advertisers are its size and composition.

There are several accepted measures of Web site audience size. The one that's currently most popular is unique visitors per day or per month. Another commonly used measure is pageviews per day or month. As either of these numbers grows, your site becomes more attractive to visitors. If your site has under 1000 pageviews a day, your chances of attracting paying advertising are slim. On the other hand, if you can deliver over 100,000 pageviews a month, you're getting into reasonable territory. At half a million pageviews a month, even the big Internet advertising networks will begin to give you a look.

Audience makeup is almost more important than audience size. Who comes to your site, and do they have money to spend? Are they part of a

demographic profile that online advertisers want to reach? How tightly focused is your audience? The more directly you reach a desirable audience, the more an advertiser will be willing to pay for space on your site. A site with a desirable, tightly focused audience may actually be able to earn more advertising revenue than a site that accrues many more pageviews, but to a wider range of visitors. In the eyes of an advertiser, the ultimate Web site provides a very large audience that is highly focused in a way that closely matches the advertiser's target market. Creating such a site will bring the frugal Webmaster the greatest profits.

But creating a tightly focused site can also reduce the pool of potential advertisers to those in a single industry or niche market. It's also rather hard to do, unless you have highly valuable, specialized knowledge in a particular area. Even then, it takes time to build up a high level of traffic in a niche market.

If you hope to sell advertising on your Web site, early on in its evolution, you should make a conscious decision about which category your site will fall into:

- General interest, high traffic
- Focused, niche audience, at the expense of a smaller audience

Sites in the first category will receive lower advertising rates, but have more space to sell, while those in category two will have higher rates, but less space available.

Types of Web Site Advertising

The most apparent form of Web site advertising is the banner ad that appears at the top of many commercial Web sites. But the top of the page isn't the only spot for sale. If it was, you'd be limited to selling only as many advertisements as you have pageviews. By judiciously placing multiple ads on each page, you can up your advertising inventory considerably.

Advertising can also be sold as banners and boxes of other shapes and sizes, placed in other spots on the page. You might wish to revisit Chapter 11, which contains the sidebar, "Standard Banner Ad Sizes," listing specific sizes recommended by the Internet Advertising Bureau. The Web page shown in Figure 15-1 displays advertising in the traditional top spot, as well as down the right-hand column.

Text links offer a less space-consuming, and faster loading, alternative to graphical banners. Sponsorships are popular as well. With *sponsorships*, an advertiser pays to be the sole, or at least most prominent, sponsor

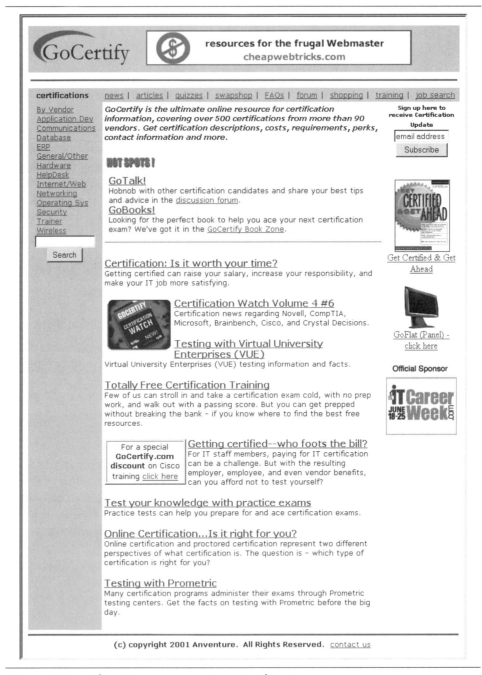

Figure 15-1 • Advertising can appear in various locations on a page.

of a particular page or Web site section. Advertising can also be sold in a newsletter associated with the Web site. I'll talk more about that in Chapter 18.

You may also encounter a form of advertising called interstitials. An *interstitial* is an advertisement that is loaded into a separate browser window that opens while a viewer is waiting for a Web page to load. An advertisement that appears on top of the page is called a *pop-up*, while one that is loaded behind the current page is called a *pop under*. Advertisers pay higher rates for interstitials because of their size, but many Web site visitors find them annoying, so use them sparingly if at all.

How Web Site Ads Are Priced and Sold

Advertising, whether banners, buttons, boxes, or text links, is most often sold on the basis of the number of people that will see the ad. Sometimes—particularly if there's no tracking mechanism in place—ads may be sold based on how long they will appear on the site, rather than how many times they will be viewed.

Cost per Thousand

Web site advertising is most commonly sold as a package of impressions. As you may recall from Chapter 2, an impression is a display of the advertisement on a viewer's screen. Impressions are sold in increments of a thousand. The price of a thousand impressions is called the CPM rate.

JARGON ALERT: *CPM is an acronym for cost per mille. Mille, also represented by the Roman numeral M, means thousand.*

A Web site that charges a $4 CPM would receive $200 for 50,000 impressions of an ad. A Web site with a CPM of $20 would earn $1000 for 50,000 impressions.

Cost per Click (CPC)

On occasion, advertising is sold on a per-click basis instead of per impression. In this case, the advertiser pays a set amount (usually a few cents) each time a visitor actually clicks on an advertisement. This is a very unreliable and not terribly fair method. First of all, it doesn't account for the brand awareness that is being created each time viewers see the advertiser's banner, even if they don't click on it. Second, cost-per-click advertising is ripe for abuse, with clicks being falsely generated by individuals who have no intention of purchasing or learning about the product. I strongly suggest that you don't offer CPC advertising as an alternative on your site; stick with the CPM model instead.

Term Pricing

The third pricing alternative is term pricing: Advertisers pay a set amount to have their ad displayed in a specific spot for a predetermined time period. This is sometimes used by Web sites that don't have ad tracking facilities in place to count impressions, but it can also simply be an easier way to sell space for specialty items like page sponsorships.

JARGON ALERT: *Your ad inventory is the quantity of impressions you have available to sell in a specific time period.*

Setting Your Prices

One of the biggest challenges in selling Web site advertising is determining what price to charge for your ad inventory. Obviously, premier spots can be sold for more than less-desirable positioning. For example, a banner at the top of the page is worth more than one at the bottom. Plus, as a general rule, the more tightly focused your audience is toward a desirable niche, the higher the CPM rate you can charge.

TIP: *Take care not to saturate your pages with too many ads. Although it might seem like you're increasing your ad inventory, you will drive visitors away with this tactic, so you may actually decrease it.*

Advertising prices vary dramatically depending on the type of products and services a Web site is suitable to advertise and the type of audience it has. As this is being written, CPM ranges from as low as less than $1 to as high as $40 or more.

Figuring out your own rates is a trial-and-error process. Start by scouting out your competitors' rates. Visit sites that cater to a similar audience, and try to determine what they are charging. Look for an advertising

link, or the words "rate card." Often the rates aren't published, partly because they can change frequently as market demand fluctuates. You may have to call or send an e-mail to inquire.

JARGON ALERT: *A rate card is a list of the published rates for various advertising spots. The rates that are actually received are often substantially lower.*

You can also find advertising pricing information online as part of industry reports. Places to look include

- **AdResource (adres.internet.com)** Articles on the state of Internet advertising, including periodic rate surveys. A fabulous resource. Shown in Figure 15-2.

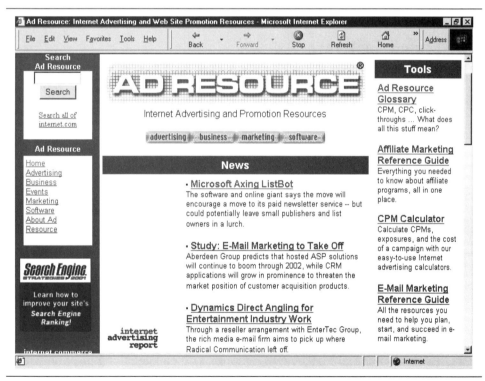

Figure 15-2 • **AdResource contains lots of useful Internet advertising information.**

- **Internet Advertising Report (internetnews.com/IAR/)**   A good source of online advertising news and information, including articles on the effectiveness of online ads.

JARGON ALERT: *ROS is short for "run of site." Run of site ads appear on every page instead of only in a particular section or two.*

The Technology of Serving Ads

The most straightforward way to display advertisements on your Web pages is to hand code each one by using HTML tags. First insert the image, and then link it to the advertiser's site. But if this is the only way you can display ads, it's going to be difficult to get potential advertisers to take you seriously. If you want to sell advertising successfully, you're going to have to implement a more sophisticated system.

Ad Serving Software

The process of displaying advertisements is called *serving*. Serving ads goes beyond simply displaying images; it includes scheduling, tracking, and reporting functions. With ad serving software it's possible to rotate multiple advertisements through a single spot, record how many times each is displayed, and tally how many users clicked on each one. The more advanced systems permit targeting to specific Web pages, days of the week, hour of the day, or to certain viewer characteristics.

JARGON ALERT: *CTR, or click-through ratio, is the percentage of ad impressions that are clicked on by a viewer. If one click is recorded for 100 displays of an ad, the CTR would be 1 percent.*

As you've probably guessed, high-end ad serving systems cost a bundle—up to thousands of dollars. But unless your Web site generates a million or more pageviews a month, you can get along just fine with much less power.

There are two ways you can get access to ad serving software:

- Obtain and install the ad serving software on your Web server, or have someone else install it for you.
- Use ad software that is installed on someone else's server.

Once you have access to the software, you will insert special coding into your Web pages each place you want an ad to appear. When a page is called up by a visitor, that code will call the ad serving software, which will fetch the proper ad and place it on the page in the desired spot.

Installing ad server software can be tricky. If you've installed scripts on your server before, you can probably handle it yourself. Otherwise, it's probably worthwhile to consider an option that doesn't require installation, or get someone else to install it for you.

TIP: *In order for someone else to install software on your server, you'll have to provide them with your login information, including user name and password. For the sake of security, change your password immediately afterward. Although the installer is most likely an honest person, it's not a good idea for anyone other than yourself to know your password.*

Sources of free ad serving software include

- **Ad Butler (adbutler.com)** Remotely hosted advertising management. Free to you, except that they get 7.5 percent of your ad inventory. Shown in Figure 15-3.
- **Ad Deliver.com (addeliver.net)** Remotely hosted, free banner serving and tracking. Offers nifty "HOT AD" button that lets advertisers sign up for advertising online, by clicking the button and answering a few questions.
- **Ad Rotator (ad-rotator.com)** Remotely hosted banner system. They get 10 percent of your impressions to start, but the percentage drops quickly if you refer others to their system.
- **OrbitCycle (orbitcycle.com)** Remotely hosted ad serving software. Takes 10 percent of your banner impressions in exchange for the service.

PART III

Figure 15-3 • Ad Butler will serve up your ads for free.

Handling Unsold Ad Inventory

Despite your best efforts, there will be times when you have unsold advertising inventory. There are several useful things you can do with this space:

- *Use it yourself.* Unsold advertising spots can be used to promote your own products, services, or other Web sites.
- *Swap it.* Consider trading extra impressions with other Webmasters. This is a cheap way to obtain advertising for your site.
- *Donate it to charity.* One of my favorite things to do with unsold space is to donate it to charity. By running free advertisements for causes you believe in, you can contribute to organizations that

will really appreciate your efforts. The AdCouncil (**www.adcouncil.org**) operates a clearinghouse service that provides professionally developed charitable advertising campaigns for free use by Webmasters. Their Web site is shown below.

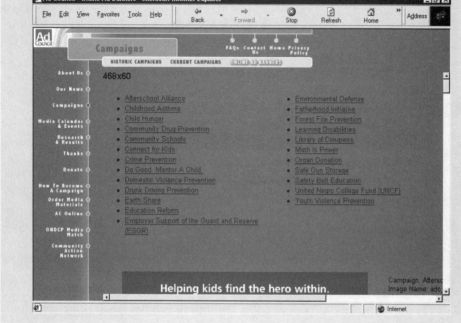

Ad Networks

Webmasters who don't want to manage their own advertising sales and support might wish to join an advertising network instead. These networks bundle sites into categories and then sell advertising on all the sites in the category as a package. They provide participating Web sites with the necessary code to display the ads.

NOTE: *Ad networks often unilaterally turn down sites that are run by free hosting services, so the most frugal Webmasters may have to use one of the other ad serving alternatives.*

PART III

This sounds so easy, why wouldn't everyone choose this route? Because the rates provided by ad networks are typically abysmally low. Huge Web sites (or networks of sites) large enough to get individual representation may get decent rates, but smaller Web sites earn only a fraction of what they might get if they were able to sell their own advertising directly.

Despite those criticisms, ad networks do free Webmasters from a task they may not be well suited for—sales. Network ads are also sometimes used in combination with other sales efforts, to fill in unsold space so that at least it's earning something.

Ad networks can be tough to get into. Here are a few I know about, and the requirements they have in place as this is being written:

- **BannerSpace (bannerspace.com)**   Pays per click and sometimes per impression (CPM). Posted rates start at three cents per click.
- **BURST! (burstmedia.com)**   Markets banner advertising and e-mail advertising. Pays a percentage of their earnings: 50 percent for a nonexclusive month-to-month arrangement. You must have a minimum of 5000 pageviews per month.
- **Content Zone (contentzone.com)**   Willing to accept small sites, but pays very low CPM rate (15–17 cents). Rate is higher for premier members (at least 250,000 impressions per month). Also serves full-page interstitials at a much higher CPM.
- **FocusIN (focusin.com)**   Provides both CPM and CPC advertising. Promises a 65 cent CPM minimum, but the small print says they sell some space below that price.

NOTE: *You might wonder why some of the ad networks you've heard of aren't on this list. It's because they require a huge amount of ad impressions—in the millions-per-month range—as their minimum.*

Additional Advertising Resources

I'll close this chapter with a list of resources that will help you get the greatest benefit and profit from your Web site advertising efforts.

- **About.com's online advertising site (advertising.about.com/ careers/advertising/cs/onlineadvertising/index.htm)** General advertising information, articles, and links.
- **ClickZ (clickz.com)** Advertising and e-commerce articles, case studies, and strategy information.
- **Internet Advertising Bureau (iab.net)** Articles on the state of Internet advertising, including revenue analysis, advertising standards, and case studies.
- **Yahoo!'s Internet advertising directory (dir.yahoo.com/ Business_and_Economy/Business_to_Business/ Marketing_and_Advertising/Internet/Advertising/)** Links to dozens of advertising networks and information resources.

PART III

16

Chapter Sixteen

Cashing Out

The ultimate goal for many frugal Webmasters is to create a successful Web site on a shoestring budget, and keep running it for as long as it holds their interest and serves its purpose. The idea of selling the site to someone else only enters the picture when someone approaches with an offer, or when the Webmaster has something else he or she wants to do and is unable to keep the current site operating at the same time.

For others, the goal of selling the site for a profit has always been somewhere in the picture, either at the forefront as the driving objective, or lingering on a back burner as an interesting possibility. In either case, it's an exciting prospect: There's money to be made, pitfalls to avoid, and a huge sense of accomplishment that comes with a few bragging rights for those who enjoy such things. If selling your site is part of your dream, I want to help you make it happen.

My experience with selling Web sites comes from the sale of GoCertify.com to EarthWeb (now Dice) in February 1999. To bring you the best advice possible, I've also tapped the expertise of David Cutler, founder and director of New Business Development at Sandy Bay Networks. He has participated in the sale of several Web sites.

Preliminary Work

You wouldn't try to sell a car before getting it in tip-top condition and doing a little research to figure out how to get the highest sales price. A Web site sale requires similar attention. The process begins by asking and answering a series of questions about the item you have to sell, and the market for it.

Do You Have a Salable Property?

What does your site have to offer a potential buyer? When it comes to buying Web sites, purchasers are looking for properties that will improve their bottom line. That means you will have to identify how your Web site can increase someone else's revenue. Be prepared to make a case for how your site will do that.

Direct Revenue
One of the first things a potential acquirer will want to know is how much revenue the site produces. This includes income from advertising, sales

of products and services, content syndication, or any other activities that produce cold hard cash.

Although potential acquirers love to see a solid, substantial influx of revenue, don't despair if your site doesn't have that yet; you may have other things of value to offer.

Indirect Revenue

Your site may have potential revenue in addition to, or in place of, actual revenue. It may sound like smoke and mirrors, but it's not. If you can drive sales of the potential purchaser's products or services, even without generating sales of your own, you have something to offer.

The most obvious way this could happen would be if the acquirer advertises and sells its own products and services through your (acquired) site; but that's not the only route to added profits. For example, suppose you have a very strong relationship with a particular market segment. In the case of GoCertify.com, the strong relationship was with IT professionals, specifically, those interested in advancing their career through certification. If your site has a similar relationship with a market that the potential acquirer wants to reach, your site can be their gateway.

You may have other relationships of value to offer. For example, you might have a well-developed information or sales network in place that would take a lot of work, expertise, or expense to reproduce. Or perhaps you have a connection to a selection of companies that the potential acquirer would love to call customers. These are all things you can bring to the table.

TIP: *Before sharing your operating secrets with another company, consider asking them to sign a nondisclosure agreement (NDA). You can find an article describing the why and how of NDAs at* **management.about.com/smallbusiness/management/library/ weekly/aa062199.htm.**

Special Technology

If you're lucky (and innovative), you may have a special technology to bring to the table. This doesn't have to be a patented design for a better mousetrap (though it could be), but anything you have that no other Web site does. For example, you might have an automated online ferret genealogy system. By acquiring your site, the purchaser will gain the renown of owning and operating the only such service on the Web.

PART III

According to Cutler, "You are ready to consider selling when either you have exclusive content that another company wants enough to pay for (they probably would just want to rent or buy you!), *or* (more likely) you can show growth in e-commerce revenue and/or subscribing customers. It's best to also have multiple and repeat revenue streams."

Is It a Good Time to Sell?

If you've gone through the earlier sections and come up with a skimpy list of what your site has to offer, that doesn't necessarily mean you can't sell it; rather, you need to build it up more first. When it becomes a more valuable property, reconsider selling.

But even if you come up with an attractive list of virtues on the first try, consider carefully whether now is the time to sell. There are several reasons you might want to hold off.

Market Condition   I'm not an expert on the economy, but Web site acquisitions seem to go in flurries. When the economy is strong, and especially when dotcoms are doing well, they're out patrolling for sites to buy. They'd rather add a ready-made site than build one up from scratch. Conversely, if stock prices are sliding downward and companies with an online presence are tightening their belts, you won't be able to rouse nearly as much interest. Waiting a few months could bring you a much better price.

You're on the Brink   Are you about to complete something that will add substantial value to your site—for example, a partnership arrangement that will add a brand-new service that's virtually guaranteed to drive your traffic up? If so, wait until you have it in place, and your total package will be more attractive.

You're Not Done   Are you ready for someone else to take over your site and control its everyday operations, even if they run it into the ground? Do you have nifty and cool things you still want to add, but haven't yet? No one will be invested in your site like you are. Although an acquirer may keep you on to run it, the site won't be your own anymore. If you're not ready to let go, wait.

Finding and Approaching Buyers

If you're lucky, buyers will come to you without any encouragement, but more often, you'll have to identify and approach them. Once you have a prospect in mind, you can tailor your approach to their needs, increasing your chances of success.

Researching Possible Buyers

In addition to the initial research you conducted before beginning, chances are that as you've progressed through building and operating your site, you've developed a pretty good sense of the marketplace you are in. It's time to put that knowledge to work in new ways.

The largest pool of potential buyers is within your own marketplace—other companies serving the same audience as yourself. By acquiring you, they can expand their market share while cutting competition, an attractive combination.

Your list of site partners—companies you already have arrangements with—is another pool of possible buyers. Instead of just working with your site, they can own it. "Your most likely buyer will probably be your best (and largest) partner or competitor," confirms Cutler.

Make a list of potential buyers. Visit their Web sites and search for information that might indicate that they're in a buying frame of mind. For example, if they have a press release page, look there for news of acquisitions or recent financing, both potential indicators they'd be willing to give your site a close look.

Keep notes of what you find. And analyze it from more than one perspective. For example, if one company has been acquiring in your market area, its direct competitor may be feeling pressure to do the same.

Opening the Door with an Alliance

Before you actually approach a potential buyer with a proposal that they acquire your site, consider building a relationship with them first. Is there a mutually beneficial partnership arrangement you could propose, such as traffic sharing, providing content, or something else? This could be a swap arrangement or, better yet, something they pay you for.

If you do manage to forge a working relationship with a company on your list of potential buyers, you will have already demonstrated your site's value before you make your formal pitch. In the event you decide to approach another company first, you can use your relationship with the first company as a demonstration of your site's value and potential.

Preparing Your Pitch

Before you approach potential buyers, attempt to anticipate their questions and have appropriate answers ready. They may want to see a business plan, for example. If you don't have one, consider creating one, to help sell your site if nothing else. You can find plenty of information on writing business plans online. Here are a few resources to get you started:

- **U.S. Small Business Association (www.sba.gov/starting/indexbusplans.html)**   Tutorial, outline, explanation.
- **Entreprenur.com (entrepreneur.com)**   Choose the Biz Startups tab; then look for Business Plan in the left-hand column. Lots of articles and advice.

In addition to a well-considered business plan, create an executive summary, and customize it for each buyer you plan to approach. Outline your SWOT: strengths, weaknesses, opportunities, and threats, advises Cutler.

TIP: *Consider hiring an accountant to crunch the numbers for you. This will allow you to present professionally prepared financial documents.*

Approaching Buyers

When you have your documents and plan in order, it's time to approach potential buyers. First you have to figure out who is the proper person to approach. In some cases, this will be as simple as visiting the Web site of the acquiring company and looking for a contacts page. If you're lucky, the contacts page will specify the name and contact information of the person in charge of business development. That is who you should approach first. In some cases, there will be no one with that title. You may have to contact a high-level manager or even the CEO in order to find the best person to connect with.

TIP: *Before sending your entire pitch, complete with executive summary, make initial contact and verify that you have identified the proper contact person.*

Your initial approach can be by e-mail; use it to get a telephone conversation. Don't go for a hard sell right off the bat. Simply broach the idea that you have a Web property that they might be interested in, and discuss the types of alliances the company is looking for. If you receive the slightest positive feedback, move forward, providing more details and information as seems appropriate.

Making the Sale

As your efforts move toward fruition, there are several aspects of any potential deal that you should consider. Have several price points in mind, including the minimum you'd be willing to accept, and an amount that you'd consider most fair. There's no need to set an upper limit—after all, it's not like you're going to turn money away.

Talking Terms

In some cases, the price paid for your site may be linked to the traffic or revenue that occurs during a specified test period. For example, they pay X amount if you get Y amount of site visitors during the specified period. Set the target amount to an attainable number, and then beat it!

Cash up front often isn't the only element of a proposed Web site deal. For example, you may be offered stock or stock options. Approach either with caution, and don't even count the first as real money. Stock prices, especially in the dotcom sector, fluctuate wildly. Any stock you receive may lose part or all of its value before you can sell it. This doesn't mean that stock is worthless, just that it's much riskier than cash.

If you will have ongoing involvement with the site, perhaps as a consultant, the agreement should specify exactly what will be required of you, for how long, and what the compensation will be.

Legal Issues

I'm not qualified to give you legal advice, and I highly recommend you have an attorney look over any proposed contract before you sign it. Remember that the buyer is going to write the contract in their favor, as much as you let them. It's your (and your attorney's) responsibility to make sure you get a fair deal. With those caveats in mind, based on my personal experiences and those I've heard about from others, I can make a few suggestions for conditions that you might want to make sure are provided for in the contract.

- If you will be staying on as a consultant, under what conditions can they terminate your employment?

PART III

- There will probably be a noncompete clause preventing you from working in particular areas or Web sites for a specific time period. Make sure it is as specific and limited as you can make it. The initial wording will invariably be too broad.
- If the Web site is shut down, will you have the opportunity to regain ownership?
- If the acquiring company is acquired or goes bankrupt, how will this affect your contract with them?
- If you are still running the site, and it is sold or transferred to another owner, will your contract remain in force or be terminated?
- Try to obtain an interest charge on payments that are late to you. Otherwise, you can be left hanging for an extended period of time at no expense to the acquiring company.

Creating and selling a Web site for a profit is quite an accomplishment, and one to be proud of. Just be certain that you are ready to part with your creation, and that you are getting the best deal possible. Most businesses operate with a reasonable level of ethics, but they are still out to make a profit and get the best deal for themselves that they can. Your job is to make sure that the deal benefits you as much as it does them.

IV

Building on Your Success

17

Chapter Seventeen

Goodies You Can Add

AWeb site that offers quality content, clean and neat organization, and dynamite design already has a lot to offer, but it can provide even more. By adding features that go beyond the basics, you can give visitors more reasons to return to your site, and make it a more valuable resource.

Many of the add-ons in this chapter supply an element that is important to any Web site—interactivity. With the exception of product and service sales, everything discussed so far provides a passive, even though valuable, experience to site visitors. They come, they look, they read, and hopefully they leave with more knowledge or goods/services than they arrived with. The problem with this is that it tends to keep visitors at a distance. They are patrons of the site, but it isn't their site. By adding features that allow for and even encourage interactivity, you can create a closer and more personal experience for your visitors.

The add-ons explored in this chapter include discussion boards, poll questions, a guest book, feedback forms, news tickers, and other interesting stuff. First I'll tell you where and how to get such things without programming ability and without spending a dime. Then we'll dive into the details and purposes of each of these goodies, along with specific sources for each one.

Where the Goodies Come From

HTML allows you to add color and shape to a page, and to connect resources together, but it doesn't provide a facility to create much more than that. Interaction requires the ability to manipulate and respond to user input in ways that go beyond displaying another page. Although it's difficult to create much interaction using HTML alone, other programming languages, such as Perl, make it possible.

Don't worry, I'm not suggesting that you learn to write computer programs using Perl or any other language (although you might decide to at some time in the future); other people have already done the programming for you. And they're willing to let you reap the fruits of their labor for free. There are two ways this can occur: by using remotely hosted applications or by installing scripts on your Web server.

Remotely Hosted Applications

The easiest way to add features and functions that require more than you can create on your own is to sign up for remotely hosted versions of them. A remotely hosted application runs on someone else's server. When you sign up for the service, you receive a bit of HTML code to insert in your pages, which effectively adds the chosen feature to your site.

There are two different ways the code may work. The first is to provide the service right on your page, by calling the program on the remote server but displaying the results on your page. This is the method most often used by online polls and features that require minimal interaction with site visitors.

The second method, which is often used for more complex add-ons such as discussion forums, is to actually transfer your visitors to the remote server, where they will be able to use the service and return to your site when finished. In this case, the pages on the remote service carry your site name and a link back so that visitors can return to your main site at any time.

There are both for-pay and free remotely hosted services. As with many of the freebies in this book, in exchange for providing you with the service, the remote host will expect a bit of free advertising in return. This may be as innocuous as a little button with the remote host's name on it, or something more substantial, such as the ability to display banner ads at the top of the pages that provide the feature or service to your visitors. Often you will be given the option to remove the advertising in exchange for a fee.

Figure 17-1 shows the home page of Bravenet Web Services (**bravenet.com**), a popular provider of remotely hosted services for Webmasters.

Remotely hosted services are generally very easy to set up, and they usually allow you to create add-ons that follow your site's color scheme. As an added plus, part or all of the traffic load created by adding the feature will be borne by the remote host, and not come out of your personal Web hosting traffic allotment. The downside is that you will have to allow the advertising in order to receive the free service (unless you pay to have it removed). You will also have less control (although often an adequate amount) over the features and functions than you will if you use the other method of adding goodies to your site—installing prewritten scripts.

PART IV

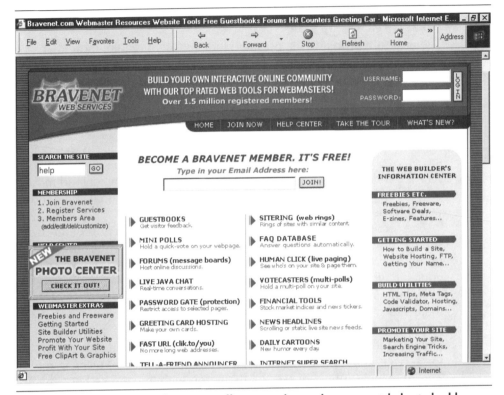

Figure 17-1 • Bravenet Web Services offers more than a dozen remotely hosted add-ons.

TIP: *Many hosting services provide preinstalled add-ons as part of the sign-up package, so you won't have to go anywhere else to get them. Just look in the "help" section of your Web host's site.*

You'll find a plentiful supply of free, remotely hosted add-ons at the following Web sites:

Resource	Add-ons Offered
BraveNet **bravenet.com**	Remotely hosted guest books, polls, site stats, chat, news headlines, search engine, and more
CGI For Me **cgiforme.com**	Message board, guest book, poll, search engine, and other interactive elements

Resource	Add-ons Offered
FreeTools **www.freetools.com**	Guest books, horoscopes, e-mail, site search polls, and a few other add-ons
HostedScripts **pages.hostedscripts.com**	Twenty-three free scripts, including message board, form mailer, site search, guest book, quote of the day display
MultiCity **multicity.com**	Remotely hosted, quick setup; runs a banner ad at the top of the pages
Site Gadgets **sitegadgets.com**	News, tell-a-friend tool, message board, guest book, and other add-ons

Prewritten Scripts

The second way to add features that go beyond HTML is to install prewritten scripts onto your Web host, or, in the case of JavaScript, into your Web pages. The former gives you more power and the ability to perform complex actions, while the latter is easier to implement.

Installing your own scripts takes a little more effort than signing up for a remotely hosted service, but the benefit is that you keep control of your visitors and your site space. Any advertising on the resulting pages will be your own, and you can modify the scripts to fit your site.

Perl

Many free (and for-fee) Web scripts are written in Perl, and it's a very common way to add special functions and features to a Web site. Perl is a scripting language that makes it possible to create the interactive processing I've been talking about. In other words, a Perl script can be used to take user input and manipulate it somehow before creating customized output.

A Perl script is a collection of computer instructions written in text using special syntax rules. For a Perl script to actually do something, it must be located on a server that has a Perl interpreter that can take that text and translate it into code the server can execute. Fortunately, almost every Web server has a Perl interpreter installed. A few Web hosts don't allow people to install or run Perl programs because they use up system resources and can be abused, so check with your Web host before adding scripts to your site.

Because Perl scripts are fairly easy to install (see sidebar), and are very popular among Webmasters, there are quite a few Web sites that collect, organize, review, and make them available for download for free. Figure 17-2 shows one such site.

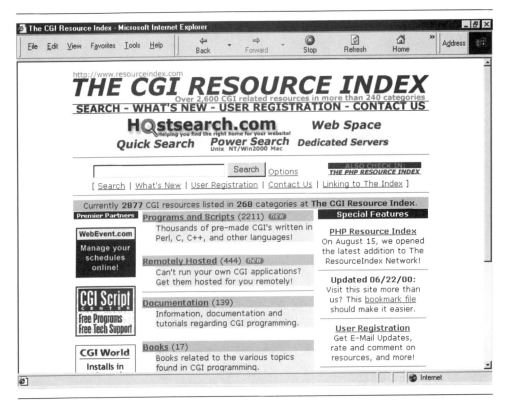

Figure 17-2 • The CGI Resource Index offers thousands of free scripts.

JavaScript

I said a (very) little bit about JavaScript in Chapter 8. Basically it provides a way to add interactivity or dynamic content to a Web page without installing anything extra on your Web server. Unlike Perl, which is executed on the Web server itself using a Perl interpreter, JavaScript is executed by an interpreter built into the visitor's browser. This means that the things you can do with it are more limited and that the visitor's browser must support JavaScript for it to work.

Despite those limitations, the fact that the JavaScript is inserted straight into the HTML pages, combined with a plentiful supply of free JavaScript, makes it a popular tool for many Webmasters.

Script Repositories

The best places to find a large collection of free scripts in a single location are online script repositories. These allow you to search for scripts that serve a particular purpose or browse through listings.

Installing Perl Scripts

When you obtain a new script, it will usually come with a file called readme.txt. This file, which can be viewed with any text-capable program, such as Notepad, contains the instructions to get the script working. There may be lines in the main script file that have to be changed to work properly with your hosting environment, and readme.txt will tell you what they are. If there is no readme.txt, open the script file itself. Often instructions are built in.

Once you've made any modifications per the instructions, the next step is to upload the script to your Web server. You can use any FTP program to do this, but be sure you upload the file in ASCII (text) mode. If you use binary mode, the script won't function properly.

The script must also be put in a special place on the server—in a directory named cgi-bin. If your Web host allows Perl programs, a cgi-bin directory will probably be ready and waiting. If not, you may have to create it yourself.

Once the file is uploaded, its permissions must be set. Permissions define who can do what to the file. If you don't specify that the script is a file that can be executed, no one will be able to make it run, even though you can see it sitting there using FTP.

The permissions on the script file need to be changed so that the file can be executed. For Unix hosts this means you need to issue the command "chmod 755," which is equivalent to rwxr-xr-x. This means that the file can be read (the *r*) or executed (the *x*) by anyone, but only the person who created the file (you) can write (the *w*) to it.

Setting file permissions can be accomplished using some FTP programs, but if your hosting service has provided you with a control panel for managing your site, you can set the file permissions with that as well.

Once you've uploaded the file (some programs will come with multiple files), and set the permissions properly, you should be able to execute it from your browser by typing the path to the script file like this:

```
http://mysite.com/cgi-bin/newscript.pl
```

When a newly added script won't run, 90 percent of the time the problem will be either

- The file was uploaded in binary rather than ASCII mode.
- The file permissions weren't set properly.

The rest of the time it will probably be a variable that you didn't set properly, so recheck that readme.txt file and try again.

This can give you ideas for new features you might install. The following resources ought to keep you busy for a while:

Resource	Scripts Offered
BigNoseBird **bignosebird.com/cgi.shtml**	Funny name, fantastic resource for CGI scripts and advice. You'll find plenty of tutorials here too.
The CGI Resource Index **cgi.resourceindex.com**	Thousands of free scripts plus a directory of remotely hosted scripts.
FreeCode **freecode.com**	Free scripts for personal or commercial use, mostly Perl and C/C++.
HotScripts **hotscripts.com**	Thousands of rated freebies in Perl, JavaScript, and other languages; includes a list of remote hosts too.
JavaScripts.com **javascript.internet.com**	Over 700 free JavaScripts.
scriptsearch.com **scriptsearch.com**	Hundreds of scripts in various languages, including Perl and JavaScript.

Popular, Useful, and Nifty Goodies

As you'll find from browsing the script repositories and other resources mentioned above, there is virtually an endless supply of add-ons you can use to enhance your site. But not every add-on is appropriate for every Web site, so choose only those that are a good match for your site's audience and purpose. Take care not to load down your pages with special features no one cares about (although if it's really nifty...). The following sections describe some of the options you might consider.

TIP: You can find links to many free add-ons, organized by category, via the Cheap Web Tricks site (**cheapwebtricks.com**).

Discussion Forum

One of the most obvious ways to create interaction on your site is to add a discussion forum (also called a message board). A forum allows visitors to post messages and questions about topics that interest them, and respond to other people's postings. Figure 17-3 shows a sample forum.

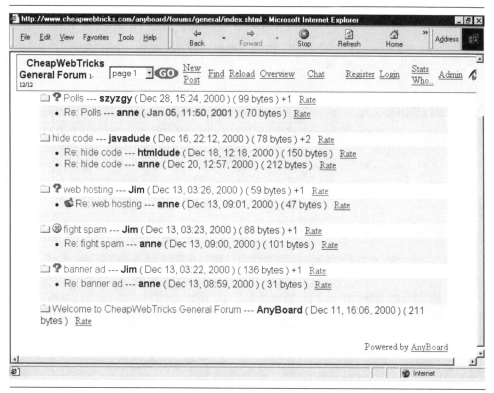

Figure 17-3 • A discussion forum using the free version of AnyBoard

Discussion forums can be a little tough to get started. If your visitors simply aren't the chatty type, the message board will remain unused, and can make your site appear as if no one visits, even if you have thousands of pageviews a day. On the other hand, once it gets going, a message board can create a steady stream of repeat visitors, so it's worth the effort to try to get one going.

JARGON ALERT: *A moderator has the ability to delete and control discussion forum user accounts and messages. Normal users do not.*

Once you have your discussion forum set up, post a message or two yourself, and call on your friends and relatives to do the same. There's a mysterious point of critical mass where people will start joining in, and the postings will take on a momentum of their own. Until then, promote the heck out of it on your home page, and make sure you provide plenty of messages yourself.

Visitor Polls

Instant polls offer another opportunity for visitors to interact with your Web pages. They also provide a way for you to learn about your visitors' interests, concerns, and plans. Figure 17-4 shows a sample poll question on a Web page, and Figure 17-5 shows the results it produced.

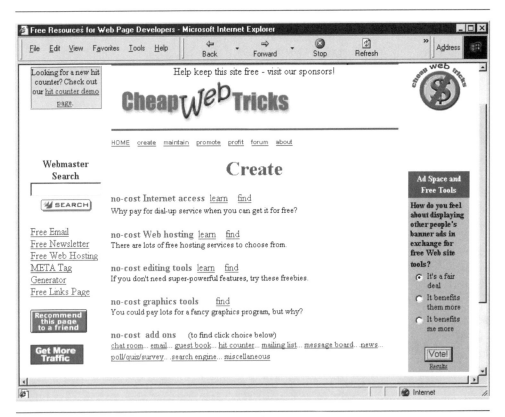

Figure 17-4 • A poll question on cheapwebtricks.com

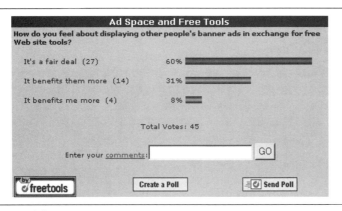

Figure 17-5 • And the survey says...

Poll questions can be humorous or serious, and should be tied to the theme of your site. Be sure to change the question from time to time to keep it fresh.

In addition to the general resources already mentioned, you can find free polls at

- FreePolls (**freepolls.com**)
- Insta-Poll (**insta-poll.com**)
- Mister Poll (**misterpoll.com**)
- PollNow (**freepoll.com**)
- Sparklit (**pollit.com/webpolls**)

These tools allow you to customize the appearance of the poll and specify the question and answer choices. To make the poll appear on your Web site, you'll have to insert a snippet of provided JavaScript or HTML where you want it to appear.

Chat Room

A chat room provides a virtual meeting place where users can type messages to each other and interact without the delay a message board inserts. It provides another opportunity to add interactivity to your site. Figure 17-6 shows a sample chat room.

Although you can install scripts to run a chat room via your own Web host, this is one add-on where a remotely hosted option is probably

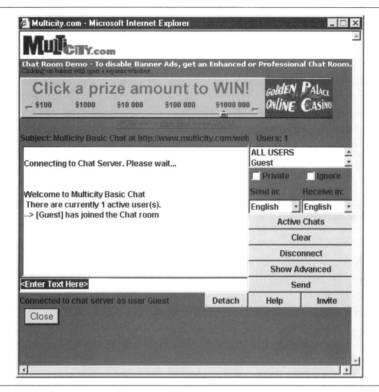

Figure 17-6 • A chat room at Multicity.com

preferable. If used heavily, a chat room can use extra system resources and run you over your account limits. It's easier to let someone else deal with the overhead.

Even more so than with discussion boards, chat rooms can suffer from "nobody's home" syndrome. When people click Chat, they may find themselves alone in a virtual room with no one to talk to. To keep this from happening, you'll either need a large stream of visitors or a very chatty group.

Another way to combat this problem is to publicize a regularly scheduled "chat hour" at a particular time each week. Then make sure you're in the room at that time too, and do what you can to facilitate discussion. Special chat events featuring an expert guest can draw visitors as well.

News Feed

One of the key things to keeping Web site visitors happy is fresh, up-to-date content. But endlessly adding new things to a Web site can be a time-consuming, never-ending process for the Webmaster. By adding a free news feed to your Web site, you can provide visitors with relevant content that changes regularly, without having to lift a finger yourself. The "Webmaster News" column in Figure 17-7 is supplied by a news feed. It updates automatically, without Webmaster intervention.

Thanks to modern technology, news feeds are available on a huge variety of topics, from showbiz in Hollywood to NHL hockey. The process of setting one up varies a bit among providers, but is basically a simple four-step process. We'll use moreover.com as an example:

1. Specify the content of the news feed.

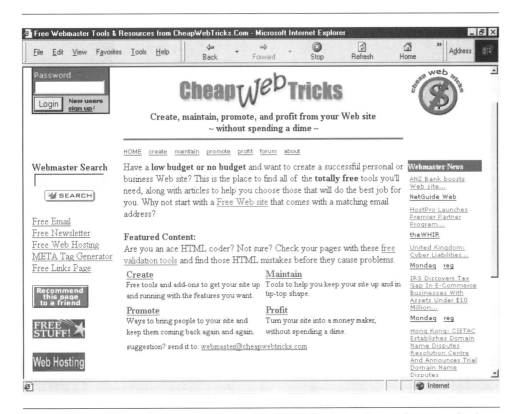

Figure 17-7 • Webmaster News is timely and always fresh, thanks to a free news feed.

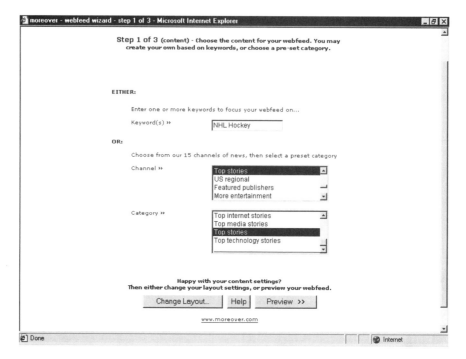

2. Specify the format of the news feed.

3. Enter any required contact information about your site.

4. Paste a bit of JavaScript provided by the service into your Web page where you want the news to appear.

Free sources of news feeds include

- **iSyndicate Express (affiliate.isyndicate.com)**   Provides changing news, weather, sports, and other content from a large variety for sources.
- **moreover (w.moreover.com/webmaster)**   Provides close to a thousand predefined categories, or you can create your own by using keywords.
- **NewsClicker (newsclicker.com)**   Provides sports, headlines, technology, and financial news. Choose from several different delivery formats.

Free E-Mail

You've seen the free e-mail accounts provided by companies like Microsoft (hotmail), Yahoo!, and NBCi (email.com). How would you like to offer the same service through your Web site? As a traffic booster, free e-mail has a lot going for it:

- You can set up the service so that visitors come to your home page to sign into their e-mail account. This brings them back to your site again and again.
- Every message that goes out via one of these free accounts has your tag line appended at the bottom.
- Users would have the e-mail address Fred@yoursite.com, which spreads your branding message.
- When e-mail users view their messages online, a banner ad is displayed at the top. This can be your banner (at least part of the time).
- You build up a pool of users that you can (judiciously) market to.

Installing free e-mail service is a bit more complicated than the other add-ons mentioned so far. First, you can't use it unless you have your own domain name (yoursite.com). Second, to get it to work, your Web host will have to make changes to the records associated with your domain name so that all e-mail is forwarded to the free e-mail provider for processing.

TIP: *Consider using a variant of your current domain name for your e-mail services. For example, if your site is yoursite.com, register yoursite.net and use that for e-mail. That way you can keep yoursite.com e-mail and yoursite.net e-mail separate, while still gaining the branding benefits of free e-mail.*

The two primary providers of this type of e-mail service are **Everyone.net** and **BigMailBox.com**. BigMailbox.com is free and gives Webmasters 20 percent of the banner space on mail pages. Everyone.net, which used to be free, now charges for e-mail service. For Webmasters, rates start at $9.99 per month. Be forewarned that both of these companies insert pop-up advertisements on or behind the actual mail pages, which can be annoying.

There are a few scripts that will let you set up a free e-mail service on your own server, but administration and traffic considerations make that a bad idea for most independent Webmasters.

Search Tools

Web surfers are a notoriously impatient lot. If they can't find what they're looking for pretty quickly, they look elsewhere within seconds. Your mission is to make it ridiculously easy for them to find exactly what they're looking for, without leaving your site. You can accomplish this by providing search functions directly from your site.

Search functions are missing from many a Web site, without good reason; there are many free alternatives you can take advantage of.

NOTE: *Some of the features discussed in this chapter are available through built-in features of certain publishing tools, such as Microsoft FrontPage. If you use those, just be aware that in order to keep those functions working, you will have to continue using the same tool. In the case of Microsoft FrontPage, it also often means that you are limited to publishing your site to a server that has FrontPage extensions installed.*

Both remotely hosted and installable scripts are available. My favorite Perl search script is KSearch (**kscripts.com/scripts.shtml**). Other search scripts are available in the script repositories previously mentioned. Remotely hosted search tools worth a look include

- **Atomz Express Search (atomz.com)**   Free for sites with less than 500 pages. Keeps track of which search terms are used, no advertising required.
- **FreeFind (freefind.com)**   Ad-supported free search engine tool. No page count limit. Tracks search terms.

Miscellaneous Add-Ons

In addition to those already mentioned, there are lots more goodies you can add to your pages. Need a currency converter? Get one free at **www.oanda.com/site/ccc_intro.shtml**. Want to add a little fun in the form of free games? Try HyperGames (**hypergames.net/freecenter/**) or HtmlGames (**htmlgames.com**).

There are lots of free goodies like these to be had. To find them, prowl around the script repositories and other sites mentioned in this chapter. And don't forget to visit **cheapwebtricks.com**, which offers a plentiful supply of freebie links of interest to frugal Webmasters.

18

Chapter Eighteen

Starting and Running an E-Mail Newsletter

Once you have your site up and running and have a steady supply (though not necessarily a large one) of visitors, consider launching a companion e-mail newsletter. An e-mail newsletter (also called an *e-zine*) is somewhat different from a traditional, paper and ink newsletter. For starters it usually costs less to produce, and mailing it is free. The cost of subscribing is usually free as well.

Even though you won't be making money via subscriptions, there are several compelling reasons for starting a newsletter. First, a regular newsletter can significantly increase traffic to your Web site. Each time you send out the newsletter, it reminds people that your site exists, and provides an easy way for them to return to it (via a link). Recipients can also forward the e-mail to friends, who might visit your site as well.

Second, the newsletter can serve as an advertising vehicle for your own enterprises. Use it to promote products and services you offer, or special events related to your organization.

Third, you may be able to sell advertising in the newsletter to others. E-mail advertising is quickly becoming a preferred method of online advertising because it carries the message directly to a targeted group.

Finally, it gives you something free to offer to your visitors. By providing them with tips and information that it takes you minimal effort to produce and distribute, you will increase your ties with your audience.

Newsletter Content and Format

There two main approaches to creating online newsletters, each with its own set of pros and cons. Which you choose will depend upon how much you want to write each month, and whether you have a lot of specialized information to offer.

The Teaser Method

The most common e-mail newsletter format doesn't actually provide substantial information in the newsletter itself. Instead it provides a

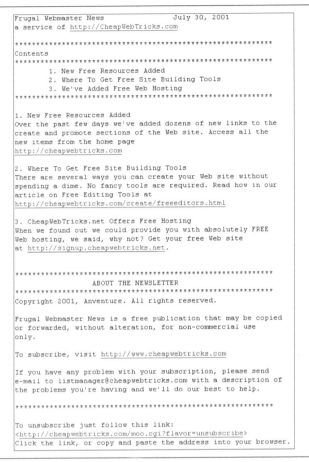

```
Frugal Webmaster News                    July 30, 2001
a service of http://CheapWebTricks.com

*************************************************************
Contents
*************************************************************
            1. New Free Resources Added
            2. Where To Get Free Site Building Tools
            3. We've Added Free Web Hosting
*************************************************************

1. New Free Resources Added
Over the past few days we've added dozens of new links to the
create and promote sections of the Web site. Access all the
new items from the home page
http://cheapwebtricks.com

2. Where To Get Free Site Building Tools
There are several ways you can create your Web site without
spending a dime. No fancy tools are required. Read how in our
article on Free Editing Tools at
http://cheapwebtricks.com/create/freeeditors.html

3. CheapWebTricks.net Offers Free Hosting
When we found out we could provide you with absolutely FREE
Web hosting, we said, why not? Get your free Web site
at http://signup.cheapwebtricks.net.


*************************************************************
                   ABOUT THE NEWSLETTER
*************************************************************
Copyright 2001, Anventure. All rights reserved.

Frugal Webmaster News is a free publication that may be copied
or forwarded, without alteration, for non-commercial use
only.

To subscribe, visit http://www.cheapwebtricks.com

If you have any problem with your subscription, please send
e-mail to listmanager@cheapwebtricks.com with a description of
the problems you're having and we'll do our best to help.

*************************************************************

To unsubscribe just follow this link:
<http://cheapwebtricks.com/moo.cgi?flavor=unsubscribe>
Click the link, or copy and paste the address into your browser.
```

Figure 18-1 • This newsletter uses the teaser method.

sentence or two, followed by a link to the Web site that the reader can click to get the full story. Figure 18-1 shows an example.

The teaser method has several things going for it:

- It's quick to produce, since it contains little original content.
- It's quick to read. A subscriber can quickly scan the entire newsletter and pick out items of interest.
- It contains lots of encouragement, in the form of links, to bring visitors immediately to your Web site.

PART IV

Full Text

The alternative to the teaser method is to provide a full-text newsletter with substantial content in each edition. This type of e-mail newsletter is much like its traditional print counterpart. Figure 18-2 shows what it might look like.

The benefits of a full-text newsletter include

- Longer shelf life. Since it contains useful information rather than just links, it's more likely to be kept longer before being deleted.
- More likely to be forwarded to friends, for the same reason as above.
- Provides more value to the subscriber.

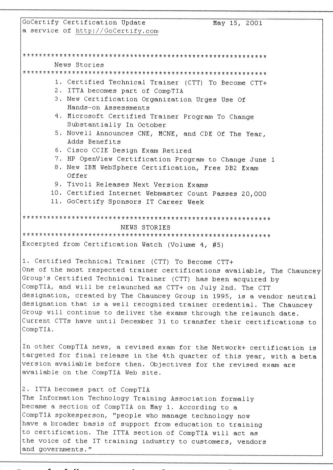

```
GoCertify Certification Update                    May 15, 2001
a service of http://GoCertify.com


************************************************************
         News Stories
************************************************************
         1. Certified Technical Trainer (CTT) To Become CTT+
         2. ITTA becomes part of CompTIA
         3. New Certification Organization Urges Use Of
            Hands-on Assessments
         4. Microsoft Certified Trainer Program To Change
            Substantially In October
         5. Novell Announces CNE, MCNE, and CDE Of The Year,
            Adds Benefits
         6. Cisco CCIE Design Exam Retired
         7. HP OpenView Certification Program to Change June 1
         8. New IBM WebSphere Certification, Free DB2 Exam
            Offer
         9. Tivoli Releases Next Version Exams
        10. Certified Internet Webmaster Count Passes 20,000
        11. GoCertify Sponsors IT Career Week


************************************************************
                    NEWS STORIES
************************************************************
Excerpted from Certification Watch (Volume 4, #5)

1. Certified Technical Trainer (CTT) To Become CTT+
One of the most respected trainer certifications available, The Chauncey
Group's Certified Technical Trainer (CTT) has been acquired by
CompTIA, and will be relaunched as CTT+ on July 2nd. The CTT
designation, created by The Chauncey Group in 1995, is a vendor neutral
designation that is a well recognized trainer credential. The Chauncey
Group will continue to deliver the exams through the relaunch date.
Current CTTs have until December 31 to transfer their certifications to
CompTIA.

In other CompTIA news, a revised exam for the Network+ certification is
targeted for final release in the 4th quarter of this year, with a beta
version available before then. Objectives for the revised exam are
available on the CompTIA Web site.

2. ITTA becomes part of CompTIA
The Information Technology Training Association formally
became a section of CompTIA on May 1. According to a
CompTIA spokesperson, "people who manage technology now
have a broader basis of support from education to training
to certification. The ITTA section of CompTIA will act as
the voice of the IT training industry to customers, vendors
and governments."
```

Figure 18-2 • Part of a full-text newsletter from GoCertify.com

> **TIP:** *Remember to put the name, issue, and date at the top of every newsletter you send out.*

Text vs. HTML

In addition to the style of newsletter, you'll need to consider its format. For a long time, text newsletters (all words, no pictures) were the only option, but now many e-mail programs can read and interpret HTML. A newsletter that's written in HTML, just like a Web page, can include fancy graphics and formatting that text newsletters can't. Figure 18-3 shows what an HTML newsletter looks like.

While HTML newsletters are much spiffier, text newsletters have the benefit of being universally readable by virtually any recipient. Sending HTML newsletters to people who can't read them may cause quite a bit

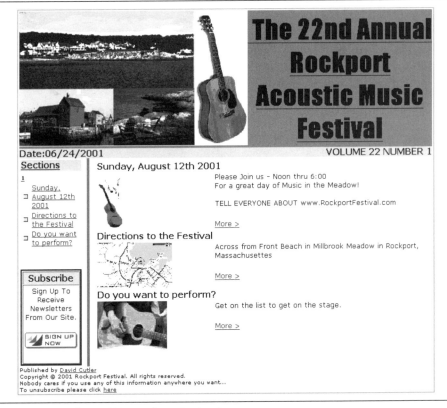

Figure 18-3 • This HTML newsletter looks sharp.

of annoyance. Some newsletter publishers handle this trade-off by creating two versions of their newsletter and letting subscribers choose which they wish to receive.

Critical Elements

There are a few elements that you should take care to include in each issue of your newsletter. For example, each issue should begin with the publication name and date. Arrange it any way that appeals to you. Here's an example to get you started:

```
GoCertify Certification Update          June 15, 2001
a service of http://GoCertify.com
```

Also be sure to include your contact information in every newsletter, along with a copyright notice, and information on how to subscribe. If you wish to encourage subscribers to pass issues along to their friends, tell them so. You can package all this information together with a few lines similar to this:

```
Copyright (c) 2001, Anventure. All rights reserved.

This free publication may be copied or forwarded, without
alteration, for noncommercial use only.

To subscribe, visit the GoCertify.com home page at
http://gocertify.com
```

As a courtesy to your readers, each issue should include information on how to unsubscribe as well. Newsletter recipients tend to get very mad if they keep getting a newsletter they don't want, and this can result in negative talk about your site. Often, unsubscribe instructions are placed at the very end, with a link users can click on to automatically unsubscribe.

Frequency

When you first create your newsletter, you'll need to decide how often it will go out. As with most other Webmaster tasks, if you don't have it scheduled regularly, it will soon fall through the cracks.

Keep in mind that managing a list and creating content is probably going to take more time than you anticipate, especially until you become proficient at it. Common choices are weekly, biweekly, or

monthly. A daily newsletter is a major commitment, although some Webmasters find it worthwhile.

Getting Subscribers

As soon as people arrive at your site, invite them to sign up for your free list. Make it as easy as possible; a box for their e-mail address with a Subscribe button, like the one below, is ideal.

| By Vendor
Application Dev
Communications
Database
ERP
General/Other | *GoCertify is the ultimate online resource for certification information, covering over 500 certifications from more than 90 vendors. Get certification descriptions, costs, requirements, perks, contact information and more.* | **Sign up here to
receive Certification
Update**
email address
Subscribe |

If you have an existing customer list, use it to invite people to join your list. Don't add anyone to your subscriber list without their permission; doing so is a big no-no. The most valuable lists consist of people who want to be on them.

> **JARGON ALERT:** *An opt-in list is one that subscribers sign up for of their own accord. A double opt-in list requires users to sign up, and then confirm their subscription by responding to an e-mail confirmation that is sent to the address they wish to subscribe from. This prevents people from signing up others without their knowledge or consent. An opt-out list, however, is one that someone was signed up for without their knowledge and must follow a specified procedure to be removed from the list.*

Building up a list of subscribers takes time and effort. Be patient and persistent, provide a quality newsletter, and your list will grow.

How to Distribute Your Newsletter

Distributing your newsletter when you've got a dozen subscribers is no big deal; any e-mail program will do it. When you get hundreds or thousands of subscribers, you can't get by without specialized mailing list software to automate the tasks for you.

PART IV

Mailing list software does several things for you. First and foremost, it sends the newsletter to all the subscribers on your distribution list, but many packages go beyond this basic service. They also allow users to subscribe and unsubscribe without your assistance, create archive copies of newsletters you send, and in rare cases, handle e-mail messages that are returned as undeliverable.

Your Own Software

If you have the ability to install scripts on your server, consider installing free mailing software that you can use and configure as you wish. This will give you the most control for the least cost. My absolute favorite package for this is Mojo Mail (shown in Figure 18-4), written by Justin Simoni. You can find other mailing list scripts at the script repositories listed in Chapter 17.

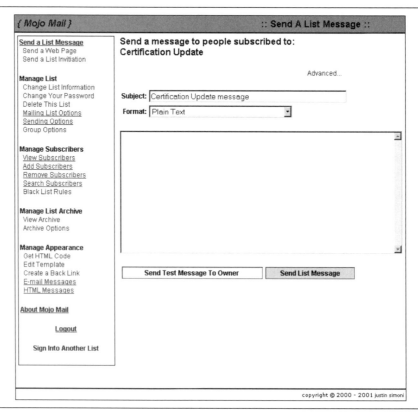

Figure 18-4 • Mojo Mail handles text and HTML newsletters with ease.

TIP: *For a refresher on how to install scripts, revisit Chapter 17.*

Your Web host may already have mailing list software installed, free for your use. This is definitely worth investigating, but in my experience, the documentation for these is very scanty, the interface awkward, and support hard to come by.

Use a Service

If you are unwilling or unable to install scripts on your server, the next alternative is to use a free mailing list service provider, like the one shown in Figure 18-5. These providers let you use the mailing list software installed on their server in exchange for some form of shared access to your list. This may take the form of adding a promotional tag line at the end of each message, or the ability to send occasional

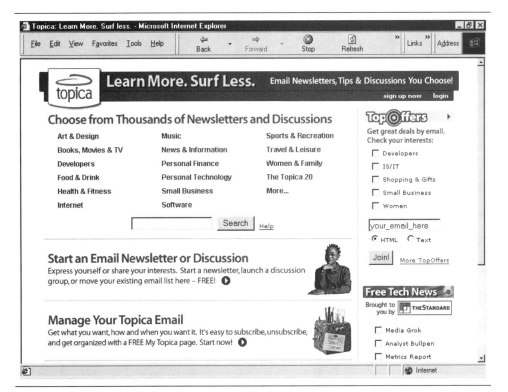

Figure 18-5 • Topica will manage your mailing list for free.

PART IV

advertising messages to your list. Be sure you know what you're giving away, and make it as minimal as possible. If your subscribers receive a bunch of junk mail from your list host, they will be upset with you and unsubscribe.

Free mailing list service providers include

- **CoolList (coollist.com)** Free list hosting. Promises not to disclose list names to others. Attaches an ad to the bottom of your list messages.
- **FreeLists (freelists.org)** Free list hosting for any technical topic. Promises not to include advertising or give out your list names.
- **ListPower (listpower.com)** Free list hosting. When users sign up, they are offered other lists to join. Revenues generated as a result are shared with you.
- **Topica (topica.com)** Free list hosting. You can join their promotion network and receive a share of revenue from paid advertisements placed in your list.

TIP: *A few free mailing list hosts actually provide you with additional revenue opportunities. They will sell advertisements in your newsletter, and share the revenue with you.*

For Webmasters who don't want to install scripts and find promotional messages appended to the end of their e-mail objectionable, there's a third alternative: paid list hosting. It's basically the same as free list hosting, except that your list is yours alone, and your newsletters go out unaltered. Most of the free providers listed above also offer a paid, promotion-free version of their service.

Whichever system you put in place, remember that your newsletter is a representative for your site. Make sure it's a quality creation with no grammar or spelling errors. If it includes advertisements, take care that they don't outnumber the quality articles. Promote your publication and protect your subscriber list, and you may find that becoming an e-zine publisher is one of the highlights of your Web site efforts.

19

Chapter Nineteen

Staying on Top

Congratulations! You've come a long way since you opened the first page of this book. You know how to build, promote, and profit from your Web site, without spending a dime, as well as when and why you might decide to open your wallet in the name of Web site success. Once you've parlayed your new expertise into a dynamite Web site, there are a few final things you need to do to keep visitors coming back.

Keep It Fresh

Like a loaf of bread, Web site content can grow stale over time, first becoming a little less tasty and eventually progressing to inedible. Consider that the first time a visitor comes to your site, everything is new and interesting. The second time, the site is just as packed with information, but they've seen it before. By the third time, the novelty is gone, they've read most, if not all, of what you have to offer, and they're off to greener pastures.

The second form of staleness also happens without you lifting a finger: Links leading to other resources go dead. Broken links can be the kiss of death for a Web site. Although most users are willing to overlook one or two dead links, if your site has more, it's unlikely visitors will return. Any Web site with external links will sooner or later have dead links, unless you have a plan in place to keep that from happening.

Content Plans

Let's take the fresh content issue first. Earlier in this book I urged you to create a site that has plenty of content of interest to your particular target audience. Now you need a plan for updating that content on a regular basis. Don't use the "when I have a few spare minutes" plan if you can possibly avoid it. Trust me on this—if you don't have a plan, it won't be long before the updates get fewer and farther between and eventually stop happening entirely. Then one day you'll check your traffic statistics and find that traffic has dropped to a negligible level. A simple content plan can keep this from happening.

The extent of your content plan depends on the amount of time you have to spend on your site balanced with the type of Web site you created. A team-focused Web site, like the women's hockey Web site

used as an example throughout this book, needs to be updated after each game, and any time new games are scheduled. A site that attracts visitors by providing updates on frequently changing information, or lots of articles, will need new content much more often, ranging from daily to once or twice a week. GoCertify.com, for example, provides certification news and program information, and falls into the frequent update category.

A content plan doesn't have to be complicated or fancy; just choose a schedule, record it in a simple text or word processing file, and keep it someplace where it will catch your eye. That might be as a file on your desktop, or as a printout hanging on the refrigerator door. Figure 19-1 shows an example.

Make your content plan mesh with your life. Don't schedule a new article every week if you don't have time to write it, unless you can convince or hire someone else to produce it for you.

When you add new content or features, make sure your visitors know you've done so. Provide a notice on the home page that highlights the new items, or place it someplace where it can't be missed. For example, you might create a "Feature Content" box on your home page that announces the latest additions.

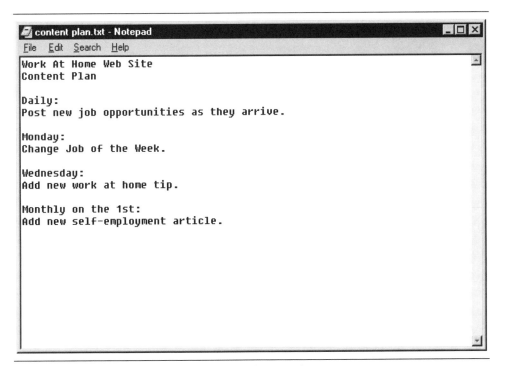

Figure 19-1 • A sample schedule for adding fresh Web site content

PART IV

Link Patrol

You can't stop off-site links from going belly up, but you can catch them right away and either remove or correct them. And you don't have to click every link on your site to see if it works; you can use an automated tool to do that for you.

An automatic link checker will follow every link on your site and create a report indicating those that return an error instead of a normal Web page. You can then investigate to see if the page has been moved, or is gone entirely.

Some Web site design tools include a link-checking capability. FrontPage and Homesite, for example, have link checkers built in. But if you're using an HTML editor that doesn't come with link checking built in, there are quite a few freebies that will do the job for you. One of my favorites is NetMechanic, shown in Figure 19-2. It will check all the links on any page you specify for free.

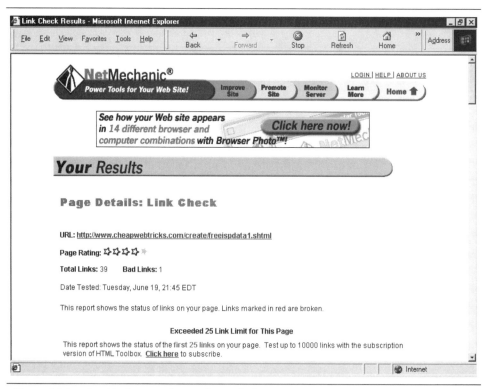

Figure 19-2 • NetMechanic will patrol your links.

Some free link checkers will perform other maintenance tasks while they're on your site. For example, Web Site Garage promises to check links, assess search engine readiness, look for HTML errors, and check your spelling. Free link-checking resources include

- **Dr. Watson (watson.addy.com)**   Free check of links, spelling, and loading time, plus a few other options. One page at a time.
- **LinkGuard Classic (www.linkguard.com)**   Plain old link checking, any time you want it. Scan up to 50 pages three times a week.
- **NetMechanic (netmechanic.com)**   Check up to five pages at a time for free, including links, HTML code, page load time, and spelling. Repeat test once a month, automatically.
- **Web Site Garage (websitegarage.com)**   Check any single page for free, for multiple potential problems, including slow loading.

If you have CGI access and time on your hands, you can also find link-checking scripts that can be installed on your server. Get them in the script repositories listed in Chapter 17.

Many of the online free link checkers (with the exception of LinkGuard Classic) are only going to let you check one page at a time. On a multipage site, this can be tedious. So if you have a lot of pages to check, you might want to consider upgrading to a paid tool that will automate the process for every page on your site. But if you only have a few pages, or more time than money, the free, one-pagers will do the trick.

Whether you choose a freebie or for-pay tool, add it to your content plan as a regularly scheduled activity. Ideally, link checking should happen once a week, but once a month is better than never.

What to Do If Your Site Goes Down

It's every Web site owner's worst nightmare: Just as a reporter from the *Wall Street Journal* types in the URL of your Web site so she can feature it in a front page story, the Web server goes down, and she gets a Page Not Found error. Instead of making you rich and famous, the reporter types in a different URL and makes your brother-in-law rich and famous. If only your Web site hadn't gone down.

Even the best Web hosting services experience brief outages now and then, but such occurrences should be extremely rare. If it happens to you, here's what you should do:

1. Wait three to five minutes and try loading your site again. Often it will be fine.

2. If it isn't fine, visit the hosting service's support page. You may find a message there explaining what's going on.

3. If there's no message, send an e-mail to your host's support address. Mark it urgent. Keep your message calm. Ask them nicely to look into the problem ASAP. Be sure to include your domain name. Make the subject something like "Urgent - site down."

4. If you don't get an answer within half an hour, or if the downtime is costing you money by the minute, call the hosting service's support phone number and ask for help.

5. If you can't reach a real person, and the site stays down for more than an hour with no reasonable explanation to you, consider moving it elsewhere.

Chances are, if your site goes down for a minute or two, you'll never know about it. Unless you happen to be calling up the page yourself when it goes down, or a user reports it to you, the event will probably pass unnoticed. For most Web sites, this is fine. A minute or two (or even ten) a month of downtime has no effect. But if you suspect your site is going down more often than that, or if you're simply curious, you can use a site monitoring service to track it for you.

Site monitoring services periodically load your page and immediately send you an e-mail, or even page you, if a page won't come up. You can then go through the steps described above to resolve the problem.

You know I wouldn't be telling you about this if you couldn't do it for free, so here's a list of free site monitoring services. Most offer a very basic free service, with a for-pay upgrade that checks pages more often.

- **1stWarning.com (1stWarning.com)** Checks your site every three hours and creates weekly reports.
- **Alertra (alertra.com)** Checks your Web site as often as once a minute (which would be excessive). You receive weekly summary reports.
- **nFinite Sentry (nfiniteweb.com)** Checks your site at the frequency you specify and sends reports via e-mail.
- **ServerRat (serverrat.com)** Checks your Web site every 15 minutes and notifies you of no-load or slow-load problems.
- **WebSitePulse.com (websitepulse.com)** Checks your site every 60 minutes and sends you an e-mail if it isn't up to snuff.

A Final Word on Security

Your Web site is only as secure as your hosting service makes it. There are many hackers out there with nothing better to do than wipe out other people's Web sites. Your best defense is to keep a current backup of your site at all times. Then, if some moron comes by and does some damage, you just repost the files, urge your host to fix the security hole, and go on your merry way.

The other security item to keep in mind is not to leave confidential customer information (such as credit card numbers) on your server if you can possibly help it. If you must store them, do it on a computer that isn't connected to the Web. It's much safer that way.

The Beginning

This is the last section of the last chapter of this book, but I hope it's only the beginning of your Web endeavors. For people who don't know much about them, the Internet and Web can be intimidating. But you're not in that category any more. You know that there are many things you can do online, without having to be a computer wizard, and without having a key to the vaults at Fort Knox.

The Web is a wide open land of possibilities. Seize this opportunity to unleash your creativity, answer your entrepreneurial urge, or obey your drive to change the world one opinion at a time. Or just build a Web page to report on the growth of your rubber band ball. It's entirely up to you.

V

Part Five

References

Appendix

HTML Quick Reference

The lists of HTML tags and attributes presented in this appendix are not intended to be exhaustive. Rather than give you every possibility, including the obscure, I've limited this reference to the most frequently used tags and their attributes.

The <HEAD> Section

Tag	Attributes	Description
<TITLE></TITLE>	none	Specifies the document title that appears in the browser title bar.
<META>	http-equiv, name (author, description, keywords, generator), content	Specifies information about the document. This information isn't displayed; it can also be used to reload or redirect a page.

The following example names this page "document_name":

```
<TITLE>document_name</TITLE>
```

The following are three examples using the meta tag. This code provides a description of the page for use by search engines:

```
<META name="description" content="Free tools and resources
 for the frugal Webmaster.">
```

The next example provides keywords for use by search engines:

```
<META name="keywords" content="free tools,
 webmaster resources, web design, cheap web tricks.">
```

Finally, this code automatically forwards the viewer to a new URL in ten seconds:

```
<META http-equiv="refresh" content="10;url="URL">
```

The <BODY> Section

Elements commonly used in the <BODY> section perform many different functions. They can be roughly organized into the following categories.

Basic Text Appearance

The following elements are used to specify how text will be displayed, for example, in bold or italics, large or small. Styles like these are usually applied to individual words or phrases.

Tag	Attributes	Description
<B></B>	none	Bolds the text between the opening and closing tags.
<CENTER></CENTER>	none	Centers the text between the tags.
<I></I>	none	Italicizes the text between the tags.
<U></U>	none	Underlines the text between the tags.
<BIG></BIG>	none	Displays text between the tags in a larger size than the default.
<SMALL></SMALL>	none	Displays text between the tags in a smaller size than the default.
<EM></EM>	none	Emphasizes text between the tags; similar to italics.
<STRONG></STRONG>	none	Strongly emphasizes text between the tags; similar to bold.
	none	Displays text between the tags in subscript.
	none	Displays text between the tags in superscript.

Text appearance can also be manipulated using the font tag:

Tag	Attributes	Description
<FONT></FONT>	face, size, color	Controls the typeface used, as well as size and color.

Here are two examples of using the font tag. The first one renders "text" in the Arial typeface (if Arial is installed on the viewer's computer):

```
<FONT face="Arial">text</FONT>
```

This renders the enclosed text in the next larger size and in the color red:

```
<FONT size="+1", color="Red">text</FONT>
```

The spacing of text is controlled with the following tags:

Tag	Attributes	Description
<P>	align (left, right, center)	Creates a paragraph break.
 	none	Creates a line break. Text following this tag starts on the next line.
<BLOCKQUOTE> </BLOCKQUOTE>	none	Text between the tags is indented.

Headings

Heading tags are used to distinguish up to six levels of heads:

Tag	Attributes	Description
<H1></H1> <H2></H2> <H3></H3> <H4></H4> <H5></H5> <H6></H6>	none	Text between opening and closing tags is formatted as a heading at the specified level. H1 is most prominent, H6 is least prominent.

Lists

The two most commonly used list types are ordered (numbered) and unordered (bulleted):

Tag	Attributes	Description
<OL></OL>	type (1,a,A,i,I), start	Creates an ordered (numbered) list.
<UL></UL>	type (disc, square, circle)	Creates an unordered (bulleted) list.
<LI>	none	List item

The following code creates a three-item ordered list using uppercase Roman numerals:

```
<OL type="I">
    <LI>text1
    <LI>text2
    <LI>text3
</OL>
```

Images

You use the following tag to insert and format images:

Tag	Attributes	Description
<IMG>	src, align, alt, border, height, width	Inserts an image into the document.

The following example inserts an image located at "URL," sized 10 pixels high by 10 pixels wide, and provides alternate text of "image_description" for browsers that don't show images. It also puts a 1-pixel-wide border around the image.

```
<IMG src="URL" alt="image_description"
 height=10 width=10 border=1>
```

Linking

There is one linking tag that can be used to link text or images:

Tag	Attributes	Description
<A></A>	href, name, target (_blank, _self, _top, _parent, anyname)	Creates links to other documents or within the same document.

The following examples show how to use the linking tag. This code links the word or phrase "text" to the specified URL:

```
<A href="URL">text</A>
```

This code

```
<A href="URL" target=outside>text</A>
```

links the word or phrase "text" to the specified URL and opens that page in a new browser window named "outside."

The code shown next defines a target location called "bookmark_name" within a document:

```
<A name="bookmark_name">
```

And this code links the word or phrase "text" to the target location "bookmark_name" within the specified URL page.

```
<A href="URL#bookmark_name">text</A>
```

PART V

Here, when the word or phrase "text" is clicked on, a new e-mail message is created with the address in the To: field already filled in:

```
<A href="mailto:address">text</A>
```

Finally, the following code links an image to the specified URL:

```
<A href="URL"><IMG src="URL2"></A>
```

Forms

You define a form with the <FORM> tag:

Tag	Attributes	Description
<FORM></FORM>	action, method (post, get)	Defines a form.

For example,

```
<FORM action="URL" method=post></FORM>
```

defines a form (with no fields in it yet) that will send its information to a form handler at "URL," using the post method.

Forms need input fields inside them to do anything useful:

Tag	Attributes	Description
<INPUT>	type (text, radio, checkbox, password, Submit, Reset), name, size, value, checked	Creates a user input field of the specified type with the specified characteristics.
<SELECT> <OPTION> <OPTION> </SELECT>	name value	Creates a drop-down box containing the items specified by the option tags.
<TEXTAREA></TEXTAREA>	name, rows, cols	Creates a rectangular text box for input.

This example creates a form with a text box named "user_name" and a Submit button. The form contents are sent to "URL" using the post method.

```
<FORM action="URL" method=post>
    <INPUT type=text name="user_name">
    <INPUT type="Submit">
</FORM>
```

Tables

The most common tags used for tables are as follows:

Tag	Attributes	Description
<TABLE></TABLE>	align, bgcolor, border, cellpadding, cellspacing, width	Creates a table.
<TR></TR>	align, bgcolor, colspan	Defines a row within a table.
<TD></TD>	align, bgcolor, height, width, rowspan	Defines a cell within a table row.

This example creates a table consisting of one row with two cells:

```
<TABLE>
    <TR>
        <TD></TD>
        <TD></TD>
    </TR>
</TABLE>
```

Miscellaneous Tags

You may find a couple of miscellaneous tags useful:

Tag	Attributes	Description
<HR>	align, size, width	Creates a horizontal rule (a line).
<!— —>	none	Treats code between the tags as a comment, and it won't appear in the viewer's browser.

Commonly Used HTML Color Values

The value for a color can be specified using its name or its hexadecimal value. Not all browsers use the same name for a color, so to be safe, use the values instead.

Aqua	#00FFFF	Navy	#000080
Black	#000000	Olive	#808000
Blue	#0000FF	Purple	#800080
Fuchsia	#FF00FF	Red	#FF0000
Gray	#808080	Silver	#C0C0C0
Green	#008000	Teal	#008080
Lime	#00FF00	White	#FFFFFF
Maroon	#800000	Yellow	#FFFF00

I'd love to provide you with a color chart of all 216 browser-safe colors, but since this is a black-and-white book, I'll have to point you to several online charts instead:

About.com color chart	webdesign.miningco.com/compute/webdesign/library/ weekly/aa061598chart.htm
HTML Goodies color chart	http://htmlgoodies.com/tutors/non_dithering_colors.html

Glossary

404 error   A Page Not Found message that is generated by a Web server when a visitor tries to access a file that doesn't exist.

above the fold   The "top" area of a Web page that appears on screen as viewers open the page, without scrolling down.

ad inventory   The quantity of ad impressions you have available to sell in a specific time period.

affiliate program   A sales relationship in which a merchant pays a Web site owner to sell and/or market the merchant's products. The site owner usually does so by posting banners, buttons, or links.

animated banner   A banner that incorporates motion. It changes while you're looking at it.

ASCII (pronounced "ask-key")   An acronym for American Standard Code for Information Interchange. It provides a uniform way for text characters (which people understand) to be translated and stored as numbers (the language of computers).

autoresponder   A program that automatically sends a premade e-mail reply in response to an incoming e-mail message.

banner exchange network   A loosely affiliated group of sites that trade free banner advertising with each other.

below the fold   The "bottom" portion of a Web page that viewers must scroll down to see.

B2B (business to business)   Refers to companies selling to other companies rather than to consumers.

B2C (business to consumer)   Refers to companies selling primarily to consumers, rather than to other companies.

caching (pronounced "cashing")   The process of making temporary local copies of frequently used files to save time. Web browsers cache Web pages on the user's hard drive so they don't have to be retransferred if the user views them again within a short period of time.

CGI (common gateway interface)   A standard for communications between programs and Web servers. Sometimes people mistakenly use the terms Perl program and CGI program interchangeably, but CGI programs can be written in languages other than Perl, including Visual Basic and C.

cobranding   The process of creating a page, site, or service that carries the brand identity (such as logos, company names, and/or color scheme) of more than one company.

cookie   A small amount of data that is passed from a Web server to a visiting browser and stored on the visitor's hard drive. If the person returns to the same Web site in the future, the data will be automatically transmitted back to the Web server. Cookies are often used to track affiliate sales, automate logins by remembering user names, or personalize a Web page.

CPC (cost per click)   An alternative method of selling advertising, which charges per user click on the ad rather than per ad displayed.

CPM (cost per mille)   The unit of measure used to price Web advertising sales. The CPM rate is the price charged for a thousand ad impressions.

CSS (cascading style sheets)   A method of controlling the appearance of Web pages by specifying how headers, links, and other elements should appear. A single style sheet can be applied to more than one page.

CTR (click-through ratio)   The percentage of ad impressions clicked on by a viewer. If one click is recorded for 100 displays of an ad, the CTR is 1 percent.

dedicated hosting   Web hosting that uses your own domain name, on a server that isn't shared with anyone else. Typically used by very high volume or mission-critical sites.

domain name   An English-like substitution for an IP address (or collection of IP addresses). Domain names are easier than IP addresses for humans to remember and type without error.

doorway page (also called jump, portal, gateway, or bridge page)   A page specially created to achieve a high ranking with a particular search engine spider.

double opt-in list   A mailing list that requires users to sign up and then confirm their subscription by responding to an e-mail message that is sent to the address they wish to subscribe from. This prevents people from signing up others without their knowledge or consent.

FFA (free-for-all)   Refers to free-for-all links pages, which allow anyone to post their site name and URL at no charge.

FTP (file transfer protocol)   A method used to send and receive files over the Internet. Often used for uploading pages to a Web server.

hit   A request for a file (document, graphic, or other type) from a Web server. Viewing a single page can cause multiple hits to be recorded in the server's log file.

hit counter   A graphic that shows the number of times a page has been loaded. It automatically increments each time someone visits the page.

impression   A single display of an advertising banner.

interstitial   Refers to an advertisement that is loaded into a separate browser window that opens while a viewer is waiting for the main Web page to load.

IP (Internet protocol)   IP (pronounced as separate letters) is the addressing scheme used on the Internet. An IP address, which consists of four numbers separated by periods, uniquely identifies each computer directly connected to the Internet.

Java   A programming language created by Sun Microsystems that is popular for creating programs that run on the Web. Java programs must be compiled into machine code before they can be run.

JavaScript   A scripting language used by Web developers to add features and interactivity to Web pages. It only works if the visitor's browser supports JavaScript, which most do.

log   A file that stores information about files that have been retrieved from your Web site, including the location of the item requested (either an HTML page, image, or something else), and the source of the request.

metajacking   The practice of copying and using the meta tags from another site.

moderator   On a discussion board or list, a person who has the ability to delete and control the forum's user accounts and messages. Other users do not have this ability.

opt-in list   A mailing list that subscribers sign up for of their own accord.

opt-out list   A mailing list that people are signed up for without their knowledge, and must follow a specified procedure to be removed from the list.

pageview   A single loading of a Web page, including all of its elements.

Perl   A programming language commonly used to create CGI programs.

pop-up   A new browser window that pops up on screen when viewers visit a particular Web page. *See also* interstitial.

rate card   A list of the published rates for various advertising spots. The rates that are actually received are often substantially lower.

reserve   An amount a credit card processing service will hold back to cover potential problems, such as customer chargebacks.

rich media   Graphics that use HTML, the programming language Java, or browser plug-ins such as Flash and Shockwave to create interactive and eye-catching displays.

ROS (run of site)   Run-of-site ads appear on every page of the site, instead of only on particular pages.

shopping cart system   Software that functions like a standard grocery store shopping cart. As visitors travel through the store they can place items they wish to purchase in the cart. When they are finished shopping, they can pay for all the items in one transaction, just as they would in a traditional store.

spider (also called a crawler or search bot)   A program that automatically fetches Web pages and follows (crawls) the links on them to find additional pages.

SSI (Server Side Include)   A type of directive that you can place in an HTML document that causes the Web server to dynamically process and insert data at that point, before displaying the page.

SSL (secure sockets layer)   The set of rules that Web server software and browsers use to make secure connections work.

static banner   A banner that is motionless, like a print advertisement.

telnet   A terminal emulation program that allows you to connect to a network (Web) server and execute commands as if you were using a terminal of that server.

TLD (top-level domain)   The suffix attached to a domain name, for example, .com, .org, .net. There are a limited number of predefined TLDs.

UCE (unsolicited commercial e-mail)   Another name for spam, the junk messages that clog your e-mail box.

URL (uniform resource locator)   The address you type into your browser to visit a particular Web page, which looks something like http://cheapwebtricks.com/index.shtml.

URL forwarding (also called domain forwarding or URL redirection)
Automatic forwarding of all traffic associated with a particular domain name to another location. Can be used to provide a shorter, more memorable address for a Web site than the one it has.

virtual hosting   Web hosting that uses your own domain name, but physically shares a server with many other domains.

vortal   A search portal that focuses on a specific market. Short for "vertical portal."

Web ring   A loosely affiliated group of sites that cover a common topic area. Each member site displays a Web ring logo and set of links that encourage visitors to visit other sites in the ring.

Web-safe palette   A selection of colors that only includes colors known to appear the same, even when viewed on different computer equipment.

XML (eXtensible Markup Language)   A language similar to HTML for creating Web documents, but with XML, developers can create and use their own tags instead of being limited to a predefined set.

Index

INTERNATIONAL CONTACT INFORMATION

AUSTRALIA
McGraw-Hill Book Company Australia Pty. Ltd.
TEL +61-2-9417-9899
FAX +61-2-9417-5687
http://www.mcgraw-hill.com.au
books-it_sydney@mcgraw-hill.com

CANADA
McGraw-Hill Ryerson Ltd.
TEL +905-430-5000
FAX +905-430-5020
http://www.mcgrawhill.ca

**GREECE, MIDDLE EAST,
NORTHERN AFRICA**
McGraw-Hill Hellas
TEL +30-1-656-0990-3-4
FAX +30-1-654-5525

MEXICO (Also serving Latin America)
McGraw-Hill Interamericana Editores S.A. de C.V.
TEL +525-117-1583
FAX +525-117-1589
http://www.mcgraw-hill.com.mx
fernando_castellanos@mcgraw-hill.com

SINGAPORE (Serving Asia)
McGraw-Hill Book Company
TEL +65-863-1580
FAX +65-862-3354
http://www.mcgraw-hill.com.sg
mghasia@mcgraw-hill.com

SOUTH AFRICA
McGraw-Hill South Africa
TEL +27-11-622-7512
FAX +27-11-622-9045
robyn_swanepoel@mcgraw-hill.com

**UNITED KINGDOM & EUROPE
(Excluding Southern Europe)**
McGraw-Hill Education Europe
TEL +44-1-628-502500
FAX +44-1-628-770224
http://www.mcgraw-hill.co.uk
computing_neurope@mcgraw-hill.com

ALL OTHER INQUIRIES Contact:
Osborne/McGraw-Hill
TEL +1-510-549-6600
FAX +1-510-883-7600
http://www.osborne.com
omg_international@mcgraw-hill.com